THE MOUNTING THREAT OF
HOME INTRUDERS

THE MOUNTING THREAT OF HOME INTRUDERS

Weighing the Moral Option of Armed Self-Defense

By

BRENDAN F.J. FURNISH, Ph.D.

Professor of Sociology
Westmont College
Santa Barbara, California

DWIGHT H. SMALL, M.Div.

Professor Emeritus
Westmont College
Santa Barbara, California

CHARLES C THOMAS • PUBLISHER
Springfield • Illinois • U.S.A.

Distributed Throughout the World by

CHARLES C THOMAS • PUBLISHER
2600 South First Street
Springfield, Illinois 62794-9265

© *1993 by* CHARLES C THOMAS • PUBLISHER

ISBN 0-398-05828-8

Library of Congress Catalog Card Number: 92-33130

All Scripture References are from THE HOLY BIBLE: Revised Standard
*Version (sec. ed.), Copyright 1971, Division of Christian Education of the National
Council of Churches of Christ in the United States of America.*

With THOMAS BOOKS *careful attention is given to all details of manufacturing
and design. It is the Publisher's desire to present books that are satisfactory as to
their physical qualities and artistic possibilities and appropriate for their particular
use.* THOMAS BOOKS *will be true to those laws of quality that assure a good
name and good will.*

Printed in the United States of America
SC-R-3

Library of Congress Cataloging-in-Publication Data

Furnish, Brendan F. J.
   The mounting threat of home intruders : weighing the moral option
of armed self-defense / by Brendan F. J. Furnish, Dwight H. Small.
      p.   cm.
   Includes bibliographical references and index.
   ISBN 0-398-05828-8
   1. Crime prevention.   2. Violent crimes—United States—
Prevention.   3. Self-defense—Moral and ethical aspects.
4. Pacifism.   5. Gun control—United States.   I. Small, Dwight
Hervey.   II. Title.
HV7431.F87   1993
364.4—dc20   92-33130
                                                    CIP

CONTRIBUTORS

Law and Criminology Consultants

Don B. Kates, Jr., J.D., currently in law practice in San Francisco; adjunct professor at Stanford University Law School; foremost author on firearms, violence, and issues of social policy relating to gun control.

Edward F. Leddy, Ph.D., formerly New York State Parole officer; Editor of the *Journal on Firearms and Public Policy;* currently teaching Criminal Justice, University of Virginia.

Mark A. Kroeker, Deputy Chief, Los Angeles Police Department.

Biblical/Ethics Consultants

William Nelson, Ph.D., Professor of Old Testament.
Robert H. Gundry, Ph.D., Professor of New Testament.
Robert N. Wennberg, Ph.D., Professor of Philosophy.

To the Many Westmont College Colleagues
Who Encouraged and Assisted the Authors
in Seeking to Apply a Moral Perspective
to an American Crime Crisis

PREFACE

The book has three major objectives, hence is divided into three parts.

Part I analyzes a critical social issue tearing our nation apart: the mounting incidence of violent crime, especially the alarming increase of violent home intruders—predators who reach not only into inner-city crime pockets but into suburbs formerly thought safe.

For those whose homes are entered, their lives are at high risk. Whatever purpose the intruder, it may be presumed he's dangerous and very likely armed. If confronted, he's prepared to assault his victim in his own defense.

We begin by profiling the diverse types of intruders and the equally diverse reasons for forcing their way into homes.

Take today's burglar. Despite the fact that burglars seek to enter homes when occupants are away from home, many are armed so as to successfully ward off anyone they might encounter. Sudden confrontation can quickly turn into a defensive tactic—often a lethal one! What follows may be a brutalizing assault, even the taking of life in order to save one's own skin in a successful escape, protecting one's own identity from some future witness, and avoiding being brought to justice.

Or take the rapist. He might be on the final leg of tracking a victim to her residence, or simply seeking a random victim in what appears an easy-access, little-protected neighborhood. Perhaps he knows the woman lives alone—a likely prey. All too frequently, rapists brutalize or kill, usually preferring to use their superior strength, or knife, putting a silent end to their victims. Not a few rapists are serial killers.

Can a rapist be successfully held at bay with a gun? Despite propaganda to the contrary, under some circumstances he can be deterred, under others physically stopped. This is not to suggest that armed confrontation is always the best decision, but it is certainly a demonstrably viable option. The popular advocacy of submission promotes what at times is the method least acceptable if one wishes to stay alive.

Or suppose the intruder is an adolescent on drugs, in desperate search of money, a mere youngster armed with knife or gun, frightened and scarcely knowing what he's doing. He's the product of peer associations, probably street-wise and daring, his life shaped by a violent subculture. In a moment of entrapment he uses his weapon without regard for the consequences, never having seriously thought through the implications of shooting a surprised householder.

One thing is common to all intruders: they're pre-inclined to weigh the necessity of having to confront a householder, and they're wary of anyone who might subdue or injure them, anyone who might shoot to kill. Unless the householder is stopped—be it a man or woman—the possibilities of arrest or of danger to life itself are always imminent. If the intruder has an arrest record, there is even greater danger of his using all necessary means to escape. Nor are his reactions ever predictable. Chances are, risks will quickly escalate for both victim and victimizer. To law enforcement people, desperate measures on the part of an intruder confronted are the expected.

We begin, then, with criminological, legal, and practical aspects of facing intruders, armed or unarmed.

For many families the issue is emotionally weighted because of trage-dies they've experienced or have known about through friends or neighbors. Of little help is conventional wisdom or the media which often badly distort facts. Moreover, today we have a liberal New Class Elite, information brokers influencing both conventional thought and social policy. How is their influence to be assessed?

Inescapably, the overall crime problem has to do with America's diverse social classes with their compelling social and economic needs. Society has deep-seated structural problems, uppermost among them America's ethnic struggles and vastly multiplying underclass.

Part II is particularly relevant to all professing Christians—Protestants and Catholics alike, indeed, all persons of basic religious morality. Beyond pragmatic questions of armed self-protection (often reflecting a utilitarian ethic), thoughtful Christians require the perspective of tradi-tional biblical ethics. Here we discover a common Protestant-Catholic ethic. Pacifism, the minority tradition, will be thoroughly examined and put to the test.

What, for example, must we think of Jesus' example of non-violence? Is this intended as a model meant to cover all instances where life is threatened? Does the Bible allow for retributive justice? Lethal defense?

If so, does this justify preemptive action on the part of a victim in his own home? Is it acceptable to take life when necessary to preserve and protect other lives? In other words, does taking life sometimes serve the cause of life?

In all these questions, the authors take a mediating position. We are selectivists, not non-pacifists. At a deeper level, concern for individual safety must be accompanied by concern for a safe, just, and ordered society.

Part III takes a look at the ongoing debate over social policy. With sharply opposing sides to the gun-control question, with powerful groups exerting national influence, Congress is debating various proposals. At the heart of contending views is the issue of the Second Amendment. Proposals now on the table will be carefully analyzed.

Research reveals that Protestant and Catholic Christians alike are sharply divided on policy issues. Curiously, they also represent a large percentage of gun owners. Whereas Catholic policy pronouncements come more directly from the Conference of Bishops, less the concern of laymen, Protestant lay people wish but seldom have a voice in the official pronouncements of their denominational bodies, often finding themselves in conflict with denominational policy commissions.

Author of the criminological and social policy chapters, Doctor Brendan F. Furnish is Professor of Sociology at Westmont College, serving as Department Chairman and having long pursued a specialty in the American gun culture and social policy. He maintains extensive association with authorities in the field. Doctor Furnish is a Fellow of the Center for the Study of Firearms and Public Policy and was 1991 recipient of the Westmont College Faculty Research Award for investigative research leading to the development of this book.[1]

Author of the chapters on ethical considerations, Dwight Hervey Small, Professor emeritus and Westmont College colleague of Doctor Furnish, Adjunct Professor, Talbot Theological Seminary, with degrees in philosophy and theology, is author of a dozen books relating biblical ethics to contemporary problems.[2]

NOTES

1. Brendan F. Furnish, "The New Class and the California Handgun Initiative: Elitist Developed Law as Gun Control," *The Gun Culture and Its Enemies.* William R. Tonso, (ed.), 1990.

2. Especially acclaimed: *Christian Celebrate Your Sexuality*. Old Tappan, NJ: Fleming
   H. Revell, 1974; *How Should I Love You?* San Francisco: Harper & Row, 1979;
   Remarriage and God's Renewing Grace. Grand Rapids, MI; Baker Book House,
   1986.

ACKNOWLEDGMENTS

Ned Divelbiss, College Librarian, research resources.

Betty Fleming, Editorial Associate and Director of Manuscript Production.

Research has been made possible in part through the generous auspices of Mrs. Sam Burd and Mr. C. Spector.

CONTENTS

THE MOUNTING THREAT OF
HOME INTRUDERS

Part I
AMERICA THE VIOLENT

INTRODUCTION TO PART I

Recently, Americans across the nation experienced a chilling sensation as they noted a full-page newspaper advertisement depicting a sinister criminal about to attack, possibly rape, a defenseless victim.

The National Rifle Association was promoting the proposition that we should *defend the right to defend ourselves.* The message came with intended shock value. Public reaction to such a proposal contained widely varied thoughts and emotions. For some it brought feelings of incredible incongruity, if not outright revulsion, that lethal self-defense should have social merit in an enlightened era. Others heartily agreed with the proposal, having no problem, actually regarding self-defense a virtual mandate. Their attitude: *We've had enough of criminals' getting their way! It's our lives or theirs! Let's put them at risk for a change! Let's take back our homes, our neighborhoods! They deserve what they get!*

To practicing Christians, this gives immediacy to the following questions: *Do we have a moral right to use lethal force in self-defense? Can this right extend as far as preemptive killing of an intruder whose possible intent is to brutalize or kill? What about protecting third-parties under our care? What* **does** *biblical ethics allow? Do we have responsibility to develop pre-planned defense strategies?*

Protestant and Catholic Christians can be found on both sides of the issue. Most readers will bring to the question their own initial set of biases. Why is it that perhaps no subject (other than abortion, euthanasia, or AIDS) generates such diverse attitudes as the propriety of armed self-defense?

To begin with, acceptance of personal armed defense means acquiring a deadly force mind-set and the weapon that can implement it, then training for the possible eventuality. Gun possession implies a readiness to kill in defense of innocent life—understandably, orientation that cuts across the grain of non-violent, peace-loving people. Especially does it threaten to desensitize people who loathe all weapons that harm or kill.

Really, should suburbanites like us be all that concerned? Aren't we ade-

5

*quately protected by the police? Won't our Neighborhood Watch program deter
this kind of thing? We haven't had violent crime in our neighborhood.*

As statistics show, even in our suburbs violent crime is rapidly increasing.
We dare not dismiss the potential danger, nor the urgency of our taking
responsibility for ourselves.

We are deceived if we take the casual view that firearms in the home
can be controlled to merely deterring, or, at most, superficially wounding,
an assailant in hopes of stopping him. While deterrence is an option, it is
not always available—or may prove unavailing, and always dangerous.
Whereas a defenseless householder may face brutalization or murder, an
armed householder is provided a viable option.

Among all Christians of conscience, the question of armed home
defense highlights an age-old controversy regarding the biblical ethics of
killing other human beings: pacifism versus non-pacifism. It is with this
issue that we shall ultimately have to come to terms.

So first, we look at the threatening circumstances we share commonly,
assessing the odds of any one of us becoming a victim. Secondly, we look
at defense measures that might be adopted for our own and our family's
safety. Thirdly, we note the legal ramifications.

To be prepared is to be informed. This involves dispelling false fears
and removing the mystery and myth surrounding guns: who uses them
and for what purposes. Our major focus shall be upon the validity and
the effectiveness of gun possession, with emphasis upon proper training
in safe usage and storage, and also upon the moral and emotional factors
involved in the actual use of a weapon.

Chapter 1

NATION UNDER SIEGE

Every contemporary culture, the world around, has its subculture of violence. World observers peg the United States as extraordinarily violent. To gain perspective on America's culture of violence, we begin with the real dangers all Americans face. Then we shall look into underlying causes.

Beyond the violence of our make-believe world of television and movies lies the real experience of men and women, notably but not exclusively in our metropolitan areas. Here, crimes against persons are taking on a violence unprecedented in modern world history. The escalating gang wars of our crowded cities (recently with the addition of extraordinarily vicious Asian gangs), the proliferation of violent predators in our neighborhoods, senseless drive-by shootings, burglaries increasingly the work of armed professionals, street violence driven by drug wars, rapists who mutilate their victims—these have become standard notices in local newspapers in towns and cities alike. A major change is that today there are no neighborhood sanctuaries.

Take one American city. New York has a population of 8 million, with more than a half million assaults each year and countless homicides. Analysts predict an infant born in this city today and living there for a lifetime has one chance in 65 of being murdered.

Review one nationally celebrated case. In April, 1989, 30 boys, most under 16, went *wilding* (their own description). They gang-raped and nearly battered to death a 28-year-old jogger in Central Park. They hit her with a pipe, hacked her skull with a knife, and pounded her face with a brick. As she lay nearly bleeding to death, they walked off, leaving her undiscovered for almost four hours.

This was not the activity of the underclass, the vengeful disadvantaged. Most of the young woman's attackers came from middle- or working-class homes, four actually living in a building with a doorman. As one boy said simply, *It was something to do; it was fun* (inflicting random brutality is *fun*).

Hardened detectives flinched at the callousness of the teenagers, noting that the parents showed little interest in their children's behavior even while those youngsters were confessing on videotape.[1]

New York Governor, Mario Cuomo, voiced his dismay by noting how teenagers today are killing "out of a grotesque insensitivity to the dignity of life and most basic requirements of civilized conduct."[2]

Behind the theorizing of social workers is a plain manifestation of what Christians call *human sin.* Nearly three thousand years ago the author of *The Book of Proverbs* saw this neverending problem:

> If young toughs tell you, *Come and join us* — turn your back on them! (Proverbs 1:10 TLB). If they say, *Come with us, let us lie in wait for blood, let us wantonly ambush the innocent. . . . Good or bad, we'll treat them all alike* (verse 11, RSV).

Then the writer advises:

> Don't do it, son! Stay far from men like that, for crime is their way of life, and murder is their specialty. . . . They lay a booby trap for their own lives. Such is the fate of all who live by violence and murder. They will die a violent death (verses 15, 19, *The Living Bible*).

Basic human propensities have not changed.

GUN VIOLENCE

Shocking is the realization that death by gunfire has become nearly as dulled in our consciousness as auto fatalities—so routine as to be often ignored by the local news media.

Our law enforcement consultant, Mark Kroeker, recalls walking into his office at the Los Angeles Police Department on a Monday morning, looking over the twenty-four-hour *occurrence logs,* counting fifteen murders over the weekend in Los Angeles. Yet, not one of these was reported in the *Los Angeles Times!* What he did find, in a section reserved for statewide news, was the notice of one murder that took place in central California!

This year more than thirty thousand persons will share the fate of death by shooting. This is about the same number to date as have died of AIDS and, over just two years, more than were killed in the entire Vietnam War! As 1990 ended, the District of Columbia registered its third consecutive annual homicide record of killings per number of population: 436 killings in the nation's capital.

Time Magazine [3] summarized a single week, May 1–7, 1989, reporting how in just seven days 464 people were killed by gunfire in the city of New York. The breakdown is as follows: Most of the killings took place with ordinary handguns and shotguns, not so-called assault rifles. Self-defense accounted for fourteen deaths; thirteen involved law enforcement officers. The victims were frequently society's most vulnerable—the poor, the young, the abandoned, the ill and the elderly. The most common single cause was suicide, with sixteen deaths, about one-quarter of which included killing someone else first, frequently spouses or other relatives. Another twenty-two deaths were preventable accidents. Less occasionally was the shooting gang- or drug-related or the final end to a fight, robbery attempt, or random shooting such as a drive-by. More often it was what Detroit psychiatrist, Karole Avila, has called *a permanent solution to a temporary problem.*

For every death, five times as many shooting victims escape with wounds. Still, a gun assault is more certain to be fatal than any other form of assault, because they have greater firepower which causes greater numbers of fatalities and serious wounds. Semiautomatics have replaced single-shot handguns as the weapon of choice for many criminals because of their availability and increasing use by drug dealers.

Incidentally, one weapon of choice among drug dealers is the TEC-9, a 9-millimeter Luger-type, semi-automatic pistol produced in Florida, advertised as *an intimidation factor.* Equipped with a 36-round magazine, these rounds can be fired in about forty-five seconds. Inexpensive and easily concealed, sales on these guns range about three thousand units per month. One of every five assault-style weapons is a TEC-9.

But where do criminals get guns such as these? In our State of California, 19,475 guns were reported stolen last year. In a sample of guns seized by the Los Angeles Police Department, just short of fifty percent were semi-automatic pistols. Since 1984, over seven million handguns have been added to the national stock and nearly four million were semiautomatic.

In February, 1992, *The Wall Street Journal* reported its investigation of the three Southern California companies most responsible for flooding U.S. cities with cheap guns, all three companies owned by members of the George Jennings family.[4] Every year they churn out 400,000 cheaply made *Saturday Night Specials.* These are considered most lethal by dint of sheer numbers in circulation, easy availability and rock-bottom prices. Selling for as little as $35 versus $600–$1,000 for higher-quality weapons, these are the starter guns for the fearful poor, the criminal poor, and the very young.

Made of cheap materials, notably die-cast zinc alloy rather than stain-less steel, these guns are notoriously unsafe and are banned in some states because of this. There are no safety requirements for U.S.-made guns, which makes them one of the least-regulated hazardous products in America. And these are the guns that figure disproportionately in robberies and murders. According to the BAF, of the six leading hand-guns used in crimes during the years 1990–1991, based on completed traces, 55 percent were Jennings family products.

On the street, the buyer may pay triple the normal retail price to avoid required waiting periods, registration, and restrictions based on age and felony convictions. As users *move up,* these guns are found in pawn shops. Interestingly, a recent editorial in the *Los Angeles Times* (5/24/92) claims that a significant number of handguns used in crime-related incidents in Los Angeles have come from federally licensed firearms dealers who sell their wares, no questions asked, out of skid row hotels. Apparently, the federal government has approved dealer license applica-tions *without ever checking criminal backgrounds or shop locations.* Because of budgetary and staffing problems, federal, state and city authorities no longer appear able to adequately supervise such businesses.

Typically, the guns are first bought by wholesalers, who in turn sell to gun stores and pawnshops for legitimate trade. Often, though, they are bought in bulk by illegal dealers, particularly in states where gun laws are lax. They are then smuggled by bus or train to urban centers for resale on the street. Thus, the Jennings family business is able to thrive on government protectionism and de facto oligopoly. Presently, the companies are expanding into high-powered weapons to sell in large volumes at low prices.

And now guns are flooding the ranks of middle and high school students, known to the police as the *kiddie arms race.* In 1991, New York schools had the bloodiest year ever, with 56 shootings. In the first two months of 1992, spot searches turned up 121 weapons in one New York school. Fully one quarter of the nation's largest urban school districts now use metal detectors to search for weapons. While there are no national statistics on the number of gun-related incidents in schools, the consensus is that with the rise of drug-related crime, drug-related money in the hands of the young, and easy availability, we can expect a steady escalation.

School children are learning a new kind of civil defense drill: hitting the dirt when gunfire erupts. According to the Ronald D. Stephens

National School Safety Center, nearly three million crimes occur on or near school campuses every year — 16,000 per school day, one every six seconds. No longer are our schools safe havens, whether in the inner city, suburbs, or rural areas. They are the newest armed camps.

In a recent article in the *Journal of the American Medical Association*,[5] Brandon Centerwall revisits a theme he had tackled previously.[6] He traces contemporary studies relating to the effect of television violence on young minds, going back to the 1968 National Commission on the Causes and Prevention of Violence. This was followed by the 1972 Surgeon General's report. In 1976, M. B. Rothenberg alerted the medical community on the effects of television's portrayal of violence on normal child development, a strategic alert for those in the pediatric branch of medicine especially. These findings were further confirmed by the 1982 report of the National Institute of Mental Health.[7] Since then, some twenty long-term studies have been published.[8]

Each of these studies, documenting a broad consensus in the scientific literature, indicated that continuous exposure of children to television violence dramatically increases their likelihood of physical aggressiveness.

In retrospect, Centerwall points to two surveys of young male felons imprisoned for violent crimes.[9] Twenty-two percent to thirty-four percent reported having overtly imitated crime techniques learned from television programs.

An interesting correlation is the annual increase in the white population homicide rate since the introduction of television into the United States, a rise of 93 percent from 1945–1975. Almost identical was the rise in Canada.

Centerwall points out that, given that homicide is an adult activity, and since television exerts its behavior-modifying effects upon children primarily, the initial television generation of children had to age ten to fifteen years before affecting the national homicide rate. This is precisely what researchers found. In turn, this leads Centerwall and others to conclude that the correlation is well established.

It is also well established that television audiences are maximized with programmed violence, a fact not lost on advertisers. Nor has that emphasis abated today. On the contrary, as Centerwall indicates, in twenty years of monitoring there has been no lessening of the amount of television programming devoted to violence or a diminishing of the nature of the violence itself. Rather, there has been an increasing intensity of violent portrayals.[10]

In 1989, the U.S. Congress passed a television anti-violence bill granting television industry executives the opportunity to confer with each other on the issue of television violence without violating antitrust laws. Unfortunately, the four networks responded that they had no intention of taking advantage of this exemption for such a purpose, nor did they expect to make any substantive changes in programming to accommodate the spirit of the bill. Today, we can say that nothing has changed for the better.

ARMED HOUSEHOLDS ARE NOT DEVIANT HOUSEHOLDS!

Ask the increasing number of people found at popular firing ranges why they have guns. Especially ask the growing number of women now seen at such ranges—or their instructors. A majority will say that an important reason is personal protection.

California firearms usage currently breaks down to some 1,740 willful homicides annually (according to Mark Kroeker, about eight hundred of these were in Los Angeles, of which sixty-seven were criminals shot to death in justifiable homicides by private citizens).

There are criminal predators waiting for hapless victims wherever they may be found, especially when isolated within their own homes and unable to secure their own safety. In many a situation where the victim faces an armed or physically superior assailant, a gun is the *equalizer*. Still, one cannot assume that guns always provide the solution.

Increasingly, people of means are living in secured residential communities, precisely as sociologists predicted over two decades ago. But what about those living in high-crime areas who cannot afford security systems, who are left to their own devices? Is it irrational that so many resort to possession of lethal weapons as their best hope for to possession of lethal weapons as their best hope for fending off violent predators? Is it a cause for wonder that there exists a market for cheap handguns that less-affluent, more-threatened inner-city individuals can afford, especially single mothers living in the poverty pockets in our cities? Where the threat of crime is greatest and protection most needed, police protection cannot be counted on for situations that require instant response. This, obviously, would require an enormous force of officers, each stationed through the night in the immediate vicinity of every person's residence.

According to Mark Kroeker, the Los Angeles Police Department's ideal average response time to emergency calls is seven minutes. But, he adds, to a victim a lifetime passes by in seven minutes! Remember, he's speaking of ideal time, not actual, to-be-counted-on time.[11]

But isn't home in a "good" neighborhood a pretty safe haven? Not at all! The danger in every neighborhood cannot be overestimated! One objective of this book is to put to rest all cause for indifference.

SEEING VICTIMS AS REAL PEOPLE

As we examine the data, we should not see victims as statistics (i.e., nameless people on police blotters) but the real people they are: wives, husbands, children, friends, neighbors. Try to imagine the terror faced by individuals who have had to submit to a violent aggressor. Imagine the added associations when this takes place in one's own home. Mentally place yourself in the circumstances of the victim. For unless we have genuine empathy for the victims who make up the statistics, crime data alone loses its power to motivate us to consider actions we ourselves might need to take if found in a similar situation.

Take one highly publicized case of reaction to fear that speaks eloquently of the instinct for survival, that of Bernhard Goetz, who shot four black youths who accosted him on a New York subway in 1984. This highly relevant, nationally reported case of self-defense is still discussed today. Although it did not involve a home intruder, it reveals a lot that we need to understand about the psychology of perceived threats of victimization.

In a recent article,[12] Arthur Eckstein, history professor at the University of Maryland, looks at Goetz's emotional trauma at being threateningly accosted. In 1981, three years earlier, Bernhard Goetz had been mugged and seriously injured by three black youths. Now, this time, he is armed — and terrified! One doesn't have to predicate paranoia to account for his reaction to danger. As Eckstein remarks, to be faced by four black youths on the subway must have seemed as though he had stepped back into the past — his own worst nightmare, a replay of the trauma he had suffered three years earlier. He had vowed back then, *The next time, I'll be ready.* Now he asks himself, *Something's up! Why are they coming my way? No, not again!*

Let's face it; he was white, they were black. In the subways, black crime is predominant. What would be your thoughts? Your fears? Your response?

The testimony of Goetz's fellow passengers revealed they too were frightened. Doesn't this suggest that Goetz clearly perceived the grim realities of New York subway life? As Eckstein points out, those realities include the fact that 13,800 felonies are committed in that subway system every year.

These youths were not children. All were eighteen or nineteen. What Goetz couldn't know, but might surmise, was that each of these young men had been arrested or convicted at least twice. At the time, each was facing trial or a hearing on criminal charges—armed robbery, assault, rape. After the trial, one juror said that one of the boys, Ramseur, had terrified them with just his viciousness in court.

So, we ask, wasn't Goetz a normally discerning survivalist? Wasn't this a wise Bernhard Goetz in his on-the-site assessment of a threatening situation? Hardly deniable.

Interestingly, six of the twelve jury members had been victims of street crime. Eckstein's observation is relevant:

> Anyone who has ever been brutalized by muggers will tell you that the main and longest-lasting psychological impact is terror—permanent terror that it might happen again. As one victim told me, "people who have been mugged have a sort of 'black hole' inside them —a terrible fear of it happening again, and an absolute fear of anyone who looks like the person who mugged them before" (italics added).[13]

Anyone whose home has been intruded, any woman who has been raped, or any assault victim knows the truth of this depiction. We must realize the psychological residue of fear, which terrible moments of confrontation with a criminal bring, and the accompanying sense of impotency in the face of the possibility that it might occur again. Those who have been victimized and have survived carry forever this same fear as a Bernhard Goetz. So there needs to be a realization that people who've had their persons violated by, say, assault or rape can never be quite the same as they were before, never completely whole again, whether it happens outside the home or inside.[14]

Crime control is more about persons than about guns or knives, single-shot or semiautomatics, more about clearing the streets of criminals than about gun shops, more about criminal justice reform—about violent personalities and the social causes leading to violence. Violence always has and always will find a way of expressing itself, regardless of the weapons available at the time; this is the record of history. Of course, access to lethal means can embolden and add spontaneity, compounding the deadly effects.

STATISTICS PAINT A GRIM PICTURE

The FBI estimates that only 40 percent of all crimes are reported, and of every 100 reported, only four criminals are apprehended, convicted and sent to prison. Shockingly, for every 100 prisoners serving life sentences, 25 are freed before their third year, 42 by their seventh year. Individuals acquitted of murder by reason of insanity spend an average of only 500 days in mental hospitals before being released. We need to ask, *How much is the problem simply the revolving door of the judicial system?*

The most reliable source of crime statistics is the *Uniform Crime Reports* published annually by the FBI. In general, the rates indicate a significant increase in violent crime over the last several years.

According to the National Crime Survey, the number of Americans victimized by violent crime rose to 2.3 million last year. Over 11 out of 1,000 people aged 12 or over were victims of violent crime. At present, a U.S. citizen has about a 1 in 10,000 chance of being murdered during any given year. And if these odds seems fairly good, consider translating this to lifetime possibilities and the chances increase to 1 in 133. Bear in mind that such data reflect the total U.S. population, with significant variance found between different population components.

In the homicide category, when charges are filed they are frequently the result of plea bargaining, allowing a criminal to avoid a more serious charge (such as manslaughter) and to stand convicted of a lesser charge. This is done in exchange for the defendant's willingness to waive a long jury trial that is costly to the state and burdensome for the court docket. But the process skews the statistical picture of crimes actually committed. Unfortunately, also affecting such decisions are state costs for incarceration along with prison cell limitations.

Last to be mentioned, the rate of reported rapes more than doubled from 1970 to 1990. In the first six months of 1990, it rose an additional 16 percent in cities with populations over 500,000, and 15 percent in cities with populations under 500,000. Some of the increase is due to the greater percentage of victims reporting.

CRIME RISK INDICATORS

One of the more useful indicators of violent crime recently developed by the Bureau of Justice Statistics is called the Crime Risk Index. What it tells us is illustrative of our plight as citizens in the 1990s. The Crime

Risk Index differs from the *Uniform Crime Reports,* in that it samples people who have been victimized and then extrapolates the information so as to estimate future victimization probabilities.

This index reveals that at the existing rate, 83 percent of males who are presently twelve years of age will be victims, or intended victims, of a violent crime within their lifetime. Furthermore, over fifty percent of these victims will be attacked more than once in the course of their lives. Most of those involved in violent crime will be victims of criminal assault themselves, frequently resulting from such activity as a robbery.

University of California professor, Franklin Zimring, is often cited as the authority for there being only a minimal likelihood of injury or death during a burglary. His own later research repudiates this.[15] Citing Chicago as an example, he now shows that victim death during burglary in occupied premises is six times greater than that in street muggings. In over thirty percent of recorded burglaries, violent crime directed against the occupants included aggravated assault, rape, and murder.

Even more disturbing, presently 1 out of 700 women are raped each year. This means that one out of every twelve American women will be raped sometime during their life span. While this includes *acquaintance* rape, the rate encompasses a high percentage of rapes that result from home entrapment by intruders.

The probability of a woman being raped relates strongly to her age and race. For example, a woman presently twenty years old has about a 72 percent chance of being raped during the course of her lifetime, while a contemporary thirty-year-old female faces a 54 percent risk during her remaining years. In other words, as the woman's age rises, her chances of being raped decrease steadily.

Not that it provides any comfort, but, curiously enough, violence balances out over gender lines; men are about twice as likely as women to be murdered!

In real terms, these data in themselves do not demonstrate the magnitude of the threat, since the Crime Risk Index excludes crimes against property as when householders who, upon returning home, surprise a burglar at work. Such confrontations can result in assault, often unintended homicide. Most frequently, this additional violence is perpetrated by a felon who has no desire to return to prison and who all too often is under the influence of drugs, alcohol, or both. Thus, an increase in the number of burglaries indicates increased risk of violence often associated with it.

The Department of Justice recently reported that urban households are most susceptible to criminal victimization, followed by suburban households. As we would expect, the lowest rates are displayed by rural households. It is reasonable to expect that population density and the anonymity of life in urban and suburban population centers are significant factors.

RACE AND SOCIAL CLASS

In our country, crime rates are profoundly affected by race and social class. Particularly alarming are the crime rates of the non-white, underclass populations in large urban centers. Interestingly, black victimization rates are almost double that for whites. In the crime of rape, the typical rapist is black and so is his victim. The rape rate for black women is one out of nine—a risk of forcible rape almost double that faced by white women. The murder rate for non-whites is also alarmingly high.

Reynolds Farley[16] points out that in the 1940s, deaths among blacks attributable to homicide were 3 percent, this doubled by the 1970s, and now is the fourth leading cause of death for blacks in general and the leading cause of death for black men aged fifteen to twenty-four. According to the U.S. Department of Justice, black males have a one in twenty-one chance of dying in a homicide in their lifetime. Moreover, blacks account for approximately fifty percent of all arrests for criminal homicide.

The majority of black murders involve the use of firearms—usually a handgun, increasingly a semiautomatic. The frightening increase in underclass crime involving firearms is one of the understated and publicly unacknowledged reasons for gun control advocacy. We suggest readers interested in learning more about this problem read William Tucker's book, *Vigilante.*[17]

We the authors realize that black activists may take exception at even the mention of crime figures as they relate to blacks, especially since we've not devoted space to the structural reasons in American society which account for this phenomenon. We record this information not only for factual accuracy but with a desire that greater attention might be directed toward the alleviation of suffering among the black population. We need a heightened compassionate regard for the entire underclass and its needs, for those who do not yet share society's benefits in equal shares, and whose inordinate rates of violent crime reflect the frustration and despair that spawns aggressive behavior against those more affluent—even lashing back against themselves.

Blacks make up 12 percent of the population of the U.S., 28 percent of all Americans below the poverty level, yet comprise 58 percent of all who are arrested for murder and manslaughter, 48 percent of all those arrested for rape, and 63 percent of those arrested for aggravated assault—the violent crime categories.

Despite the record of black progress, this 12 percent of the nation's population remains subject to both blatant and subtle forms of discrimination and stigma. But whether black or white, underclass crime is often only the more radical expression of the boiling cauldron of emotions which have been provoked to the limit by unfair practices, neglect, or outright rejection. Is this not a reasonable expectation in a nation where so many have so much and others so little? The have-nots see on TV the things which entice all who aspire to a decent life. Not only do they chafe for access to these things, but they have understandable hatred for those who have this abundance yet are seen as keeping it from them. Intrusive crime is one way to get what they otherwise cannot have.

Yes, violent crime is real, is on the increase, and can touch your life and mine. As Boston Police Commissioner, Francis M. Roache, said recently, "It's time for this country to face up to the fact that we are a violent society."[18]

There is indeed in the U.S. a frightening culture of crime; our task is to understand it as best possible, especially as it enables us to understand the phenomenon of violent home intruders.

NOTES

1. George F. Will, "Hear and See No Evil—Inflict No Punishment," *Santa Barbara News Press.* April 30, 1989; G. F. Krayche, "A Nation Afraid," *U.S.A. Today,* May 1989, p. 98.
2. Will, op. cit., p. 98.
3. "7 Deadly Days," *Time Magazine* (special report). July 17, 1989. pp. 31–60.
4. Alix M. Freedman, "Fire Power: This Family Makes the Cheap Guns that Flood United States Cities," *The Wall Street Journal.* Feb. 28, 1992, pp. 1–7.
5. Centerwall, Brandon, "Television and Violence," *Journal of the American Medical Association,* 267, 1992, pp. 3059–3063.
6. Rothenberg, M.B., "Effect of Television on Children and Youth," *Journal of the American Medical Association* 234, 1975, pp. 1043–1046.
7. Pearl, D., Bouthilet, L., Lazar, J. *Television and Behavior: Ten Years of Scientific Progress and Implications for the Eighties.* Rockville, MD: National Institute of Mental Health, 1982.
8. Centerwall, Brandon, "Exposure to Television as a Cause of Violence." *In*

Comstock, G., ed. *Public Communication and Behavior.* Orlando, FL: Academic Press, Inc., 1989, pp. 1–58.

9. Heller, M.S., Polsky, S., *Studies in Violence and Television.* New York: American Broadcasting Co., 1989.

10. Gerbner, G., et al, *The Violence Profile: Enduring Patterns.* Philadelphia: Annenberg School of Communication, 1989.

11. *See* "Firearms Use and the Police: A Historic Evolution of American Values," in Kates, Don, Jr. (ed), *Firearms and Violence: Issues of Public Policy.* San Francisco: Pacific Research Institute, 1984; (*see Police Marksman,* July–Aug., 1986, pp. 489–513).

12. Arthur Eckstein, "The Revenge of the Nerd," *Chronicles.* March, 1988, pp. 26–27.

13. Ibid., pp. 28–30.

14. "Violent Crime by Strangers and Non-Strangers," *Bureau of Justice Statistics* (special report). United States Department of Justice, Washington, DC, Jan. 1987.

15. Franklin E. Zimring, "Violence and Firearms Policy," *American Violence and Public Policy: An Update of the National Commission on the Causes and Prevention of Violence.* Lynn A. Curtis (ed.), New Haven, CT: Yale University, 1985.

16. Hawkins, Darnell F. (ed), *Homicide Among Black Americans.* Boston: University Press of America, 1986, pp. 13–25.

17. Tucker, William. *Vigilante: The Backlash Against Crime in America.* Briarcliff Manor, NY: Stein & Day, 1985, pp. 301ff; Staples, Robert, *Black Masculinity: The Black Male's Role in American Society.* San Francisco: Black Scholar's, 1982, pp. 137–151.

18. "The Bloodiest Year Yet," *Newsweek.* July 16, 1990, p. 24.

Chapter 2

THE MEDIA'S PACKAGED VIOLENCE

I s there a link between violence in all its forms and the impact of violence drummed into the home by the media? Let's start by taking it from 1988. *Time Magazine* chose to summarize one week in our national life as TV watchers—Halloween week.

Halloween did more than cast its expected spell. On NBC, the mini-series "Favorite Son" showed sadomasochistic bondage, even a dog lapping up the blood of a murder victim. An ABC made-for-TV movie focused on a psychotic father setting fire to his sleeping son. On Fox Television's "The Reporters," an airline pilot disposed of his wife by shoving her body through a wood-chopping machine. Fox also aired "America's Most Wanted," offering lurid re-creations of rapes, shootings, and stabbings—all in slow motion and freeze frame. Maury Povich's syndicated, "A Current Affair," proved that any violence goes.

Is there a link between the mental processes of those who get ideas from such TV shows and those who commit crimes of violence? It doesn't take a psychologist to recognize how the media is desensitizing a generation of Americans to violence. It began with fresh-from-the-scene TV newscasts from Vietnam with its pictorial body counts. But the acceleration of violent content on TV and theater screens in every hamlet in the land has only compounded as we enter the 1990s. Who would have imagined that one of the 1991 season's top grossing films would be about a psychopath who not only murders women but skins them!

In 1990, all this was made easier when the X rating was arbitrarily changed to NC 17 (no one under seventeen)—a decision made without public consultation and condemned by religious leaders of all major faiths. Now, not only do we, the nation, devote inordinate hours to prime-time TV where the central motif is violence, but we export our fixation to the world community (Big bucks, you know!).

For audiences at home and abroad we created a national hero—Sylvester Stallone as Rambo. His *First Blood, Part Two*, recall, focused on burning, impaling, carving, bludgeoning, exploding—no violent act overlooked.

The accent was upon the capacity to not only endure pain but inflict it—the apparent means for establishing America's macho man.

Other popular programs included "The Equalizer," "Miami Vice," and "L.A. Law," along with the endless tradition of emotionless killing represented by the "Make my day" syndrome of Clint Eastwood, Charles Bronson, and Eddie Murphy. These, however, were only baby steps to the current *new standard* poised to take violence even further in the 1990s.

Roy M. Anker, who teaches film at Calvin College, incisively details the trend in media violence aimed at the youth market.[1] A 1984 survey by the Motion Picture Production Association showed that 54 percent of the movie-going public was between ages twelve and twenty-four. Between twelve and seventeen, 51 percent went to a theater at least once a month. No wonder movies are dominantly created for younger movie goers.

Among the most popular teen-oriented films is the genre known as the horror movie, commonly called *slasher* or *slice-and-dice*—sociopathic exploitation of teen curiosity about the darker side of life.[2] With large doses of carnage and sexual mutilation, these films evolved from milder versions of the 1980s. By 1987, one of every six films classified as a true horror film, called by Morris Dickstein, "...hard-core pornography of violence made possible by the virtual elimination of censorship. Typical of all forms of addiction, it requires more and more while achieving less and less— not the single film, but the appalling accretion of violent entertainment."[3]

Invariably, the plot has an abhorrent male figure stalking his victims, whom he then proceeds to mutilate and kill. The viewer is taken on the hunt through the eyes of the stalker. Slash! Gouge! Dismember! Eviscerate! (camera pause, freeze-frame depict gore splayed everywhere). Then when the sadist has stretched the pain and butchery to the point of satiety, the plot ends . . . for now (*Return soon to your favorite local theater for the next in the series—guaranteed even better!*).

As Anker shows,

> Until they [the victimizers] are permanently dispatched, they will inflict an abominable amount of pain and violence on teens, mostly girls. With unfathomable malice and relish, which the audience participates in vicariously . . . the body count in these films ranges from four to twenty.[4]

Thus is brutalization mainstreamed as an evidently established way of life.

Psychiatrist Thomas Radecki, Director of the National Coalition on Television Violence, observes that violence in small doses regularly administered produces harmful effects.[5] He contends that statistical evidence supports the linkage of 25 percent to 50 percent of contemporary social violence with violent entertainment.[6] University of Illinois psychologists Leonard Eron and L. Rowell Huesmann studied one set of children for over twenty years. They found that those who watched significant amounts of TV violence at the age of eight were consistently more likely to commit violent crimes or engage in child or spouse abuse at thirty. In 1991 they wrote, "Serious aggression never occurs unless there is a convergence of large numbers of causes, but one of the very important factors we have identified is exposure to media violence."[7]

As Anker sees it, even youthful rebellion, rampant in all social classes today, is no longer cast in terms of social idealism—the attempt to right social ills (as in the 1960s rebellion against the status quo) but is a seething resentment of most every facet of life, together with a desire for hurt and retribution for its own sake. It is no less than a lust for gaining power over others when all other avenues of personal dominance remain dormant.

The American public can be said to have an advanced, focused addiction to this kind of sensory entertainment. Thus is violence an ingrained part of our culture, with the children of America being nurtured on a diet of violent images made commonplace. To them, it is becoming "normal" life, "real" life. Our society scarcely recognizes it is being brutalized both outside and inside the home.

As for children's TV watching, recently our local newspaper, the *Santa Barbara New Press,* cited a local survey, *The Wired Bedroom.* In our affluent city, over thirty-nine percent of children from kindergarten through sixth grade have TV's in their bedrooms, children from seventh to twelfth grade just under fifty percent. Dare we refer to this as "supervised TV"—or: "sneak preview"? What better reinforcement for teen crime is there than the parade of violent images on personal screens?

A glance at the lists of most-wanted films of teens shows them including, for example, the Indiana Jones series. One sequel, *Indiana Jones and the Temple of Doom,* grossed the eighth-largest box office receipts ever. Interestingly, it showed the incineration of a boy. As Anker observes, the film is amply stocked with torture implements: whips, chains, knives, along with body parts, blood drinking, etc. Yet curiously, this film is rated PG—acceptable for children eight years old!

While only random examples, these are nonetheless representative. Strangely, adults by and large defend these films on the ground that we need greater acknowledgment of the place of fantasy. But, really, is not reality and fantasy being excessively blurred in the minds of impressionable young people, at the same time giving ever-greater credence to the place of violence in life?

Exacerbating it all is the percent of American households that now have VCR's. Thirty percent of these homes have pay-cable movie channels, combining viewing with rental video cassettes. According to Gallup, American teens see roughly ninety movies each year, 90 percent on video cassettes at home.

More significantly, in our major cities video rental stores are found within a mile of each other. Rarely do they enforce the rating code except for X-rated movies (the now questionable NC 17). These outlets, inadequately monitored (and in existence for profits), make it easy for junior high schoolers to obtain the worst of the lot. Just about anything they wish to see, they see.

The outrageous motif today in teen-targeted films is coercive sexual violence against women. Now, in the 1990s, add the emphasis upon sexual violence against women in the rap lyrics of such musical groups as 2 Live Crew.[8] These rap lyrics, seldom heard and little understood by the average parent, brought the comment from syndicated columnist, George F. Will: "Words," said Aristotle, "are what set human beings, the language-using animals, above lower animals." Will adds: "Not necessarily so!"[9]

Sociologically, what is taking place is the informal aspect of socialization —in negative ways enhancing how we become the social products we are.

In the growing underclass where supervision is scant because both parents (where there are two) are working to keep things together, excitement can be vicariously experienced through the video screen. Hard-working adults turn their minds from drudgery and anxiety to rented X-rated movies which titillate their jaded emotions. But all too often its the kids who watch these movies while their parents are at work (ever seen a lockable video cabinet?). Moreover, for adolescent drug dealers and their friends it's a cinch to secure an adult drug buyer's help in obtaining X-rated movies or violent pornography in exchange for drugs. Thus, among the disadvantaged underclass, the violence motif is exacerbated by private exposure to videos. Driven by youthful curiosity and the desire to do what adults do, is it any wonder teens are voracious consumers of these films?

Are we, then, becoming a nation inured to violent "entertainment"? Is it not disturbing that commercials for TV films so frequently portray the most violent aspects of their offerings to entice future watching—the commercials we see at the dinner table each evening?

Scientific studies by Donnerstein, Van der Voort, Singer and others,[10] have shown conclusively that violent sexuality depicted in slasher films increases the willingness of late-adolescent males to coerce women sexually. One way they do this is through break and enter—be it a college dorm (high profile news today), a suburban home (shockingly on the increase), or an inner-city apartment complex (veritable crime wave!).[11]

Over three-fourths of adolescent homicides are firearm related, with the majority the result of handguns. For every firearm fatality, there are 24-fold more non-fatal firearm injuries, often with serious morbidity. This grim reality led two members of the Department of Pediatrics at the University of Washington to conduct a research study of handguns and urban high school youth in Seattle. The research was funded by the National Institute of Health and Human Services and the Centers for Disease Control.[11] The study was conducted during a six-week period in the winter of 1990–1991 and comprised a cross-sectional survey with eleventh-grade students in the Seattle Public School District.

Doctor Charles M. Callahan and Doctor Frederick P. Rivara found that 34 percent of the students perceived handguns to be easily accessible. Thirty-one percent said they could acquire a handgun from a friend, 18 percent said they could readily buy it on the street, 8 percent specified a gun shop, and 7 percent could obtain it from home, while 13 percent already owned one.

Handgun ownership was reported by 6.4 percent of the students. Eighty-five percent reported personal ownership, the remainder sharing ownership with friends. Handguns were reported gifts by 29 percent of owners, all but one having been received from parents, 22 percent from a friend, with 19 percent purchased on the street and 6 percent from a gun store. Four percent of all eleventh-grade students had carried a gun to school at some time, and 33 percent of handgun owners indicated they had shot at another person.

Handgun ownership was more common among the lowest social class, least common among the highest social class. Ownership was also highest among students reporting hearing gunfire in their neighborhood at least one or two times per week, a strong environmental factor. Ownership was also highest among students who reported problem behaviors, the strongest associations being among gang members, high also where there was drug selling, violence associated with robbery, assault and battery on a teacher, and expulsion from school.

A recent report from the centers for Disease Control and its 1990 nationwide school-based Youth Risk Behavior survey noted that 20 percent of all students in grades nine through twelve reported carrying a weapon to school at least once in the month preceding the survey; for 20 percent it was a handgun.[12] The Seattle study is consistent with surveys of other metropolitan cities.

It seems conclusive that as individuals are socialized by means of every social impact in their unique social environment, so the culture of violence which surrounds them in the grim realities of U.S. crime, and by the media's constant diet of violence, has its lasting effect. Every protective agency in every community knows that at times only counter-violence can deter or stop criminal violence. But as with every game the human creature is called upon to play, there are rules which govern it. It is the moral dimensions of these rules which shall occupy us as we proceed.

NOTES

1. Anker, Roy M. (ed.), *Dancing in the Dark: Youth, Popular Culture, and the Electronic Media.* Grand Rapids, MI: Eerdmans, 1991.
2. Waller, Gregory A. (ed.) *American Horrors: Essays on the Modern American Horror Film.* Urbana: University of Illinois, 1988; Twitchell, James B., *Dreadful Pleasures: An Anatomy of Modern Horrors.* New York: Oxford University, 1985.
3. *American Horrors,* op. cit., 3.
4. Roy M. Anker, "Yikes! Nightmares from Hollywood," *Christianity Today.* June 16, 1989, pp. 19–23.
5. Thomas Radecki, "American Culture of Violence," *Action,* Nov.–Dec., 1987, p. 7.
6. Ibid., p. 8.
7. Huesmann, L. Rowell, and Eron, Leonard D. (eds.), *Television and the Aggressive Child: A Cross National Comparison.* Hillsdale, NJ: Erlbaum, 1986.
8. *Dancing in the Dark,* op. cit., pp. 146–210.
9. George F. Will, "America's Slide Into The Sewer," *Newsweek.* July 30, 1990, p. 64.
10. On Pornography, *see:* Donnerstein, Edward I., and Daniel G. Linz, *The Question of Pornography: Research Findings and Policy Implications.* Free Press, 1987; Edward I. Donnerstein, and Daniel G. Linz, "The Question of Pornography: It

is Not Sex but Violence That Is An Obscenity in Our Society," *Psychology Today.* Dec. 1986, p. 56; Wendy Bowers, "Violent Pornography," *Humanist* 48 (Jan. –Feb., 1988) pp. 22–25. On Television's impact on Behavior, *see:* Van Der Voort, T. H., *Violence: A Child's Eye View.* New York: Elsevier Science, 1986; Bouthilet, Lorraine, Lazar, Joyce B., and David Pearl, *Television and Behavior: Ten Years of Scientific Progress and Implications for the Eighties.* Washington, DC: United States Department of Health and Human Services, 1982.

11. Callahan, Charles M., and Rivara, Frederick P., *Urban High School Youth and Handguns: A School-Based Survey. Journal of the American Medical Association,* 267, 1992, 3038–3042.

12. Centers for Disease Control. *Weapon-Carrying Among High School Students – United States, 1990.* MMWR, 1991, 40, 681–684.

Chapter 3

PROFILING VIOLENT PREDATORS

To understand what kind of intruders householders risk facing, we must use available data, representing a wide variety of types, each capable of the threat of violence. Once we distinguish these types, we can target appropriate self-protection strategies.

Sociologists James Wright and Peter Rossi[1] report a research program on criminal violence undertaken by the Social and Demographic Research Institute of the University of Massachusetts. Data consists of questionnaires administered to nearly two thousand convicted felons serving time in state prisons around the country. The central topic is how and why criminals acquire, carry, and use firearms.

A comparable study by the Rand Corporation by Chaiken and Chaiken[2] shows that violent predators rarely specialize in one particular type of crime. Rather, they tend to be opportunists, committing various crimes, depending upon what opportunities present themselves. In the light of such research, we're mistaken to categorize criminals too narrowly. For instance, a burglar may also be a rapist when opportunity arises, a rapist may also be a killer. Today's non-violent drug abusers may resort to killing to get what they desperately need to support their habit. Daily the newspapers carry stories of senseless forms of violence where one type of crime is accompanied by another. Both professional and non-professional home intruders span a wide range of criminal types.

We've come to accept the conventional understanding that professional burglars do not ordinarily carry guns because they enter homes thought to be unoccupied at the time. If apprehended, they don't want an additional gun charge brought against them. Yet, the Wright-Rossi survey shows that about thirty percent of incarcerated felons acknowledge their practice of carrying a gun at all times. One reason: they live among peers who carry guns, making them vulnerable to assault from criminal acquaintances. Packing a weapon is a matter entirely aside from needing it to accomplish their intended crime.

Additionally, the professional burglar has little regard for the legal

27

consequences of carrying a gun. He knows add-on gun charges can often be plea bargained. About fifty-eight percent of surveyed felons made the point that they carry guns for self-protection. So, among criminal predators, the single most important reason to carry a gun is that "when you have a gun, you are prepared for anything that might happen. There's always a chance my victim will be armed."

Three-fifths of all felons interviewed agreed that they worried more about meeting an armed victim than about running into the police. This is backed up by the fact that about two-fifths reported at least one armed-victim encounter at some time in their career, while over one-third said they had personally been scared off, shot at, wounded, or captured by their victim. According to Wright and Rossi, more criminals nationwide are killed by armed victims than by police—a statistic never cited by those who seek to ban all handguns. This is confirmed by Gary Kleck's studies as well. Incidents by the dozen from across the nation are reported monthly in *The American Rifleman.* All this does much to put the question of police protection versus self-protection in better balance.

What weapons do professional criminals choose to arm themselves with? Data confirms that felons do not prefer the cheap handguns which Handgun Control, Inc. would ban. It's more important to them that their weapon be a quality one with accuracy, reliability, and untraceability. They prefer well-made large-caliber handguns, and more often today the semiautomatics. As Wright and Rossi point out, "serious criminals prefer serious equipment." It is generally agreed that criminals would be unaffected by any gun ban, while for poor householders it would remove their ability to own their only affordable means of protection.

Career Criminals

In the aggregate, the profile of prison populations shows the following. Felons tend to be young males from socioeconomically disadvantaged backgrounds. Most are under age thirty, about half are non-white, only thirty-nine percent have finished high school, most having dropped out around the tenth grade. When employed, they work at jobs close to the bottom in wage and skill levels. Fewer than two-fifths have ever been married, although roughly a fourth are living with a woman. On the average they come from families where they were one of six children, while a substantial number come from families of ten children or more. Over one-half have brothers or sisters arrested at one time or another.

About thirty-nine percent have brothers or sisters who've served prison or jail sentences. Many have fathers who've *lived outside the law,* have served time, and are men of violent tendencies (wife and child beaters). The great majority of fathers owned guns, one-third carrying their guns outside the home, although virtually none had ever had a permit to carry.

The profile shows that felons, on the average, have fired a gun by age thirteen and have a first-ever weapon before age sixteen. Initial arrest is experienced by age sixteen. Early in the seventeenth year (or younger) come hard drugs (one-third of these men were destined to become addicts, another third alcoholics). Before nineteen the average felon has seriously wounded or tried to kill someone, received his first felony conviction and been sent to prison. Most of his twenties are spent in prison, having been convicted on the average of three to four separate times, spending over eight years in prison by the time he is twenty-nine. All share the characteristic of having committed frequent, serious crimes while still juveniles. About ten percent begin their criminal career with an assault, six percent with a homicide.

At a time when most young men are completing school, entering the job market, getting married and raising children, the typical felon is in prison, his social development vastly retarded, his life totally unconventional, and in the eyes of ordinary citizens a total deviant. At the time of arrest, about two-fifths are unemployed. Among those employed the previous year, weekly take-home pay is regarded insufficient to make ends meet. More than a third commit crime because they need drug money which their low wages or partial employment cannot supply. At least half their earned income is spent on drugs. Over fifty-seven percent are either drunk or high on drugs when they commit the crime for which they are imprisoned.

Non-Career Criminals

Not all home intruders are career criminals—or violent predators. While some young suburban males get hooked on drugs and need money to support a growing habit, still others are simply seeking thrills or acting on a dare. To such young people it seldom occurs that a life of crime lies just ahead. Burglary is seen almost as a lark, not high risk, but a *smart* way to get what one wants. Little do they think of the possibilities of armed confrontation.

A sketchy look at the diversity of home intruders alerts us to the breadth of personal types. Inasmuch as home intruders are for the most part career criminals, our attention focuses upon this category.

VIOLENCE AS STATUS ACHIEVEMENT

Sociologists Robert K. Merton in the 1950s and Lewis A. Coser in the 1960s pointed out that certain categories of individuals are so placed in the social structure that they are barred from legitimate access to personal achievement. Criminal activity then becomes the ladder to *achievement status.*

As difficult as it may be to understand, one means to underclass achievement status is through a show of domination through violence— first among competing peers, then by marauding in other sections of the city with increasingly bolder activity. So what we have is a criminal subclass that achieves social status through violence.

One environment conducive to criminal activity is the home that can be entered under cover of night—especially homes of unsuspecting people who live in neighborhoods not used to intrusion, hence less prepared for intruders.

Violent intruders, then, are persons in whom none of the socially inhibiting factors are active (factors internalized in more conventional personalities). In the assailant's background of social learning there are characterological developments conducive to violent acting out. Economic deprivation and its resultant frustration translate into anger, often to uncontrollable rage that smolders within, seeking an outlet. Felons sometimes describe themselves as driven by forces outside themselves, the unexplainable "I had to do what I had to do." This compulsion is accompanied by distorted perceptions of one's power over other persons. In a twisted way, power and status seeking drive such individuals.

Erich Fromme, in *The Heart of Man,* reminds us that it is psychological impotence that drives some individuals to violence and sadism. There are some people so vacuous, so dead inside, that they only feel alive when manipulating, controlling, or destroying other life.

What we have is a hunger for status and power that cannot be satisfied in other ways, often accompanied by a generalized paranoia as a result of having been shunned by others—perhaps at first by parents. If in early childhood one has not known the attention of caring people, one is incapacitated in terms of becoming a caring person. Instead, one becomes cold, calculating, insensitive to the value of other people. Understandably, there develops a complete distrust of society and everyone who is a part of it. Sometimes such persons carry deep scars from the hurts and embarrassments they've received at the hands of various authorities—home, school, job. It is easy to see how early victimization generates compensating violence in approaching others.

Prominent New York psychiatrist, Willard Gaylin,[3] explains that the feeling of inferiority in relation to peers can turn toward increasing non-acceptance of oneself. Self-rejection renders it impossible to respect others, making it easy to victimize people who thus have no significance whatsoever to one's own life. Then, as is so often the case in the subclass, if one has himself been the victim of brutality, often unjustly so, this confirms violence as conventional behavior. Moreover, should police brutality be experienced, the message already entrenched gets further reinforcement.

Because such individuals are part of a peer group with similar backgrounds and tendencies, friends being violent predators who brutalize others. They do not see themselves as deviant; rather, just fully conforming members of a familiar social group. For them, identification with violent types is but the living out of normal association.

Unfortunately, TV and videotape watching reinforces the code of violence in a way it does not reinforce violent behavior in the more socially constrained members of society. So violence becomes a "legitimate" method of resolving disputes and of gaining what otherwise is beyond one's grasp. In this kind of unevenly rewarded society, guns are equalizers and knives are silent reinforcers. To a predator's sense of logic, physical assault is a fairly assured way to get many jobs done quickly and efficiently—indeed, a pretty slick way to distribute society's benefits.

This mentality makes it easy to engage in assaults with no sensitivity for the victims' well-being. Where no matured sense of compassion is developed, no regrets are later engendered. Should an outcome be grave bodily injury or death, well, this "just has to happen." Thus, the life of others is held indifferently. The concept "sanctity of life" lies quite beyond the mind of the criminal predator. People are like other "things" in life, simply effective means for the accomplishment of desired ends. People are "used" instrumentally. People become expendable whenever necessity requires it. Here we understand the code which prompts violent predators to break and enter homes—to rob, rape, and kill.

We see, then, that there are members of a criminal subclass for whom killing itself brings reward. Rapists, for example, as we shall see in our next chapter, are not driven by sexual desire but act out an impulse to attain superiority and self-importance through having overwhelmed another person, sometimes destroying that person in the process. Their victims are not viewed in terms of personal relationships, not valued as persons, but as necessary objects in the rapist's destructive grasp for dominance. Nothing about the victim has real significance apart from what can be stripped away. Any quality of personal being is totally missing. But whether the intruder is a rapist, burglar, deranged predator, or desperate adolescent, so far, as risks and costs to himself are concerned, his single most important need is to get what he wants, survive the event and get away unscathed, all tracks covered. He himself calculates whether this requires only quick exit, brute strength, a silent weapon such as a knife, or equalizer—a gun.

If the world of violent intruders is peopled by a variety of types of individuals, so also is the world of householders. Neither group is predictable in terms of response to a critical confrontation. No definitive counsel can be given that covers all situations, personalities, and backgrounds. A householder has a great number of considerations to sift through in determining how he or she may prepare to meet the threat we are examining. In the face of risk, the intelligent householder will want to know all the facts and weigh the options.

NOTES

1. Wright, James D. and Peter H. Rossi, *Armed and Considered Dangerous: A Survey of Felons and Their Firearms.* Hawthorne, NY: Aldine de Guyter, 1983, pp. 141–159.
2. Chaiken, Jan M. and Marcia R. Chaiken, *Varieties of Criminal Behavior.* Santa Monica, CA: The Rand Corp., 1982. *See* Gary Kleck, "Crime Control Through the Private Use of Armed Force," 35 *Social Problems* No. 1 (Feb. 1988) pp. 1–21.
3. Gaylin, Willard, *The Rage Within: Anger in Modern Life.* New York: Simon and Schuster, 1984. (*See* Petersilia, Greenwood, Peter W., and Marvin Lavin; *Criminal Careers of Habitual Felons.* Santa Monica, CA: The Rand Corp., 1985; Wilson, James Q., and Hernstein, Richard J. *Crime and Human Nature.* New York: Simon and Schuster, 1985).

Chapter 4

WHAT IF HE'S A RAPIST?

> I'm not going to tell you why I'm a rapist, but I'll say this: I do it because I like it. It's like hunting, but easier. Working women are my game, and they're usually pretty easy targets. Mostly that's because they travel by themselves, work by themselves, and are so dumb about taking care of themselves.
>
> I live in a big city, but I often hunt in the suburbs. . . . Most of the time a simple lock on the door stops me, and I stay away from places where I see people coming and going. I don't take stupid chances. Most often I can walk right in—or she lets me in. The thing is that I look pretty harmless and pretty ordinary. In fact, I try to look like I belong wherever I am. I'm deliberately clean-cut. Nobody who knows me would think I'd do such a thing.
>
> Darkness is my friend, but I don't always hunt after dark. I pick my women because of their situation, which I've studied before I move. Looks don't mean a lot to me, but she's always alone in a place where nobody else will come, or I get her to go to one. You'd be amazed how easy that is!
>
> About self-defense for women: Don't make me laugh. I don't go after a woman who looks like she'd be able to whip me in a fight. The best protection from me you working women have is company or a locked door you're smart enough not to open when I ask. Remember, there are a lot of guys out there like me who are looking for you.

So, in part, reads a letter to Ann Landers from an anonymous rapist.[1] Scary? You bet! Especially when the most frequent place a forcible stranger-rape occurs is the victim's residence. According to the Bureau of Justice Statistics, more than one-third of all rapes occur in the victim's own home, an extraordinarily high rate, even allowing for the percentage that are not stranger but acquaintance rapes. The sad fact is that predatory rapists are not at all surprised at finding houses unsecured, inadequately protected, easy targets to make a surprise entry.

The 1990 midsummer hearings of the Senate Judiciary Committee on Violent Crime concluded that rape has increased four times as fast as the overall crime rate over the last decade. A recent issue of *Crime Control Digest,* a Washington-based crime news service,[2] states that a woman is raped every six minutes, or sixteen women confronted by rapists every hour. In the past fifteen years, assaults against women ages twenty to twenty-four have increased by over forty-eight percent. All categories of violent crime against women are rising at the highest rates.

We can now expect that three out of every four women in the United States will be the victims of at least one violent crime in their lifetime — ten times the number that die in automobile accidents. Despite the higher number of reported rapes each year, it is estimated that only 50 percent of all rapes are ever reported (some experts peg this far lower). As indexed in the FBI's annual *Uniform Crime Reports,*[3] rape has been called *the most underreported crime of all crimes.* Reasons for this are generally said to be fear of reprisal by rapists who threatened them, humiliation or rejection by the court system, and public misconceptions of the victim's character ("she must have asked for it; women aren't always blameless, you know").

More than ever before, rapists are getting away with their crime. Of the increased numbers of cases reported, in recent history less than forty percent of all cases are closed with arrests, as few as five percent of these go to court, and only about two percent end in conviction. Over the past twenty years, the percentage of cases closed with conviction has declined from over seventy-two percent to less than forty-nine percent. This translates to one conviction for every 500 cases reported!

SURELY, NOT IN THE SUBURBS!

Of course, people immediately surmise that the statistics refer to inner-city, high-crime areas. But from 1986 on, there has been an estimated average five percent annual rise in rape cases in America's suburbs, compared with a two percent crime rise nationwide. Today, that increase continues at an even higher rate.

Changing factors contribute to this rise. For instance, more women are choosing to remain single and live alone or with one other woman. There are greater numbers of single-parent households. More women, in other words, are living in the suburbs, alone, with one other woman, or with young children. For rapists, suburbs are happy hunting grounds, especially because rape is least expected there and because, in general, precautions are fewer.

A Denver study found that the major proportion of rapes occur between midnight and 4 A.M., while the victim is asleep in her easily entered bedroom. Weekends account for the highest rape days in the week, with summer months having a higher incidence than any other period of the year. As to the rapist's age, more than half are under twenty-five. Most are likely armed with a screwdriver which is used to break in, a knife, or less frequently a gun. Besides rape, the intruder may brutalize, even murder, simply selecting some blunt object in the house as a bludgeon.

This is the point made by Detective Ellen King of the Sex Crimes Division of the New York City Police Department. She believes that frequently robbery and rape are jointly practiced because they are closely related in the psychological makeup of the criminal. She explains that short of murder (which takes the whole life), rape is the ultimate "taking" crime. And because violence is always an element, rape is always a life-threatening situation. Precisely for this reason, any method employed for deterring rape may backfire with deadly consequences. And, so far as burglars are concerned, rape is often an extension of the burglary for the simple reason that opportunity is there to be seized. Rape supplies an exciting supplement of personal achievement. From an opportunistic occasion, any violence can follow.

Contrary to popular opinion, rape poses a threat to all women, younger and older alike, of every class, every walk of life, and in every location. *But,* you say, *rape is something that happens to women who are careless, sexy, who flaunt their sexuality—you know, the inviting type.* Not so.

While no doubt some rapes are committed by men who find themselves with an opportunity they cannot resist, these are fewer in number and least worrisome. Driven by sexual deprivation, fantasies of ever-more exciting sex, or simple opportunism, these men are not the dangerous, more violent types. Common also is so-called acquaintance rape, but neither does this concern us primarily. Our focus is upon the compulsively driven predatory rapist whose career evidences a high incidence of sadism, brutality, and murder. By their own frequent admission, these rapists are motivated by violent non-sexual impulses.

THE PERSON WHO RAPES

In 1985, the National Center for the Analysis of Violent Crime was founded at the FBI Academy in Quantico, Virginia. While it is a relatively new weapon in the war against violence, it is already highly successful, its expertise having assisted police in every state and in several foreign countries. A major objective is to make the results of its work available to the 17,000 separate police agencies in the United States.

Through the means of interviews with incarcerated criminals fitting any number of diverse categories of violent crime, through consultative work with specific police cases in various state locations, and assisted by courses at the University of Virginia employing psychologists, sociologists and criminologists, profiles of violent criminals are being established.

Incidental to the concerns of this chapter, special agent Roy Hazelwood of the Behavioral Science Services Unit is now recognized for his success in creating psychological profiles of rapists. Numerous investigators who have studied rapists in recent decades, of whom some shall be cited, form the background of Hazelwood's work.

Doctor Pauline Bart, sociologist and rape specialist at the University of Illinois, in a study based on interviews with 94 women who either were raped or were victims of an uncompleted attempt, says that it is not possible to categorize the physical or personality traits of rapists; they are beyond stereotyping. For instance, a rapist may be dressed in the same suit as the banker who lives next door. A woman who observes a man following her may be deceived by his appearance, saying to herself, *He's carrying a briefcase; he can't be dangerous.* For some rapists, it is *fun* to disguise themselves for purposes of additional surprise.

Joyce Mallman's studies also show it to be almost impossible to identify a potential rapist in advance. Although emotionally disturbed persons, they are not obvious *mental cases.* Found in all walks of life, they often lead otherwise normal lives and work in conventional occupations. Most unexpectedly, many are family men with stable marriages, attesting to a normal sex life. In general, however, there is a deeply hidden loathing of women—all women, or one woman in particular. Rape is the acting out of this hostility. One writer characterized it *From rage to rape.*

A large percentage of rapists are repeaters, serial rapists, raping again and again. Nothing is ultimately satisfied in their repeated acts, only stimulated. When apprehended, what they tell interviewers is not about being sexually satisfied, even sexually motivated. Rather, their need, although an insatiable one, is not sexual, but that of needing to gain control over another person, a person who most likely can be dominated and humiliated by the one act the rapist is capable of accomplishing.

Researchers have compared rapists of this character with arsonists. For both arsonists and rapists, what is done is secondary to the meaning of what is done. It is exhilaration (the *high*) for what the accomplishment means—becoming a powerful achiever, against which no successful preventive stand can be taken. As the arsonist brings about submission of a whole community to his single act, so the rapist brings about the submission of an individual to his act.

In a recent study entitled *The Mind of a Rapist,*[4] an investigative team asked the question, *Why do men do it?* The answers were varied, no single profile emerging. Opportunity, psychological need, lust—it happens for all of these reasons, yet often for none of these predominantly.

Convicted rapist Roger Smith, twenty-six, interviewed in Atlanta's Metro Correctional Institute, replied, "I never thought about it. I don't know what the hell I was looking for. The opportunity occurred and I just took advantage of it." Roger, a married mechanic, had stopped to help a woman whose car had broken down. Lingering, he unexpectedly found himself assaulting her.

Bill, a serial rapist, methodically sought out his victims in their own apartments, attacking seven women at knife point before being caught. He had no other criminal interests or activities.

James, a forty-two-year-old business man in middle management, a man with a fine family, was aware only of a vague *frustration* in his life. He liked to pick up females in pairs and rape one of them in the terrified presence of the other. *Inside is a rage,* he said. *I've a need to have what I do witnessed.*

Anger, deep and dark, is a common thread. Something invariably has gone wrong in a life, affecting self-esteem. A 1982 study of rapists in Oregon found that as many as 80 percent were abused children, their own victimization resulting in a kind of emotional death, incapacitating them for feeling compassion. Thus, many rapists depersonalize their victims, making them mere objects. Rape authority Eugene Porter, California psychologist, said, *I haven't seen a rapist who didn't have a childhood horror story.* Exaggeration perhaps, but it makes a point.

We are told that one to three percent do murder their victims, another fifteen to eighteen percent inflict serious bodily harm. Menachim Amir, however, puts physical violence as high as eighty-five percent.

There is a growing body of opinion expressed by Richard Seely, director of Minnesota's Intensive Treatment Program for Sexual Aggressiveness, *It's his thinking that's dysfunctional, not his sexuality.* Current thought seems to be that rape is both an act of sex and an act of violence, not purely one or the other.

Psychologist Nicholas Groth, director of Forensic Mental Health Associates,[5] who has seen more than three thousand sex offenders in fifteen years of practice, says, "We look at rape as the sexual expression of aggression, rather than as the aggressive expression of sexuality." He adds that most of his patients were not sexually deprived at the time they committed rape.

About ten years ago, Groth established a typology of rapists that is still standard with many treatment centers, although considered by others outdated. Three types of motivation are anger, power, and sadism.

(1) Anger Attack-Rape

The rapist is getting even for some wrong he feels was done to him, although perhaps not by the person he rapes. Anger attack-rape is usually unpremeditated, impulsive, and ruthlessly violent. The desire is to vent anger by degrading the victim, at the same time employing the most violent power at the rapist's command.

(2) Power Attack-Rape

This also is a form of compensation, usually for unsureness of personal competence or adequacy. Rape gives a sense of power, of control, of achievement. The victim is subjected to the rapist's overwhelming power.

Power, said Voltaire, *consists of making others act as I choose.* Max Weber, pioneer sociologist, saw power as present *wherever I have the chance to assert my own will against the resistance of others.*

Under a twisted impulse to power, the rapist, when resisted, becomes all the more excited and violent. There is an accompanying loathing of women as inferior, together with the need to strike back for some humiliation or rejection (real or imagined), experienced at the hand of a woman. In his ability to overcome resistance, he finds, as someone once put it, *the elixir of power.* So it is easy to understand why the woman who resists must be very sure she's in control and confident of her ability to master her assailant. Otherwise, she invites an escalation of brutality. Strangely, it is reported by some women who submitted without resistance that the rapist seemed provoked to even greater brutality when he found he wasn't getting the excitement which resistance had the power to provoke.

In the same vein, Bertrand de Jouvenal wrote ages ago that " . . . a man feels himself more of a man when he is imposing himself and making others the instruments of his will," something which gives him *incomparable pleasure.* Add to this the word of Hannah Arendt that "the implements of violence, like all other tools, are designed and used for the purpose of multiplying natural strength until, in the last stage of their development, they can substitute for it."

(3) Sadistic Attack-Rape

This is eroticized aggression, not aggressive eroticism. The rapist is excited by forcible rape in ways that consensual sex cannot excite him. To create the new excitement, the rape tends toward sadistic sexual distortion. All too often this leads to the inadvertent (although sometimes subconsciously desired) death of the victim.

Now we understand that if the rapist's physical strength is unavailing, only then will he turn to a weapon; what he wishes put to the test is personal power. His demonstration of strength first comes through overpowering his victim, followed by violent rape which forces from his victim the sick pleasure he seeks (not always so pleasurable at that). This adds up to a total demeaning of her person in relation to his and a degrading of everything she has to give. Then occurs the final obliteration of any symbolization of the victim's ability to resist his *superiority;* he brutally beats her into complete incapacitation. This may or may not end in homicide—the unretractable evidence of his total domination.

Doctor Gene Abel, professor of psychiatry at Emory University, who has studied hundreds of rapists over the past twenty years, believes that rapists suffer from a form of cognitive disorder that allows them to justify their actions as well as commit them. It is also the consensus of treatment centers that few rapists seek treatment on their own because in their eyes they are not deviants at all, hence not in need of treatment. They can accept punishment easier than treatment.

THREE CATEGORIES OF RAPE

It may be helpful to review the three categories of rape: (1) acquaintance rape, (2) forced-consent rape, (3) stranger-attack rape. In acquaintance rape, the situation involves a familiar person with whom there is presumed willingness but where the woman has either given a mistaken signal or, having first encouraged sex, changes her mind and resists. In stranger attack-rape, the woman is an unknown person whom the rapist randomly selects as his victim. Our concern is only with stranger attack-rape that takes place in the woman's residence by an intruder.

Although not a general rule, rapists generally seek women who will submit under force. Single women are preferred as being generally the most vulnerable and without the possibility of assisted resistance. Single women are least likely to represent a complex set of circumstances to deal with. Highest at risk are women who appear trusting, unlikely to be threatening, easy to frighten, hence most subject to intimidation.[6]

Guided by these probabilities, the rapist usually studies the routines of his intended victim, noting habits of travel, social contacts, and general awareness—how careful she is in controlling or not controlling her situation. If she appears to be an assertive type, in command of her surroundings, a *take-charge* woman likely to resist with utmost determination and skill (perhaps even armed as a safeguard), he's not interested. Some resistance, yes, but no all-out effort to thwart and hence overcome him.

LEARNING FROM IMPRISONED RAPISTS

A survey of rapists incarcerated in California's State Hospital at Atascadero[7] provides information about rape motivation: Over 50 percent raped to achieve *dominance, humiliation, and/or revenge;* 27 percent reported enhanced excitement when the victim resisted; fully 34 percent said that overcoming their victim's resistance made them feel *powerful* or *good.* On the day of their crime, more than three-quarters confessed feeling frustrated, upset or depressed, ending up by venting their hostilities on a helpless victim. (Consider the potential here among the underclass, the socially and economically frustrated.) Mark Kroeker recalls supervising the investigation of a Los Angeles suspect who burglarized, raped, then burned eight elderly women.

Victims need not necessarily be attractive, and although over 60 percent of the rapists interviewed at Atascadero had been upset over a particular woman, they chose instead to brutalize some other female— whoever was most accessible, be it an acquaintance, stranger or whatever.

A national victimization survey by Matthew Yeager[8] reports that only 11 percent of all reported rapes involved guns, 6 percent involved knives. A much higher weapons' involvement was reported by studies in both San Francisco and Philadelphia. In San Francisco, nearly twice as many rapists carried knives as carried guns. Whereas 75 percent of the rapists surveyed at the Atascadero facility had a weapon with them during the rape, only 16 percent actually used it to inflict injury. Most injuries were caused by sheer physical force. Yeager's study of seventeen

American cities shows nearly 19 percent of serious injuries inflicted were by physical force. In the Philadelphia study, over 20 percent of the victims had been *beaten brutally* before, during, or after the rape. According to Menachem Amir,[9] over 85 percent of reported rapes involve some sort of violence. Thus, women can reasonably assume that a rapist, whoever he might be, is likely to cause great bodily harm, if not actual death.

The FBI *Uniform Crime Reports* probably underestimates the incidents of rape-murders (less than 2 percent), since these are routinely treated indiscriminately as homicides, not specifically as rape-murders. As Susan Brownmiller points out, it is often impossible to determine whether a murder victim was also a victim of attempted rape, since the rapist-murderer may have killed out of frustration with his own impotence or inability to satisfactorily complete the rape. Thus, the higher probability of a far greater number of murders being in fact *rape-murders*.

In the class of rapes termed *acquaintance rape*, the rapist is a familiar person, perhaps a former husband, boyfriend, business associate, neighbor, or casual social acquaintance. At the time a familiar person makes his sexual advance, the possibilities of brutality are exceedingly difficult for a woman to assess. It might seem unlikely to her that she will suffer brutality at the hands of a socially acceptable acquaintance. Yet, one exhaustive study by Amir[9] indicates that acquaintance rapes are frequently more brutal than those perpetrated by strangers. Sometimes a hidden grudge over rejection, or former humiliation, seethes within that acquaintance until *friendly advances* become driven by a desire to get back in a passionate way.

Amir found that slightly fewer than half of all rapes are committed by people familiar with their victims. In contrast, the Atascadero facility recorded 21 percent with acquaintances (most of those only seen casually), while nearly 80 percent were with strangers. Of course, the probability is that most acquaintance-type rapes are among those least often reported. Still in all, the percentage of stranger rapes is alarmingly high.

According to *Uniform Crime Reports,* slightly more than half of all murder victims are acquaintances. Neighbors and acquaintances are especially dangerous, even though least suspected. When seduction or attempted manipulation prove unsuccessful, the resultant frustration provokes these men even more. There is the factor of vengeance which follows a failure to seduce.

WHAT IS *GREAT BODILY HARM?*

Kates and Engberg[10] identify four types:

(1) **Physical Pain.** This refers especially to injury to the sexually abused areas of the body. While often brutal, this kind of injury seldom produces permanent effects. Does this, then, qualify as *great bodily harm?* A difficult point to make.

(2) **Venereal Disease.** Sex offenders are roughly twenty times more likely to transmit venereal disease than other sex partners. Still, venereal disease can be medically treated so as not to threaten great or permanent harm. Thus the common question whether venereal disperser qualifies as "great bodily harm." But what has changed the picture drastically in our day is the threat of death by AIDS should it be the transmitted disease.

(3) **Pregnancy.** Granted, pregnancy poses a special type of threat, inasmuch as there is no prior opportunity for contraceptive protection, and a child constitutes a long-term burden and responsibility that may do permanent damage to the mother. But does this constitute *great bodily harm?* Pretty "iffy." The consequences of having a child are more serious than the physical aspect, but only a threat to that small percentage of women for whom pregnancy under any circumstances is a risk. The real threat is upon her future, her possible need for psychological therapy, even social welfare aid. This leads to the fourth and final consideration.

(4) **Psychological Trauma.** This personal damage is not subject to measurement. However, post-rape psychiatric evaluations consistently show patterns of serious and lasting effects—what the U.S. Supreme Court has described as *the ultimate violation of the self.* Does this qualify as *great bodily harm?* In the opinion of many experts, the answer would be yes.

With respect to relative harm, sexual humiliation and loss of self-esteem may prove more damaging than other aspects of rape. As Kates and Engberg point out, the sheer horror and terror of such an experience, the fear of possible consequences, and the perceived beastliness of the act can create ineradicable mental images of the most fearful type.

Rape trauma syndrome,[11] as it is technically referred to, can create an uncertain and frightening world, a disastrously negative self-image, strong feelings of shame and worthlessness, paranoia—all conditions which tend toward depression and withdrawal and, in turn, to all the social and economic as well as psychological handicaps that may attend a woman the remainder of her lifetime. Thus, whatever the circumstances and however little physical damage, the woman may tend to blame herself and thus lose her sense of self-worth.

While numbers of women apparently come through rape experiences relatively unscathed, those with previously unstable personalities, or unsettled social connectedness, are likely to become seriously psychotic and socially damaged. Understandably, a significant number will attempt suicide, some successfully.

The more the severity of rape is understood, the easier to grasp why the Model Penal Code authorizes the use of deadly force when necessary to prevent it. An armed woman will at times be a viable deterrent.

COMMUNITY RAPE-DETERRENT PROGRAMS

Impressively, some localities have had dramatic reductions in crime following highly publicized defensive-use handgun training programs. Best known is Orlando, Florida's program undertaken because of an abnormally high rate of rape in that city. For six months, Orlando police trained women in the use of handguns, making it widely known throughout the city. Rape incidents fell roughly 88 percent. Interestingly, immediately adjacent areas—even Florida statewide—continued to experience their previous high rates, even increased rates in some localities, as was true of the United States as a whole. The Orlando effect was indeed dramatic!

To close this chapter, a personal note by Mr. Small is relevant. One day while writing this chapter, I found my devotional time occupied with reading the third chapter of St. Paul's letter to Timothy. There the Apostle predicts the following: *There will be terrible times in the last days.* He envisions the conditions using such words as *unholy, without self-control, brutal, treacherous,* etc.. I was especially struck by the following: *For among them are those who make their way into households and capture weak women* (verse 6 RSV). The word *capture* is literally *gain control over.*

NOTES

1. Ann Landers, "A Rapist Issues Warning on 'Easy Targets'," *Los Angeles Times,* July 6, 1987.
2. *Crime Control Digest.* Washington, DC: Washington Crime News Service, July 2, 1990.

3. "Crime of Rape," *Bureau of Statistics Bulletin*. United States Department of Justice, Washington, DC, March 1985.
4. "The Mind of the Rapist," (Special Report) *Newsweek*. July 23, 1990, p. 46; Neil M. Malamuth, "Rape Proclivity Among Males," *Journal of Social Issues* 37, No. 4 (1981) pp. 138–157.
5. Groth, A. N., *Men Who Rape: The Psychology of the Offender*. New York: Plenum Books, 1979. *See* Sussman, Lee and Sally Bordwell, *The Rapist File*. New York: Chelsea, 1981; Baron, Larry and Murray Strauss, *Four Theories of Rape in American Society*. New Haven, CT: Yale University, 1989; Tobach, Ethel, and Suzanne Sunday (eds), *Violence Against Women: A Critique of the Sociology of Rape*. New York: Gordion, 1985; Linz, Daniel G., Donnerstein, Edward I., and Steven Penrod, "Effects of Long-term Exposure to Violent and Sexually Degrading Depictions of Women," *Journal of Personality and Social Psychology* 55 (Nov. 1988) pp. 758–759.
6. Carol Ruth Silver, and Don B. Kates, Jr., "Self-Defense, Handgun Ownership, and the Independence of Women in a Violent, Sexist Society," *Restricting Handguns: The Liberal Skeptics Speak Out*. Kates, Don B. Jr. (ed), Croton-on-Hudson, NY: North River, 1979.
7. Wright, James D., and Peter H. Rossi, *Armed and Dangerous: A Survey of Felons and Their Firearms*. Hawthorne, NY: Aldine de Guyter, 1986.
8. Yeager, Matthew G., Alviani, Joseph D., and Nancy Loving, *How Well Does the Handgun Protect You and Your Family?* Handgun Control, Inc., Staff Technical Report 2, Washington, DC: United States Conference of Mayors, 1976; Herbert Koppel, "Lifetime Likelihood of Victimization," *Bureau of Justice Statistics, Technical Reports*. United States Department of Justice, Washington, DC, March, 1987.
9. *See* Amir, Menachim, *Patterns of Forcible Rape*. Chicago: University of Chicago, 1971. See Beneke, Timothy, *Men on Rape*. New York: Anchor Books, 1987; Brownmiller, Susan, *Against Our Will: Men, Women, and Rape*. New York: Random, 1976.
10. Kates, Don B, Jr., and Nancy Jean Engberg, "Deadly Force Self-Defense Against Rape," 15 *University of California Davis Law Review* (1982).
11. Burgess, Ann W. and Lynda L. Holmstrom, *Rape Trauma Syndrome in Forcible Rape*. New York: Prentice-Hall, 1974. *See* Burgess, Ann W., *Rape and Sexual Assault: A Research Handbook*. Garland, 1984; Silberman, Elaine, *The Rape Victim*. Washington, DC: American Psychiatric Press, 1976.; Rose, Deborah S., "Worse Than Death: Psychodynamics of Rape Victims and the Need for Psycho-Therapy," *American Journal of Psychiatry*. July 1986; E. Salholz, "A Frightening Aftermath: Concern About AIDS Adds to the Trauma of Rape," *Newsweek*. July 23, 1990, p. 53.

Chapter 5

CAN WE COUNT ON PROTECTION?

Inasmuch as any one of us is a potential victim of intruders, where do we look for protection? The conventional answer: *To the police, of course.* But this is not really the case.

HOW SURE IS POLICE PROTECTION?

Conventional wisdom assumes that the police will protect and defend the individual citizen in an expeditious manner whenever he or she is in need of such assistance. To a point this is true, and we owe an extraordinary debt to the men and women who constantly risk their lives on behalf of citizens. Nevertheless, police departments are burdened by limitations that can prove fatal to an individual in need of immediate help.

In an era of budget-cutting and holding the line on tax increases for public services, even having to cut back, many municipal budgets have become severely strained, resulting all too frequently in a significant reduction in the quality of police services, notably in their ability to respond promptly to emergency calls. Personnel are stretched beyond capacity. Increasing population density adds to the problem.

In some metropolitan areas, a call to the 911 emergency number may be greeted by an answering machine asking the caller to stay on the line until his or her call can be processed—hardly response to an emergency! If one actually gets through promptly to an emergency operator, particularly in a city such as Los Angeles, one is going to have to wait, on average, something over eight minutes for the police to arrive at the scene. Note that this is average response time. In some instances, response will be quicker than average, slower in others. If one is attempting to hold off a criminal intruder, waiting an indeterminate length of time is not particularly promising when time is of utmost importance to victim safety. The assailant usually knows time to be to his advantage, especially since the most vicious crimes are carried out in seconds, not minutes!

45

Newsweek looked at the reality of 911, calling it *a logjammed nightmare.*[1] A study by the Police Executive Research Forum shows that in less than three percent of the time does rapid police response lead to an immediate arrest. Harvard University criminal justice professor Mark Moore, says that calling 911 is not all that effective in dealing with crime. Los Angeles police estimate that only 30 percent of the 2.5 million calls they answered in 1989 were top-priority emergencies, in Boston less than 10 percent. The very diversity of calls is causing police commanders to lose control over how to allocate police services. Ironically, slow response time occurs when dispatchers seek to interview the caller sufficiently to determine if a real emergency exists, a necessary means to sort out urgent from non-urgent.

Paxton Quigley quotes Ed Davis, former chief of the Los Angeles Police Department: "Crime is so far out of hand, we can't protect the average citizen. He must protect himself."[2] Davis doesn't say how, but this points to the use of lethal instruments—to guns. The TV images of Korean merchants protecting their shops with semiautomatic *Uzis* during the recent Los Angeles disorder sent a powerful message to the American public. This message was all the more forceful in light of the disorganization and apparent impotency of the Los Angeles Police to quell large-scale anarchy for almost twenty-four hours—and then only with help from the military. This situation again raises the question with many people as to whether or not police can effectively protect the average citizen.

Another uncertainty in relying upon the police as one's sole protection has to do with expected police responsibilities over against actual legal responsibilities. Mr. Average Citizen believes that the police are obligated to provide protection to individual citizens, a reasonable conclusion if you are paying taxes for such services. But is it true?

CASE IN POINT

A notable example is *Warren et al.* v. *the District of Columbia* (1981).[3] The U.S. Supreme Court invoked the *fundamental principle* of American law that "a government and its agents are under no general duty to provide public services, such as police protection, to any particular individual citizen."

Briefly stated, three women who shared a two-story apartment had their rear door broken in by two violent male intruders. Two of the women managed to hide from the assailants and during this time made two calls to the police for help. The police, other than knocking on the front door, made no effort to enter the house as the result of the first call. They completely ignored a second call. Eventually, the hiding women were discovered by the assailants, who then proceeded to rob and rape all three women, forcing them to perform perverted acts upon each other. Finally the criminals left the scene. The women sued the District of Columbia for gross negligence. They lost! The court held that the police existed to protect society, not necessarily any particular member of society. Incidentally, the very strict gun laws in the District of Columbia are designed to make it impossible for private citizens to keep a firearm for defense purposes!

CAN WE RELY UPON GUNS?

The question comes down to whether to employ measures equally effective as those of the armed criminal. Given the problems inherent in reliance upon the police as a first line of defense, a great number of people have opted to own a personal firearm. Some choose a handgun, some a shotgun—both effective weapons (several significant studies indicate that almost one-half of the households in the United States presently possess a firearm which they regard as a defense weapon).[4]

In the authors' state, one in eight Southern California households were victimized by crimes involving guns between 1990 and 1991. In a *Los Angeles Times* poll taken between April 9–15 (before the riots escalated), three out of four residents said they planned to buy a gun in the coming year for self-defense. Similar reports are coming from other large metropolitan areas. Gun shops are being emptied.

A Gallup poll found that between 1983 and 1986, gun ownership among women rose to more than twelve million, while women considering a gun purchase had quadrupled. In a *Ladies Home Journal* survey, half the respondents reported owning guns, 40 percent saying possession was primarily for personal protection.

Reputable independent national surveys consistently estimate handguns are used more often in repelling crime than in committing it, Gary Kleck claiming approximately 645,000 defense uses versus 580,000 criminal misuses. Of those captured or scared off, it is estimated attackers were captured or driven off without a shot being fired fully half the time—an impressive argument for deterrence, despite the fact that those driven off are rarely reported. In 43 percent of the instances, attackers were wounded or killed, while just 7 percent escaped. Kleck's figures show that citizens nationwide lawfully kill two to five times more criminals than do police. For example, in California the figure is twice as many; in Chicago and Cleveland three times as many.[5]

In the popular media, a lot of spurious information has been disseminated. Since for Christians the issue is an ethical one, they of all people need to take a sober, objective look at both sides of the question. They, if any, ought to weigh the social factors and then put it all within a biblical, ethical perspective. We'll undertake this later on. In the meanwhile, the task requires that we look at two fairly mundane aspects, namely, both the dangers and the effectiveness of firearms ownership for home defense.

EVIDENT PERILS OF FIREARMS OWNERSHIP

A consistent media theme in recent years has centered around the idea that firearms are inherently dangerous to own, especially if they are readily accessible. A fairly typical statement in support of this theme comes from Michael Nagler's book, *America Without Violence*. The University of California professor makes this claim: "Statistics show that if you keep a gun in your home, it is five times more likely to harm someone in your own family than an intruder. People who keep guns are twice as likely to meet with murder or accidental death or injury or suicide than those who do not."[6]

In similar fashion, Pete Shields, chairman of *Handgun Control, Inc.* writes: "The home handgun is far more likely to kill or injure family members and friends than anyone who breaks in, and is especially harmful to young adults and to children."[7]

But wait. Massad Ayoob, recognized authority in the field of personal protection, himself a longtime professional police figure and teacher, has referred to this as *the evil talisman* orientation towards firearms.[8] The idea is that somehow the very ownership of a weapon will almost magically bring misfortune to the house in which it is located. Three variants of the theme buoy up this opinion: first, that firearms ownership invariably leads to accidental death or injuries. Second, that guns in the home are an open invitation for bringing domestic violence to a lethal end. Thirdly, the *evil talisman* theme perceives armed defense as ineffective. A corollary is that home defense guns make violent intruders more likely to attack, with the assailant disarming the homeowner, then turning the gun against him or her. Let's briefly consider each of these claims.

(1) Firearms Accidents

What about the danger of accidents posed by firearms ownership, especially those involving children? Here emotions run high because to lose a loved one through any kind of accident is a major blow, but death by a gun accident is particularly bitter.

After giving careful attention to this problem, Wright and Rossi concluded that a large proportion of such injuries are unreported and that estimates of such injuries vary so widely as to afford only general estimates. Nor are injuries discriminated as they should be, some being very serious, others only superficial.

Information on accidental death is more obtainable, more reliable. To most people it comes as a surprise to discover the death rate from firearms accidents is relatively low. The National Safety Council in 1989 reported that out of more than 20,000 deaths from all causes of children ages one to fourteen, over 4,000 were due to motor vehicle accidents, compared to about 250 due to gun accidents. For example, gun accidents involving children ages five to fourteen occur at a rate of seven per million children. In the last year for which data is available, the actual number of children in this age bracket who died from this cause totalled 235. (Every summer upwards of one thousand toddlers drown in swimming pools.) Most children killed by guns are victims of hunting accidents, not handguns kept for self-defense.

Although natural sensitivities decry the death of even a single child (or adult for that matter), one wonders if this relatively small number of gun deaths might better be prevented through serious safety education (perhaps mandatory for gun purchasers, as the State of California decided), rather than through attempting the wholesale banning of all firearms from public possession.

Curiously, we do not hear a similar cry for a total ban on swimming pools! Or ladders! Or bicycles! Or bathtubs! But individuals are acculturated to loathe guns as dreaded objects, seeing them only for the worst they are capable of.

Among fifteen- to twenty-five-year-olds, firearms death rates are somewhat higher, understandably because more teenagers are being introduced to guns; hence, the risk of their getting to them is much greater.

Unfortunately, teenagers are often trusted when they're not ready for such trust. In this age bracket, firearms accidents account for a death rate of twelve per million. By comparison, in the latest figures, the annual number of drowning deaths in this age group was 479—the next highest cause of accidental death.

More to our concern, fewer than two percent of fatal gun accidents involve a person accidentally shooting someone mistaken for an intruder. Actually, on average fewer than twenty-eight such incidents or this sort occur annually, compared with nearly 700,000 defensive gun uses. This translates into about 1 in 26,000 chances of a defensive gun use resulting in this kind of accident.

MANIPULATING FIGURES

A frequent ploy of anti-gun advocates is to include firearms suicide in their accident summaries, thus giving a highly inflated view of the total number of accidental deaths, when the only common factor is the instrumentality, a gun. Apparently, Nagler, cited earlier, relied upon a spurious study by Rushford et al. which is widely quoted in popular anti-gun literature.[9] As Silver and Kates point out:

> The authors of this study manufactured their statistic by an unannounced transfer of gun suicides into the tiny category of gun accident deaths. Since the number of yearly handgun suicides is about forty-four times the number of accidental handgun fatalities, the effect of this sleight-of-hand is to exaggerate the number of accidents by upwards of 4,400 percent, rendering the accident-to-self-defense comparison worthless.[10]

To further muddy the waters, coroners and medical examiners have been known to list suicides as accidental deaths in order to spare family members the compounded grief of induced feelings of remorse. Careful researchers, however, have reason to ask just how high a degree of probability there is that a person will in fact accidently shoot himself or herself (or someone else) while "cleaning" a gun or showing it off. We need only compare the accidental injuries and death to mechanics who have had an automobile slip off a shop jack. The conclusion of researchers is that accidental death by gunshot is in fact an explanation highly manipulated. This subject, so highly confused in the popular media, is thoroughly addressed by Don Kates in a recent book.[11]

ON BALANCE

In general, the rate of accidental death related to firearms has remained remarkably stable for many years at about two percent of all accidental deaths. Between seven to eight times as many of these are attributable to long guns, not handguns, and mostly through hunting accidents. Yet, mainly as a result of state-mandated hunter-safety courses, the death rate for firearms-related accidents has dropped appreciably over the past two decades.

As to the annual number of fatal handgun accidents, the National Safety Council began recording separate figures in 1979. Through successive years there have been an average of 246 identifiably accidental handgun deaths out of an average of 1,825 fatal gun accidents overall. What skews the picture is that some deliberate killings are successfully claimed to be accidents.

The comparative safety of handguns is demonstrated by the fact that although they represent 90 percent or more of all guns kept loaded and accessible at any one time, in less than one in seven of all fatal gun accidents is a handgun identified as the weapon.

What information we do have indicates clearly that firearms need not be a source of accidents if the householder and other occupants of the home are adequately trained in their proper use and care, and especially in the manner in which they are kept inaccessible to others besides the owner, with special attention to the safety of naturally curious children. Like many other things, this is a matter of personal discipline.

The question, of course, is how to instill responsibility? People who are generally irresponsible will be irresponsible in the matter of gun safety.

In California, the Children's Firearm Accident Protection Act went into effect on January 1, 1992. The first such law was passed in Florida in 1989. Since then, Connecticut and Iowa have passed similar measures, with other states considering bills. The California law states that it was the legislature's intention that only *grossly* negligent parents or guardians should be punished, one section stating that the prosecutor should consider the effect of a child's death on the parent or guardian who owned the gun. Prosecution is bound to be difficult. The law may unduly punish what may be a single act of carelessness by an otherwise responsible gun owner. The parent is already grieving the loss of a precious child, having to live forever afterward with that act of negligence.

Wisely, the law is intended for those proven grossly abusive of the privilege.

Researchers are agreed that those who cause gun accidents are not the average gun owner, but individuals disproportionately involved in other accidents, and most notably those into heavy drinking, drug abuse, and violent crime. Of course, carelessness will always exist. For this reason we seek to properly manage all kinds of material objects that can cause accidents.

We look upon automobiles as being lethal weapons in the wrong hands. Through the use of door and ignition keys, we maintain care not to allow automobiles to be accessible to unqualified drivers. Still, with every precaution, automobiles still account for an appalling number of accidental deaths each year. But we don't ban them.

(2) Available Guns Lead to Homicide

Does the mere presence of readily accessible firearms in the home lead to higher levels of domestic homicide? Does it cause normal people to become crazed murderers under certain provocations?

Psychiatrist Bruce Danto cites the report of a task force on gun control:

> Psychiatric study of homicide indicates that the majority of homicides are committed by law-abiding citizens, perpetrating the act in a state of altered consciousness against some emotionally significant person. The presence of a firearm in such a state is usually the most significant factor since in the absence of a lethal weapon, a less destructive discharge can take place.[12]

Notice the last phrase particularly—*can take place* (not *will*), also the words *most significant factor*. Like many similar assertions, this is short on data. In the interest of brevity, we are limiting our discussion to homicide involving spouses, the most commonly acknowledged murder situation within the home. Here we need to point out that the term *spouse* is used loosely, with little attempt to differentiate between the lawfully married and those pairs who have been living together for some length of time.

INTRA-FAMILY HOMICIDE

Professor Murray Strauss reported a U.S. total of 4,408 cases of intra-family homicide in 1984.[13] This is equivalent to a rate of fewer than two per 100,000 persons, about one-quarter of the overall homicide rate. Of this, spousal murders accounted for 2,116, about one-half the intra-family murders. But when a firearm is the weapon involved, it is difficult to determine how many of these murders might actually have been committed had another weapon besides a firearm been used.

The best estimate comes from studies analyzing homicides in Philadelphia by Marvin Wolfgang, and another in Detroit. What they tell us is that about fifteen percent of the husbands were killed by a wife's using a firearm. A significant number of spousal deaths were the result of stabbing or beating.[14] More recent investigators of intra-family homicide indicate that spousal homicide does not commonly succeed an isolated quarrel between husband and wife. Rather, it is part of a pattern of abnormal, violent behavior that escalates to murder, a process increasingly predictable. The popular notion that these are normal couples who commit murder in a solitary *fit of passion* is simply a canard. In over half of these murders at least one of the spouses (usually the husband) had been drinking heavily or abusing drugs.

In the vast majority of spousal murders, sometime prior to the homicide the police had been called to intervene in altercations involving these same couples—in many cases summoned frequently. Records consistently show that, on the average, police intervention occurred more than twice previously. The most generally identifiable pattern seems to be that with each round of hostile arguing, the strife becomes progressively intense, culminating in one partner's inability to any longer control the anger and frustration. The succession of violent disputes ends with the ultimate violence: murder.

Perhaps the most significant fact is the number of spousal murders committed in self-defense. But as first shown by the 1980 Crime Survey Index, this number is obscured because by best estimates spousal victimization is reported less than half the time.

One investigator, Margaret Howard,[15] points out that women who kill their mates are usually frightened, desperate individuals who feel inextricably trapped. They see no way out, only a violent end. It is either fight back effectively or be killed by the mate's increasing violence. As 1992 opens, many such cases of imprisoned wives in Texas are being reviewed with a number already overturned.

What we do know, as Don Kates points out, is that an overwhelming majority of murders are committed by career criminals, persons with lifelong histories of violence. The typical murderer has a prior criminal history extending over at least six years. Even people who accidentally kill with guns, or passionately kill in other than spousal defense against violence, tend to have similar felony records. These aberrant individuals are characterized by a consistent indifference to human life, including their own.[16]

Now, you see, to equate such homicides with stable, non-violent couples who have quite normal relations (albeit with occasional harsh disputes) is to make an entirely false generalization. In light of this, to propose that guns per se are to blame for the killing in domestic quarrels is a proposition unsupported by fact.

BLAME GUNS, PEOPLE, OR BOTH?

Violent people will gravitate to the best weapon at hand. When a gun is not handy, data suggests they will resort to brute strength, a knife, or to whatever blunt instrument is at hand. How often does one read an account of murder only to find it stated *the coroner determined cause of death was a result of blows from a blunt instrument.* Perhaps we should seek to ban all blunt instruments!

It is the violent person, not the weapon, that is the critical element. The suggestion that a weapon other than a gun might be less destructive is not borne out by the evidence and is really quite beside the point. Remember, guns are used only fifteen to twenty percent of the time. In a nation where at least half of all households contain a gun, it is less than rational to conclude that gun ownership represents a deviant status!

(3) Are Firearms Effective for Home Defense?

A final assumption widely held by opinion makers in our society is that personal ownership and use of firearms for home defense is ineffectual and not worth the risk. Their argument is meant to cover deterrent use as well as actual use when that is deemed necessary. This is completely refuted by experts.

A personal illustration by Doctor Furnish illustrates the falsity of this assumption. He tells how a gun served as an effective deterrent in his own family's experience. He recounts the following:

> A number of years ago, my wife and I lived in quite a sparsely populated area in the hills overlooking a small city. There were no street lights and the distance between houses was considerable. Although we lived in rustic surroundings, we were in close proximity to a major urban area. This was cause

for concern since frequently we were troubled by marauding rowdies, especially on weekends. These were young men in their late teens who came into our area to smoke marijuana and to get drunk. This quite naturally led to some uncontrolled behavior, often at the expense of the residents. In coming to this particular neighborhood they could avoid police harassment, since this area was under the jurisdiction of the sheriff's department and very few deputies were available for patrol duty.

At the time, I was going to graduate school, and because I had a wife and three small children to support, I worked nights. I was always troubled by the fact that most nights of the week my wife was home without another adult for companionship or protection. To help assuage my worries and hers, I rigged up floodlights around the house and purchased a used handgun. It was an old, large-frame .38 caliber Smith and Wesson—a ponderous but impressive weapon. I gave her some rudimentary lessons on how to fire it, then put it high in the closet where our toddlers couldn't get to it.

Over time the rowdiness changed to crime. A gang of ruffians set one of the neighbor's houses on fire. There was increasing trouble. The sheriff's office seemed unable to deal with the growing problem.

One night I was trying to sleep. I had been in school all day and then was scheduled to work graveyard shift from midnight to 8:00 a.m. Along towards 10:30 in the evening the gang set up a great commotion, even rolling someone's automobile off a nearby precipice. I called the sheriff who responded and actually arrested some of the young men. Unbeknown to us, the deputies gave the arrested hoodlums our names as the residents who had complained.

The following Saturday evening, while I was working swing shift, about 9:30 in the evening, and while my wife was reading Bible stories to the kids, someone began to pelt our house with rocks. Our dog began to bark frantically and a chorus of angry male voices chanted, *Come on out! We know you're in there!*

My wife was terrified and realized she was on her own. As I had previously instructed her, she turned on the outside floodlights, grabbed the old revolver and opened the door. There about fifteen feet from her was a circle of hostile young men, determined to extract revenge from the people who had *finked* on them. She held up the .38, cocked it (a very audible sound in the night air!), and pointed it at the mob. She then said in a quiet but determined voice, *There is nothing here you want. If you come any closer I'll shoot!* Without any further action, even much sound, the suddenly somber mob melted into the night, never to personally trouble us again.

What the outcome might have been had my wife not had a gun we do not know and are thankful we never had to find out. Incidentally, what the outcome might have been had my wife relied only upon a call to the sheriff's office is equally frightening to conjecture.

Many cases are of the type experienced by Mrs. Furnish. The mere display of a firearm was sufficient to deter a crime, resolving the case without further action on anyone's part. Then, since the problem was resolved, no record was made, there is no entry in the statistical tables.

EVIDENCE FROM ANOTHER QUARTER

An anecdotal source of information about civilian use of firearms is found in the column entitled "The Armed Citizen" in *The American Rifleman,* the monthly publication of the 2.5 million membership of the National Rifle Association. This column is a compilation of articles giving local accounts of instances of successful armed home defense, as reported in newspapers around the country. Each issue carries upwards of a dozen or so separate accounts. While this is anecdotal in nature, it does provide a legitimate source of information often dismissed.

According to criminologist Edward Leddy, the NRA began to publish this column in the 1920s and has more or less continuously carried it ever since then. The recently retired editor of the column, Walter Howe, claims that in the course of the last thirty years almost 3,500 cases were cited where armed citizens successfully prevented a crime from being completed. This also represented a total of 5,285 individual assailants. Of these, 19 percent were killed, 22 percent wounded, and 34 percent apprehended, leaving 25 percent driven away.

These figures are even more significant when one realizes that this is a relatively small sample—consisting only of newspaper accounts of cases involving local citizens. It does not represent any kind of broad census. What is clear from the information in these columns is that effective armed civilian defense is much more common than people have been led to believe, clearly more common than most people apparently have imagined, certainly more than is recorded in statistical tables.

SEEN THROUGH THE EYES OF FELONS

Some very significant studies concerning armed civilian defense have been forthcoming in recent years. One of the more important is the large-scale survey of incarcerated felons by James Wright and Peter Rossi, research referred to in a earlier chapter.[17] Intriguing to note is the fact that of the felons surveyed, 37 percent had at some time encountered armed victims. Of those, two-thirds admit to having been thwarted or scared off by the victims—successful deterrence on either count. Furthermore, 40 percent of the incarcerated felons reported having decided at some time not to commit a crime because of the knowledge (or at least strong intimation) that the intended victim was armed.

FIREARMS EFFECTIVENESS SUBSTANTIATED

Possibly the most definitive work on this topic to date is that of Gary Kleck, a Florida State University criminologist, published in 1991.[18] Elsewhere Kleck generalizes that firearms ownership is *a very routine aspect of American life with obvious relevance to criminals.* He then goes on to compile a variety of surveys and victimization studies. His summary conclusion is that because of armed citizen defense, violent crime is *reduced to a degree that could rival the effect of the criminal justice system.* An extraordinary conclusion.[19]

Kleck also ascertained the following: "Being threatened or shot at by a gun-wielding victim is just about as probable as arrest, and substantially more probable than conviction or incarceration."[20] Significant acknowledgment indeed for the deterrent effect of armed home defense.

From a careful analysis of the data, Kleck comes to some other startling conclusions. Using 1980 as his base year, he finds that between 1,527 and 2,819 felons were legally killed by civilians in defense situations in that one year alone. Rather astounding when one realizes that despite the extreme danger their crimes impose on victims, the penalties handed down by the criminal justice system are often minor compared with the possibility of death or severe injury through encountering an armed civilian.

Take the extreme penalty, execution for murder. Between 1967 and 1984 only twenty murderers were legally executed in the U.S. Is life at high risk for killers? No. To this category of criminal the odds must look quite good. In the last several years, various states have begun to execute a few of those presently being held in various prison death rows. Compared to the murder rate, the probability of being executed for murder is almost statistically insignificant.

But a far more threatening aspect to violence-prone intruders is their realization that *the death penalty* is more likely to come at the hands of home defenders than through the criminal justice system. Thus, for example, when it is known that a neighborhood has taken up arms to meet such threats, the worst possibilities are very real for the criminal who thinks about entering a home.

Further confirming the unexpected, Kleck estimates that in 1980 there were from 1,527 to 2,819 felons legally killed by gun-wielding civilians in self-defense or other legally justified cause. For the same period there were from 8,700 to 16,600 non-fatal, legally permissible wounding of criminals by gun-wielding civilians. The remaining 98 percent of estimated defensive gun uses involved neither killing nor wounding but warning shots fired (or criminals driven off without any shooting).

The best available estimates, extrapolated from the *Uniform Crime Reports* and National Crime Survey victimization surveys, shows that handguns were used about as often for defensive purposes as for criminal purposes (aside from metropolitan gang shootings), and guns of all types substantially about as often used defensively than criminally. In a 1990 national survey, Gary Mauser found that 3.9 percent reported a defensive use of a gun of one kind of another. He estimates an average annual defensive gun use of 691,000 between 1985 and 1990. Kleck concludes: "Thus the best available evidence indicates that guns are used about as often for defensive purposes as for criminal purposes."[21] The same report found that the gun was fired in less than half the defensive uses; the rest of the times it was merely displayed or referred to in order to frighten away the criminal.

A *Time/CNN* survey found that 80 percent of gun owners thought that they would get their guns ready if they thought someone was breaking into the house, and 78 percent said that they would shoot an intruder if they felt threatened by that person.[22] Since many such episodes are unreported, the number may be far greater. It is not unreasonable to assume that in many of those cases only the victim's possession of a gun prevented death or serious injury to an innocent person. Of course, there is no way of knowing the full impact of deterrence because there is no way to measure it. It is conjectured quite reasonably that underreporting of defensive users is not only due to the fact that there was no injury or property loss, but some victims might doubt the legality of their gun use. Since the result was satisfactory, why complicate the situation with a report? It is common talk in state prisons that the intruder runs an ever-increasing risk of getting shot.

Kleck argues that gun use by private citizens against violent criminals is about as frequent as arrests for violent crime and burglary, while being threatened or shot at by a gun-wielding victim is about as probable as arrest and substantially more probable than conviction or incarceration. It is a negative consequence more promptly experienced than legal punishments. Predatory criminals say they perceive a risk from victim gun use roughly comparable to that of criminal justice system actions. This perception unquestionably influences criminal behavior at least some of the time.

Kleck's conclusion: "Gun ownership among prospective victims may even have as large a crime-inhibiting effect as the crime-generating effects of gun possession among prospective criminals. Guns are a source of both social order and disorder, depending upon who uses them."[23]

To close with an illustration, Gilbert Alston is a judge in the Los Angeles County Superior Court in Pasadena. The fifty-eight-year-old judge, like more than two dozen other judges in Los Angeles County, has a permit to carry a concealed weapon, and often does. As an advocate of strict gun control, he says, "Once we have formulated some rational kind of arms control in our society, I will be the first to turn in my gun. . . . You could say that I don't believe in unilateral disarmament." He was speaking of more than legislation, pointing to an effective reduction of arms in criminal hands.

SUMMARY

We conclude that citizens' deterrent use of firearms can indeed be achieved with a high degree of safety, and the use of weapons by citizens in potential crime situations (especially against home intruders) can be highly effective. Furthermore, the threat is not lessening.

Lest we become complacent, recall that about one in eight residential burglaries occurs while a household member is present. National Crime Statistics data indicate that when a residential burglary is committed with a household member present, it results in an attack or threat of attack over 30 percent of the time. In 1985 over five million household burglaries were counted, with over 200,000 resulting in assaults on the victims. In crimes reported in the U.S. just within the last year of reported statistics, a murder occurred every twenty-eight minutes, a rape every six minutes. Over 8 million households like yours and mine will be touched by *crimes of high concern* —rape, robbery, assault by strangers— with violent crimes alone leaving their mark on more than 4,500,000 families—about twenty-eight percent of all American households. Nearly one of ten will suffer either a burglary or a violent assault by strangers. In all, a total of over 86 million Americans—almost three-fifths of the population—will be affected. At current rates, a citizen is more likely to be a crime victim than a victim of fire, auto accident, or cancer. Statistically, every American household can expect to be touched by serious crime at least once every four years!

What do law enforcement organizations have to say? Two of the nation's most distinguished are on record as favoring private gun ownership. The largest is the American Federation of Police. Speaking of Americans who fear for their lives, they ask, *Should these people be disarmed?* Their reply, *No, we don't need to disarm our loyal citizens, our friends and our neighbors.*[24]

The National Police Officers Association of America agrees:

> We feel that an American citizen of voting age and of good character should have the right to purchase without restriction a handgun, pistol, revolver, rifle, shotgun, or like item without interference by a governmental body.... For every criminal that uses a gun to rob and kill, we have ten times that number of armed citizens who are able to assist the police in capturing these potential killers because they are armed.[25]

With Kleck we conclude that whether we like it or not, and whether control measures can deter crime considerably or possibly little at all, guns are here to stay (criminals will see to that). Guns are a source of both social order and disorder, depending upon who uses them. Furthermore, if civilian use deters crime, as is becoming evident, reductions in general civilian gun ownership would be tantamount to a reduction in one major source of crime control at least equal to the source of crime itself.

As reassuring as these words are for defense-minded readers, this leaves questions. First, that regulation itself is implied in the two conditions mentioned—*voting age and of good character.* It is one thing to permit gun ownership to those of voting age and of good character, quite another to answer *What is good character?* or *How is it determined?* and *Who determines it?*

The pragmatist will simply conclude: *Until criminals can be disarmed, the citizen must not be.* Especially, that is, when the citizen is threatened in his own place of residence by an intruder who by his very act is on a criminal mission. But, of course, for Christians, the matter goes far deeper than what is legal, even what is pragmatic. The issue comes down to the degree to which the Christian is willing to subordinate the defense of personal and family to the test of theological ethics—not ethics of his own *theologizing,* but ethics based upon Scriptural principles. This we shall review in due course.

NOTES

1. "The Curse of 911," *Newsweek.* Nov. 5, 1990. pp. 26–28.
2. Quigley, Paxton. *Armed & Female.* New York: E. P. Dutton, 1989, p. 56.
3. Warren v. District of Columbia, 444A.2d 1 (DC Ct. of Apr. 1981).
4. Wright, James D., "Public Opinion and Gun Control: A Comparison of Results from Two Recent National Surveys," 455 *Annals of the American Academy of Political and Social Science* 24 (1981).
5. Kleck, Gary, "Guns and Self-Defense: Crime Control through the Use of Force in the Private Sector," 35 *Social Problems* 1 (1988), pp. 2, 4.
6. Nagler, Michael N., *America Without Violence: Why Violence Persists and How You can Stop It.* Bainbridge, WA: Island CA, 1982.
7. Shields, Pete, and Greenya, John. *Guns Don't Die — People Do.* New York: Arbor, 1981.
8. *See* Ayoob, Massad, *In the Gravest Extreme* (1980); Also: *The Truth About Self-Protection* (1983). Concord, NH: Police Bookshelf.
9. Norman B. Rushford et al., "Accidental Firearms Fatalities in a Metropolitan County (1958–1973)," *American Journal of Epidemiology* 100 (1975), pp. 499–505.
10. Carol Ruth Silver and Don B. Kates Jr., "Handgun Ownership and the Independence of Women in a Violent, Sexist Society." In Kates, Don B. Jr. (ed.), *Restricting Handguns: The Liberal Skeptics Speak Out.* Croton-on-Hudson, NY: North River, 1979.
11. Kates, Don B. Jr., *Guns, Murders, and the Constitution: A Realistic Assessment of Gun Control.* San Francisco: Pacific Research Institute for Public Policy, Feb. 1990, pp. 57–63.
12. Danto, Bruce, *The Human Side of Homicide.* New York: Columbia University, 1982.
13. Murray A. Strauss, "Domestic Violence and Homicide Antecedents," *Bulletin of the New York Academy of Medicine* 62, no. 5 (June 1986) pp. 446ff.
14. Wolfgang, Marvin E., *Patterns in Criminal Homicide.* Philadelphia: University of Pennsylvania, 1958. pp. 82–83; Wolfgang, Marvin E., *Studies in Homicide,* New York: Harper & Row, 1967.
15. Margaret Howard, "Husband-Wife Homicide: An Essay From A Family Law Perspective." 49 *Law and Contemporary Problems* (1986) pp. 63–88.
16. Don Kates, Jr., "The Value of Civilian Arms Possession as a Deterrent to Crime or Defense Against Crime," *American Journal of Criminal Law.* Vol. 18, No. 3 (1991).
17. Wright James D. et al., *Under the Gun.* Hawthorne, NY: Aldine de Gruyter, 1983.
18. Kleck, Gary, *Point Blank: Guns and Violence in America,* Hawthorne: Aldine de Gruyter, 1991.
19. Kleck, Gary, "Guns and Self-Defense: Crime Control Through the Use of Force in the Private Sector," 35 *Social Problems* 1 (1988), p. 12.
20. Ibid. p. 17.
21. Ibid., pp. 17–18.

22. *Time/CNN Poll of Gun Owners,* Feb. 6, 1990. New York: Yankelovich, Clancey, Schulman Survey Organization.
23. Kleck, Ibid., p. 103.
24. Quoted in Quigley, Paxton, op. cit., p. 56.
25. Ibid., p. 56.

Chapter 6

SELF–DEFENSE: UNDERSTANDING THE LAW

The original draft of the Declaration of Independence, as penned by Thomas Jefferson, differed from its final wording at one significant point. Initially, Jefferson had it say that all men *derive rights inherent and inalienable, among which are the preservation of life. . . .* The final draft replaced *preservation of life* with *right to life* —an entirely different idea. The original notion—the right to preservation of life—indicates taking action, rather than mere status, a notion that reappears, at least implicitly, in the Second Amendment to the Bill of Rights.

This chapter is about the preservation of life: the right to defend this precious gift of life against any who would destroy it, in particular against a home intruder. As householders, it's important we understand how this self-preservation principle is established in American law, noting the special features relating to *a man's castle,* where life is threatened within one's own habitat.

When we inquire about legal liabilities that may accrue to a person who kills another as a result of a householder-intruder confrontation, we meet unexpected possibilities. For example, the law of self-preservation can be invoked by whichever party survives a killing, householder or intruder.

The ordinary citizen needs to know just what constitutes justifiable homicide, who can invoke it, and under what specific conditions. The question is discussed by Daniel D. Polsby, professor of law at Northwestern University; Lance K. Stell, professor of philosophy at Davidson College; more recently by Stanford Adjunct Professor Don B. Kates, Jr.[1]

THE LAW OF SELF-PRESERVATION

How does the law of self-preservation apply to the victim who kills an intruder in an attempt to stop a threatened attack or to the intruder who kills his victim for whatever reason?

While the householder has the more obvious claim to take up lethal measures in the interests of self-preservation, under certain circumstances the intruder also has a legitimate plea. Fundamentally, the law permits a person to stand his or her ground, providing he or she has a right to be there in the first place. In most jurisdictions this makes the right of the householder all but automatic.

Basic to any explicit right is an implicit one—in this case the right of protection against helplessness. This right has ancient roots, for it is recognized as essential to the enjoyment of all other rights.

For these reasons, should a householder kill a dangerous intruder (assuming certain stringent conditions have been met), he is under the law's protection and can plead justifiable homicide.

LIMITS OF THE LAW

Remember that the law, while appropriately broad, is not unduly so. For example, it does not entitle a householder to use lethal force to protect property, only his own life and those whose safety is dependent upon him. With this assumption every Christian ought certainly to agree.

The Model Penal Code gives a broad dispensation for the use of lethal force against intruders. The standard, however, is less objective than might be desired. For instance, to have *a reasonable belief* that one's life is endangered is highly subjective, fraught with ambiguity and uncertainty. All the more so seeing that victims act under duress. Other implications, too, are left unclear.

In general, we may say that the law, as it now stands, allows the householder deadly force privilege under limited circumstances—basically, when there appears no non-lethal alternative to neutralize what is perceived as a life-threatening situation.

Stephen Morse, professor of criminal law at the University of Southern California, agrees that the *reasonableness* required by the deadly force privilege is vague, but nonetheless believes it to be a satisfactory standard inasmuch as it allows a jury to express a moral judgment within a specifically defined case. What is judged *reasonable* thus fairly accurately reflects current social attitudes. While the *reasonableness* criterion allows juries to act somewhat arbitrarily, a more stringent criterion might serve even less adequately, since it would not allow for the variety of cases.

DEADLY VS. NON-DEADLY FORCE

American law differentiates *deadly force* from *non-deadly force.* Deadly force is deemed impermissible in defending against a non-deadly threat. But there's a catch to all this. In a life-and-death situation, if the house-holder believes he is facing non-deadly force, so reciprocates with non-deadly force, he runs the risk of being mistaken, of facing grave harm, even death. What he cannot know is whether the assailant might have a deadly force option (concealed weapon) which will be manifest should he be alarmed at the householder's defensive stance, or when anger or fear have been provoked.

On the contrary, if the householder faces nothing more than non-deadly force, yet mistakenly supposes otherwise and responds with deadly force, his only legal recourse is an understanding court. He can only then attempt to justify what he thought was *reasonable use* of the greater force.

Understandably, the householder's perceived risk may cause him to act beyond whatever concern he might have for legalities. It is a practical dilemma, for he sees his life on the line. Can he be expected to correctly assess whether the force encountered is non-deadly or potentially far worse? If it appears deadly, he must decide, and quickly, what maximum force to employ—the law notwithstanding. He pits the risk to life against risk of legal liability.

We can assume that a proportion of all intruders will be dangerous, another proportion not (like the current joke that the Soviets have one hundred prominent economists; two are smart, but no one knows which two). In view of this, it appears reasonable that the law allows the victim the legal privilege of lethal force against any intruder where he is unable to distinguish with certainty the dangerous from the non-dangerous. It may be assumed that the intruder will act on fear that the householder will be armed (even the elderly or invalid might be armed). This is why, according to Stephen Morse, the condition attached to *reasonable belief* is that of *an average reasonable person.*

At the root of the matter, the privilege to kill in self-defense derives from the universal judgment that there can be no social interest in preserving the lives of aggressors at the cost of their victims' lives.

A logical extension of this rationale is the requirement that intruders bear the cost of any ensuing violence, the reasoning being that they are guilty of forcing the potentially dangerous situations to begin with, whereas victims have forced nothing. For his own part, the householder conjectures with good reason that the intruder is most likely a felon (perhaps even then in violation of parole or wanted for another offense), one who wishes to avoid apprehension at all costs.

Looked at from the felon's perspective, not only does he face the possibility of losing his own life, or apprehension, but also the *violence* of a possible heavy sentence if convicted and, too, the very real violence that accompanies life in prison. In other words, he has every reason to take defensive action, even if it means the employment of deadly force. From his view of things there appears more to gain than to lose.

Back to the question of lethal action. Daniel Polsby contends that if the householder is permitted to shoot *only when he has cause to know with certainty that his action is reasonable,* the argument to shoot is weak. If he is permitted to shoot *unless he has cause to know that his action is unreasonable,* there is strong argument in favor of his shooting.[2]

In our hypothetical situation, the householder's decision to shoot is not because the intruder has taken first action, but the reasonable assumption that a lethal assault is imminent, hence the need to respond preemptively before it can begin. This is called *anticipatory reciprocation.*

Here we recognize the familiar essence of game playing, where not only is the next most likely move anticipated, but there is reciprocation in advance (reciprocation by anticipation), so as to cancel any possibility of the next likely move taking place.

Two principles stand in opposition to each other. The defense rule says, *Use proportional, minimally sufficient, repellant force.* Antithetically, common sense says, *Better to take him out before he takes you out.* The pragmatic issue is: Which response is least risk-inducing? Which less dangerous? You can be legally *safe* —and dead!

Long experience shows that if the intruder is not stopped at once, forcible aggression will likely escalate. Only preemptive use of lethal force (reciprocation by anticipation) can assure full avoidance of grave consequences. If in fact the threat appears dangerously high, the only natural response is a preemptive attempt to stop the aggression then and there.

Construed in this manner, the defender's privilege is not dormant until the intruder has fired the first shot or struck the first blow. That might well be too late. Immediate judgment is called for. With these subjective factors in view, the law gives the defending householder the privilege of using lethal force the instant he has good reason to believe the intruder himself intends to use lethal force.

It is equally important to understand that the privilege ceases the instant the threat has been repelled, not a moment later. At that point in the encounter, no further shooting can take place.

For example, the householder has shot and incapacitated the intruder who is now lying on the floor, his weapon some distance out of reach. For the householder to pump shots into him merely to satisfy a desire that this individual suffer as much as possible for the wrong he has occasioned (or to make sure he's dead) would legally be wrong. The one legitimate aim is to stop the assault, but with as minimal harm as necessary. The intent at that point is to apprehend and bring to justice.

SELF-PRESERVATION—THE PARAMOUNT VALUE?

Our natural presumption is that this principle would hold universally, almost the same as saying *sanctity of life is the paramount value.* Actually, neither is paramount. For self-preservation to be paramount law, it must be applicable whenever life is threatened. This is not the case. The presumption of universal applicability does not hold up.[3]

Look at it this way: a householder lethally defends himself or herself against what appears to be a deadly assault. Is this not an obvious example of the paramount law of self-preservation?

Wait. Can we also presume that the law holds the same for the intruder, he who initiated the lethal confrontation? As Polsby points out, while the law of duress excuses most crimes committed under great compulsion, it does not hold for homicides considered unjustifiable. No householder has carte blanche to kill an intruder just because he's presumed dangerous. On the other hand, the intruder, if attacked, may himself have legal ground to use lethal force in his own defense.

The law of self-preservation is thus conditional and relative. Extenuating circumstances must be taken into full account in order to determine whether a *defensive* homicide is justifiable, *everything considered.* For whether victim or victimizer makes the claim, the question is one of *just cause.*

Take this example. The intruder finds himself unexpectedly defending his own life against an armed householder. The fact of his having entered the house uninvited has not automatically disqualified him from invoking the law of self-preservation on his own behalf. Still, he cannot invoke that law simply because he has a critical need to defend himself. There are specific conditions under which he too can claim this right.

Suppose the intruder confronts a householder who is armed and has clear advantage before the intruder can get his own gun in readiness. Seeing his complete disadvantage, the intruder decides the wisdom of the moment is to desist from the crime for which he entered the residence. Saying he'll leave immediately, he throws down his weapon. Despite the offer, the householder—enraged, frightened, or both—pulls the trigger just as the intruder is pulling back. The intruder drops dead.

While the householder's firing may have been impulsive, a consequence of fear, done under duress, the killing clearly inadvertent, nonetheless the intruder is dead when it might have ended without a death at all. The householder, having heard that defensive killing falls within the scope of justifiable homicide, invokes the reasonable presumption of imminent grave harm.

Unfortunately, not everything in this scenario is well-defined. To be sure, the intruder brought upon himself the dangerous situation. This suggests that he himself bears responsibility for bringing about his own death. No one in court is likely to press the point as to whether he might have reconsidered, called it quits, and only then was killed. He can't plead his case, his voice forever silenced. The only testimony is that of the householder, and he contends he acted in self-defense while being threatened with a gun.

The law may have been violated by the householder. If the intruder is in a state of retreat, he cannot at that moment be regarded a lethal threat; a householder is not permitted to shoot when this is evidently the case. The dead intruder may well have suffered a monumental injustice, but further consideration is beyond all possibility. So far as the householder's action is concerned, culpability is an unlikely determination of the court.

Now suppose it turned out quite differently. Say the householder, feeling his life threatened, shoots but only wounds the intruder. The intruder in turn defensively fires his weapon. This time the householder is killed. The intruder, later apprehended, invokes the law of self-preservation; he intended no harm, was threatened with being shot by the householder, and simply defended himself. Will his plea stick? Possibly.

American law has an interest in the self-preservation of all persons, criminals as well as non-criminals. However, in the case of a criminal intruder, that interest is understandably circumscribed. The presumption of criminality is present by virtue of his having entered another person's home uninvited; after all, the habitat where the encounter took place isn't his, and he comes as a threatening force. Despite an interest in his own self-preservation, the court may have little reason to believe his story or give him the benefit of the doubt.

There is no question that the intruder is guilty of having initiated the threatening situation, hence little question that he is liable to criminal charges. But if it can be proved in court that he killed in self-defense, he will not be found guilty of murder—at worst, manslaughter.

So far as the law applies to an intruder, clearly he cannot claim that a *paramount law* of self-preservation should automatically come to his rescue, permitting him to shoot simply because he felt threatened.

Take another scenario. A householder reasonably believes an intruder has placed him under threat of attack. By law he is privileged to respond with lethal force, whether his belief of imminent danger turns out to be correct or not. His sole interest is in preventing his being the victim. The critical issue is not that his perception is right or wrong; the sole question is *reasonable perception* and whether he then made a proportionately justifiable move to remove that risk.

Although at the time his decision seemed reasonable, it turns out that he is mistaken; he kills a person who in fact was not intent upon taking life. Perhaps the intruder had no weapon at all. The greater likelihood is that the court will judge the victim's belief, however mistaken, to be reasonable, hence the killing justifiable. It is the rule of reasonable mistake; the prerogative of the law is to forgive those mistakes it judges reasonably made. And what may not be altogether justifiable is excusable.

Polsby contends that this raises a serious question: Shouldn't the householder have to assume at least some liability for having been mistaken? Shouldn't there be some liability for having killed a person who, according to later evidence, was apparently innocent of intending a lethal attack? Is the burden of culpability entirely the intruder's? Legitimate question!

To the authors, it demands of conscientious Christians that they ask these questions in all seriousness, for there is merit in any suggestion that would impose reasonable restraints. There are also deep moral implications as well.

There are circumstances in which the rule of reasonable error is relatively uncontroversial. Take the scenario where an intruder pulls a gun on the householder. The gun is not loaded, the intention being merely to frighten the householder and coerce his cooperating in the crime. But the householder doesn't know the gun is unloaded and has no way of even surmising that the intruder's intent is merely to intimidate.

Sensing a momentary opportunity, the householder's decision to shoot is not unreasonable. By shooting, he preempts any further threat. His hope is to stop the intruder's attack, hopefully with minimal physical damage, but nonetheless stop him for sure.

Inadvertently, however, he kills the *gunman* (gunman with unloaded gun) who only intended to intimidate, not harm. Tragic of course, but the householder's act is nonetheless justifiable before the law. After all, who knows what tragic consequences for himself were averted?

In cases of the death penalty, we demand that it be imposed only after exercising every procedural safeguard. By contrast, the private use of lethal force is more a matter of having to act expediently, an act impossible to buttress with thorough safeguards. Under this state of duress, the law expects occasional mistakes, finding them excusable if judged to have been reasonably made.

Having enquired of legal scholars, the authors' judgment is that no liability should attach to the victimized householder who inadvertently kills the threatening assailant, whether his perception of grave danger is correct or not, and if it is evident he acted upon the dictates of reasonable perception.

It would appear that the law as it now stands is acceptable. As for any restraints that might be engendered, this must be balanced against the greater risk that could result if the defending householder hesitates to act upon his perception of grave danger. With due Christian concern, we give the nod to the pragmatic demand for quick, decisive and adequate defensive response.

THE RETREAT RULE

Further complicating the issue is the Retreat Rule.[5] In the minority of American jurisdictions which follow this rule, a person threatened with a deadly confrontation must, if it appears completely safe to do so, retreat rather than respond with lethal force.

The condition attached—an assured belief that retreat can be safely completed—is of course subjective, a judgment made in a split second. Herein lies the difficulty with the rule. To retreat with complete safety is automatically ruled out when an armed individual is close at hand. Thus, the retreat rule has limited appropriateness, say (a) when the weapon brandished by the intruder is presently out of range (e.g., knife or bludgeon at twenty feet), (b) when the threat is physical strength (not a weapon) and distance from the intruder indicates a superior chance of escaping. Note both (a) and (b) assume a safe place to go and a relatively certain route all the way.

At an instant's notice, all relevant factors must be assessed by the householder—no easy task! Time works against assuredness. Two other difficulties arise: (1) The critical assessment is made in the grip of crisis mentality. (2) A jury, not in the grip of a crisis mentality, might later have to judge the reasonableness of response, giving due consideration to the extreme conditions under which the householder acted.

In most jurisdictions the law does not place a stringent requirement to retreat, even when it seems possible with complete safety. The majority of American jurisdictions permit victims to stand their ground within their own habitat. Moreover, when an intruder is perceived to be dangerous, the householder may shoot without warning. That is, unless a reasonable threat does not exist (say, the intruder is a mere youngster). Neither must the intruder display a lethal weapon; the privilege is granted the defender whether the intruder is observed armed or not. This correlates with the assumption that anyone breaking into a home has already used force, knows he will likely meet armed occupants, and has come prepared to defend himself.

Now, of course, a householder may choose to retreat for no other reason than overriding fear. For many individuals, confrontation would be too fearful. Even an armed and fairly confident householder might at some moment panic and flee, his retreat having nothing to do with the retreat rule.

Any mistake could cost a life or make one individual liable for the life of another. At best, the retreat rule offers only a tenuous possibility of escaping without having to take rear-guard action. So however one looks at it, the retreat rule imposes hazardous conditions.

ADDITIONAL PRECAUTIONS

Never may a householder start shooting simply because he or she is armed, angry, or has a *make my day* mentality about intruders; surely not because of a hatred for criminals or because one is upset about *one more neighborhood break-in;* not in order *to get even* or *to punish;* and not because of one's confidence of the satisfaction of taking one more criminal off the streets.

None of these grounds are adequate for permitting victimized householders to inflict summary punishment. Self-defense has nothing to do with handing out punishment. Indeed, as Polsby asserts, "there is no self-evident justification for subjecting the intruder to the risk of death by expediency where, with the full apparatus of due process, he would not risk death by punishment."[4]

Granted, the average person is not likely to give much if any attention to legal nuances. Critical decisions are more likely to be pragmatic—how to save oneself when the situation requires it. But for thoughtful Christians, these issues ought to command consideration. For them, what is moral should take precedence over what is pragmatic. How important (if it can possibly be avoided) not to make the mistake of unnecessarily shooting another human being, even though one might be legally justified in doing so.

In society's judgment of what comprises rightful self-preservation, it is evident that much is left to the intuitive moral sense of the community. We are very much creatures of community values. In practical terms, this boils down to decisions made under duress, subconsciously influenced by our social environment. Upon Christian consciences, however, there exists additional moral requirements that go beyond mere community consensus.

ANTICIPATORY RECIPROCATION

As Professor Lance K. Stell observes, what we are talking about has very much the nature of an elimination contest. Everything depends upon skills of perceiving what lies ahead, especially what might involve preemptive action. Perceptive anticipation particularly includes weighing risks unacceptably high. In Stell's words, "A lethal self-help rule permits those who reasonably believe themselves under deadly threat by an aggressor to 'trump' the aggressor's threat by killing him."[5] From the game-playing analogy we recognize trump moves as coming from an advantaged position, giving an edge to the player making the move. It is a winning position—at times a game-saving one!

What Stell refers to as *trump moves* brings us to what is called *anticipatory reciprocation.* The average person probably finds it easier to think of this as *advance retaliation by anticipating the worst.* How does this form of reciprocation work?

In a game where there are two opponents, one party reciprocates following the other's most recent move. This is the conventional mode of reciprocation (reacting rather than acting). But another possibility is reciprocation in advance of the opponent's next move (anticipate, take preemptive action, stop the opponent from carrying out his intended move). In other words, anticipating and acting in advance is a substitute strategy. It takes the place of waiting for a next move before reacting.

In terms of resolving our quandary, we are attracted to this strategy of getting the jump and securing one's own safety by preemptive action.

What we need first of all is skill in assessing whether the intruder's threatened violence seems sufficiently certain to indicate taking immediate measures. That assessment will be based upon knowable facts, present perceptions, plus reasonable inferences. Caution: What so often are assumed to be facts are in reality only superficial intuitions, at times altogether incorrect. In this deadly game, both perceptive skill and a willingness to risk come into play.

Reciprocal moves which react to an adversary's latest move do not make for a winning strategy; it is only as one reciprocates by anticipation. The one requisite to preemptive use of lethal force is having a reasonably grounded anticipation of an opponent's deadly move, sensing that to wait further would only enhance the risks. The nagging question always is whether one's perceptions can reach the level of certainty sufficient to make a correct decision. If so, then defensive use of lethal force is privileged by law.

Stell makes a sound case for anticipatory reciprocation. He also concedes that inherent uncertainties make for an unstable strategy. Still and all, we can agree that in the real world this is probably the best we can hope for.

Take an example. A householder finds himself confronting an intruder. On the intruder's jacket is a recognizable symbol identifying him with a neighborhood gang known for break-ins, for fairly frequent violence, and for preferring silent switchblades to noisemaking guns. At this very moment, he is reaching inside his jacket. Alerted by these known facts and inferences, the householder surmises that the man is probably reaching for a weapon. Perceptive anticipation transmits the signal: *Shoot! Shoot first!* The bottom line is that two individuals pit their anticipatory skills each against the other in a grim game played for keeps! Only one will win!

INNOCENT THIRD PARTIES

The householder represents the protection of the home—often wife and minor children. Unless family members have been given reason to believe otherwise, they confidently assume that he shall protect them against any danger, be it fire, storm, potential accidents, or violence of any kind.

In a middle-of-the-night encounter, the householder has full reason to believe his family's lives are at risk. He himself now bears a huge responsibility for whatever happens, although he has not initiated it. Under the Model Penal Code, the use of force is justifiable to protect a third party when "the actor would be justified . . . in using such force to protect himself against an injury he believes to be threatening the person whom he seeks to protect. . . . "[6]

Attempting to wound, not kill, places responsibility on the householder for possibly failing to stop the criminal. This translates to responsibility for possible deaths of people under his care, yes, and of others whom at some future time the intruder might menace.

If the intruder has any hesitancy about killing his victims, aggressive resistance might well decide the issue in favor of his doing just that. Ironic as it seems, he could end up in court only having to plead guilty to a charge of break and entry or, at worst, possession of a gun in the conduct of a crime.

CITIZEN POSSESSION OF DEFENSIVE FIREARMS

If the law allows a person the right of self-preservation, can the same law say with consistency, "Yes, you may protect yourself, but you are prohibited from using the one weapon universally considered adequate to secure this protection, the one certain means for putting you on an equal footing with the criminal intruder?"

There is a fundamental illogic in this. Disarming the citizenry, disallowing guns in the home for self-protection, has the obvious effect of raising the householder's risk immeasurably while at the same time lowering the *occupational hazard* of professional housebreakers. It puts the threat of grave bodily injury or death solely at the mercy of the criminal. Plainly, as the householder's life is the first placed at risk, his life ought to be given first consideration for the self-preservation privilege. So long as there are guns *out there* in criminals' hands, there is logic to possession of guns *in there*.

Along with many criminologists, the authors agree that total restriction of citizens' gun possession for self-protection would undeniably lead to increased burglaries, rapes, assaults and killings. Reducing the criminal's risk would only lessen whatever precautions he tends to take. Unavoidably, the increased number of housebreakings would lead to accompanying confrontations and to increased injuries and deaths.

What would be the predictable end of such escalating events? Surely, a newly aroused defense mentality would arise, together with an insistence that the best way to deter housebreaking and preserve life intact is to be armed. Society would return full circle to demanding self-protection in the home.

WORD OF CAUTION

A defending householder's case cannot rest upon any testimony referring to previous threats of a similar kind, or to fear some earlier experience had engendered. However relevant, this is not the issue. Nor does a past threat serve to define a present threat. That was Bernhard Goetz's contention and it went against him. He argued that a previous assault and its residual fear was cause for his shooting his subway accosters. That argument didn't stick.

IN CONCLUSION

Any home occupant who takes up a gun for self-defense owes it to himself or herself to know the laws of the jurisdiction in which he or she resides and to check with the police for any precautions they need to know. Laws and how they are honored differ from one jurisdiction to another. For example, Colorado's so-called *make my day* statute permits householders to kill housebreakers even if they pose no imminent danger. Obviously, this is a privilege most jurisdictions consider far too broad. Certainly, it is remote to the thinking of a conscientious Christian. Never forget that whatever you choose to do in defense against a home intruder, there are complex and serious legal ramifications. Don't rely upon conventional wisdom or the opinions of your friend, Mr. Average Citizen.

THE PURPOSE OF IT ALL

We reiterate that the best hopes in possessing a defensive weapon is that it might be used to deter a criminal and hold him for arrest so that he might be brought to justice and taken off the streets. The next best hope is that he might be stopped but not killed, then apprehended. Nonetheless, if in the process of stopping him he is killed, the court will most likely render a verdict of justifiable homicide.

NOTES

1. Daniel D. Polsby, "Reflections on Violence, Guns, and the Defensive Use of Lethal Force," 49 No. 1. *Law and Contemporary Problems* (Winter, 1986) pp. 89–110; Lance K. Stell, "Self-Defense and Defensive Resources," *Journal of American Culture,* 1986; Don B. Kates, Jr., "Precautionary Handgun Ownership: Reasonable Choice or Dangerous Delusion?," *Gun Control and Criminal Homicide,* Bruce, L. (ed), 1990.
2. Polsby, op. cit., p. 105.
3. Ibid., p. 90.
4. Ibid., p. 91ff.
5. Stell, "Close Encounters of the Lethal Kind: The Use of Deadly Force in Self-Defense," op. cit.
6. Model Penal Code 3.05 (2) (a).
7. *See* Gary Kleck and E. Britt Patterson, "The Impact of Gun Control and Gun Ownership Levels on Violence Rates." (Unpublished paper available from the School of Criminology, Florida State University.)

Chapter 7

HOW SHALL SHE DEFEND HERSELF?

We move directly to practical questions surrounding the issue of women's armed self-defense. A woman may assume any intruder is a violent predator. Take a case where this is true and where, before he can get anywhere near her, she's aware of his presence and has time to make a quick decision concerning her chances to protect herself.

Since possible rape poses a life threat and since he's a man and she's a woman, the only effective defense may well be the use of deadly force.[1] With this forethought, she has a loaded handgun somewhere safely but conveniently at hand. She knows that while a lesser response could possibly dissuade and deter, that's the least likely assumption, more often than not only precipitating extreme brutality, even killing.

Despite the current vogue for training women in physical resistance, these means are far from guaranteed, actually regarded by many experts as the most dangerous route of all. In all candor, resistance is a stimulator of greater brutality. So while we would be careful not to recommend armed resistance as the single most-guaranteed way, it's considered by many authorities the most effective preventive of potential brutality.

To find oneself facing any potential rapist is always an uncertain prospect. Statistics show that half have been drinking prior to their crime, with many today on drugs. According to the 1980 Department of Justice report on rape victimization, handguns are used by only 5 percent to 12 percent of rapists, the threat being their possession of a knife, the use of bare physical force, or picking up something nearby as a bludgeon.

Don Kates writes that no estimates exist as to the rate at which rapes are foiled by an armed potential victim since these are rarely reported. But neither can statistics indicate how many rapes are never attempted because there was good reason to believe the victim is armed.[2]

For years the regular column "The Armed Citizen" in *The American Rifleman* has summarized news accounts of rapes and other assaults thwarted by armed victims. Of course, the value of these accounts is purely anecdotal, but they do tell us that in numerous instances armed defense has been successful.

Some sexual attacks begin with an explicit verbal threat of brutality, others with an implicit threat—as when a weapon is brandished in order to produce the perception of superior advantage. Admittedly, in the event of non-compliance, superior physical strength of most men over most women is grave enough to make for a reasonable perception of deadly threat.

Inasmuch, then, as evidence shows that rapists often kill, mutilate, or otherwise seriously injure their victims, it is congruent that in every instance deadly force defense is appropriate. With these assumptions, the courts generally are sympathetic.

In most rape situations the victim's opportunity to defend herself is very short—mere moments to determine whether he may also intend to brutalize. Unless the assault is stopped at once, she may be unable to continue any effective resistance whatsoever. With this understanding, it is not required by the law of self-defense that she wait before shooting until either death or serious injury seems absolutely certain. Even though no harm other than rape is threatened, this privilege applies, the perception of peril being the sole issue.

Now, as to the more pragmatic issue of a woman defending herself with a lethal weapon, the following are some important considerations.

WOMEN'S TENDENCY TOWARD RELUCTANCE

Unfortunately, our cultural history gives women the self-perception of being unable to defend themselves against male assault. This contributes to their general disregard for self-defense training. Susan Brownmiller notes that "a show of force is the prime requisite of masculine behavior that she, as a woman, has been trained from childhood to abjure.... Femininity has trained her to lose."

By cultural tradition, women are socialized to have an aversion to violence in general. It is this that inhibits ready use of lethal means. Not that this is the whole story, however, for it predates recent times when women have greater self-confidence and wider access to firearms. Women may very well assume that they are completely disadvantaged when it comes to physical strength and the ability to successfully resist. But in a day of handguns suited to women's use and with firing range instruction available and socially accepted, it's a different matter altogether.

It is worthy of note that today most homicides committed by women are generally the end result of violent assaults continuously initiated against them. They are restrained until the moment when further submission becomes intolerable.

Evidence to date indicates that most women will not likely abuse the tactic of violence, normally considering it to be *a means of last resort* even when life or great bodily harm is threatened. Unfortunately, this bias prevents too many women from being prepared emotionally or strategically to make a deadly force response. What women need to know, as Yeager and his fellow researchers discovered, is that while rapists have the advantage of physical strength, most are unarmed (or armed with knife only), giving victims with guns the greater chance of successfully thwarting an attack.

NEVER RISK-FREE

Here we sound a warning. Gun ownership for protection against rape carries considerable risk. Possession can induce women into making unwise decisions to resist where they might more appropriately have submitted to a lesser danger. To be demeaned is not the worst thing that can happen. Whenever a woman trusts her ability to defend herself simply because she is armed, she puts her life on the line in doing so. Having a gun does not guarantee that in all circumstances it is safe to resist. But as Kates suggests, perhaps people who own guns also tend to give more serious thought to the implications of resisting, recognizing times when they would best consider submission rather than shooting.

Curiously, Pete Shields, chairman of Handgun Control, Inc., advises women to submit to rape in instances where they cannot escape, saying that *the best defense against injury is to put up no defense — give them what they want.* But the data does not confirm this except when women are unarmed. Gary Kleck, confirming Lizotte, finds those who resist with a gun are only half as likely to be injured (and far less likely to be raped) than victims who, as Shields advises, do not resist at all (or in fact attempt any other mode of resistance).[3]

Since a rapist is not interested in shooting his victim, what about retreat? In practical terms (and actually in most instances), retreat is not feasible. Rarely does a victim confront a would-be rapist at anything like a retreatable distance. And the rapist, totally unlike the burglar, is not primarily interested in theft. He may have secondary thoughts about burglary, but his primary design is to trap a woman and overcome her. His farthest desire is to shoot, only to seize and physically dominate his victim.

A late decision to retreat might afford the attacker opportunity to seize his victim's gun, especially if while in flight she cast it aside. In those tense moments, what's to stop him from using it to at least threaten that she return or be shot? But armed, she can safely prepare to take the initiative, and if she has the advantage of surprise, then armed confrontation appears less risky than retreat. An attempted retreat only quickens within the rapist his urge to seize and overcome her.

Incidentally, Gary Kleck's analysis of National Crime Survey evidence suggests, at most, one percent of defensive gun uses result in the offender taking a gun away from the victim. For the most part, these are opportunistic thefts which do not involve turning the gun upon the victim.

In his conclusion, attorney Kates suggests that even should some criminal penalties be mandated for women who resist rape with deadly force, very likely these would be all but unenforceable. Neither judges nor jurors are likely to convict a woman who used deadly force which she reasonably considered necessary to assure her protection against a crime that so outrages public conscience.

Sometimes a woman is tempted to accept partial blame by thinking, *I must have asked for it. I guess I aroused this man sexually.* Such faulty thinking can only inhibit a woman's resolve to effectively resist. She must see herself as victim and act accordingly. This is no occasion for self-blame.

So, then, what realistic options does a woman have, and how does she assess which is best? As someone facetiously commented, *Remember, Handgun Control, Inc. will not be there to save you!* We can add, *and neither will the police.*

What about attempts to verbally dissuade a rapist? On occasion these have been known to be successful. However, in most instances this is futile. Pleading is a natural response, but pleading can prove not only ineffective but provide something additional for him to reduce to submission. It can fuel the power trip that drives him to overcome a resistant woman.

Or it might appear possible to successfully struggle physically against the rapist—kicking, scratching, biting, hitting (we've all heard about having a hat pin). Generally, however, this only invites greater brutalization.

Nor should a physically small rapist be thought any less dangerous, since he usually finds something he can use as a weapon to compensate for lack of physical ability.

What about screaming? Screams of alarm are natural enough but are thought by most authorities to have little value; in fact, they almost certainly will provoke attempted strangulation to stop the cries of alarm. Or the rapist falls back on a sharp *silent silencer.* On the contrary, some counselors do believe that any loud commotion may scare off the attacker, since the last thing he wants is attention directed to a possible rescuer. The questionable value of crying out must be balanced against its dangers.

One way, of course, is simply to submit in hopes that the assailant will be satisfied with the violence of the rape itself. Submitting is quite generally agreed to be a sensible response *in certain appropriate instances.* But it's difficult to know these *appropriate instances,* especially since there is no guarantee of survival. Talk-show participants who advise submission as the only way (or any other non-lethal defense for that matter) must be heard with a great deal of caution. Just deciding what is an appropriate circumstance for submitting or resisting is far from easy. There are just too many unpredictables.

The classic illustration is a case that gained notoriety several years ago. Caroline Isenberg was a 21-year-old Harvard graduate. She was raped while on the roof of her building in New York's Upper West Side, allegedly by her superintendent's 24-year-old son. She resisted physically and screamed her terror into the night. Neighbors phoned the police, although they themselves did not attempt to come to her rescue. Brutalized, she died the next morning, barely able to utter the words *I should have let him do it.* But who knows for sure whether the outcome would have been different? There is no guarantee whatever that had she *let him do it,* she might still be alive.

Can anyone say unequivocally that any single response is guaranteed to be successful? We contend only that the armed woman has better chances, not that use of a lethal weapon is the guaranteed way to go.

There are occasions when submission may be the correct response. For instance, ethicist Lewis Smedes offers this: "If a mother could save her children by letting a rapist have his way, love would probably tell her to yield."

Now, such a situation as Smedes envisions is somewhat difficult to imagine inasmuch as we wonder in what way children would be threatened.

Perhaps in killing her he would succeed in removing any witness to his crime.

ARMED, TRAINED, PRACTICED

The final option is for a woman to be armed. Then, if she clearly has the drop on the assailant and is confident in what she is doing, there is a good chance she can successfully deter or repel him. A reliable estimate claims that only three percent of rape attempts are completed against armed victims, clearly a reasonable option for women who consider themselves psychologically prepared to use the weapon if necessary.

One recent study stands out.[4] In 1986, statistics for the State of Louisiana revealed that in female-headed households throughout the entire social class spectrum of Louisiana, 40 percent possessed guns. That same year, four sociologists from Louisiana State University studied a large sample of these households, investigating the possible correlation between handgun ownership and the fear of rape. Previous studies from other geographical sectors of the nation had been inconclusive.

G. Newton and Franklin Zimring had long been cited as supporting the theory that fear is a major reason for gun possession. In 1983, James Wright and Peter Rossi concluded that the wave of handgun ownership was, generally, a defensive measure against violent offenders. Decision Making Information, Inc. found fear to be the reason 40 percent of gun owners had purchased their weapons. In 1985, M. Warr demonstrated the fear of rape to be a salient feature in women's fear of crime, providing a specific link that included fear of rape.

In support of these conclusions we note a Gallup poll made for the gun manufacturer, Smith and Wesson. Between 1983 and 1986 there was a 53 percent increase in female gun owners, an increase that has continued steadily until the present. Jumping to 1988, in the wake of metropolitan street violence, there was a surge of women gun purchasers who proceeded to take lessons and practice on local firing ranges, a ready acknowledgment that they were preparing themselves to confront any intruder who might threaten them. The sheer numbers currently found on firing ranges, together with interviews with instructors, affirms this substantial increase and its motivation.

In 1986, the Louisiana team found a positive correlation between handgun ownership and those reporting previous victimization, but, surprisingly, the fear factor was less significant. How conclusive is this particular study? Not at all is the consensus of other experts, or the testimony of women flocking to firing ranges. So it appears that reasons for defensive gun ownership unquestionably include fear of violent assailants, also past victimization, abetted by the media push for safe, independent living through prudent self-protective planning.[5] Kleck points to another element, however, equally important. It may not be fear but simply recognition of the possibility of becoming a victim and rationally wishing to give oneself another option.

What must we think of the danger of a vengeful ex-husband or rejected suitor returning—or the triangle shootings which are often based on jealousy and the impulse of vengeance? Oftener than not, these take place in the woman's residence. Some of these men still have access to the women's residence before she's had the locks changed. Usually a former husband or rejected boyfriend knows if *his woman* is or is not armed and capable of using the weapon. He has a pretty good idea if she would use it if she had to.

Whenever a seriously ruptured relationship takes on a threatening nature, an armed and trained woman ought then to have her gun at the ready. If she lives alone, the nearness of a loaded handgun does not carry quite the danger it would in a family setting with young children present. Still, there must be great caution when visitors are present.

Although conventional wisdom agrees with the Eisenhower Commission report that women are *generally less capable of self-defense,* it can be said with confidence that the one thing capable of making men and women equal is a gun. It provides a woman the highest likelihood of successful deterrence together with the lowest likelihood of suffering serious injury or death.

Police Instructor, Massad Ayoob, suggests that women are more reluctant than men to use lethal force. Women sometimes protest, *Oh, I'd use my gun to try to scare him off, but I'd never really shoot anybody.* But while deterrence is one hopeful possibility, the woman who counts on it may be better off not owning a gun. From long police experience, Ayoob contends that a professional criminal can tell when a person isn't going to shoot *"in somewhat the same way a dog can read fear in a human being."*

Criminologist Ronald Cruit advises: "Before you decide to keep a gun in your home, you must be prepared to kill an intruder if necessary. If you don't believe you can actually bring yourself to shoot someone, then you have no business ever getting a gun in the first place. . . . You should never point a gun at anyone unless you are fully prepared to kill him."[6]

The fact that a woman has a gun at home does not, of course, require that she use it. Possession doesn't dictate use! A weapon kept for self-defense merely increases a person's options.

Of all intruders, a rapist is easily infuriated by any sudden frustration and may instinctively counter with a brutal attack. We know how little separates frustration from anger—explosive anger. It is anger that opens the door to spontaneous, unreasoning, latent brutality. Rage leads to unthinking brutalization.

Unfortunately, there are rapists who predetermine to kill their victims. In fact, according to Mark Kroeker, there are serial rapists/murderers who in doing this again and again gain the added courage and thirst for the *next time.* Nor can any woman have a way of knowing this in advance. Neither is any response she may choose guaranteed to change his intention.

Carol Ruth Silver puts it in balance: "Faced with such an attacker a woman can only be better off for having a gun, whereas with a less brutal rapist she is no worse off." And Don Kates offers this counsel:

> I suggest the following as a more realistic assessment of the opportunities and risks which are actually involved in the option to resist which a gun provides when a woman is menaced by a rapist in her home: if she becomes aware of him as he breaks in, a gun allows her to frighten him off or capture and hold him for the police; but if her first knowledge of the threat is awakening to find a weapon pressed against her, nothing compels her to reach for a gun. Properly secreted, it remains available for use if, for instance, believing her cowed, the rapist becomes distracted in disrobing or by a police or fire siren or some other external event; or if it becomes clear that he intends to mutilate or kill her regardless, so that it is rational to resist no matter how slim her chance of success.[7]

In fairness, let it be noted that very different counsel is given by other well-known authorities. One example would be that of Ira A. Lipman in his highly touted book, *How to Protect Yourself Against Crime.*[8] To the authors, however, the counsel of Kates and Silver seems better grounded.

The victim herself is more likely than the rapist to use an available gun, and since his first objective is rape and not injury (that may well follow), he has nothing to gain from the noise of a gun being fired, whereas she has everything to gain from possibly attracting a rescuer. If she uses her handgun, chances are it will immobilize but not kill her attacker. Over ninety percent of all handgun wounds are non-fatal. The point is to stop his attack and make his capture possible.

Mark Kroeker sounds a warning here. A victim should never attempt to *just wound* the rapist (aiming at his legs in hopes of stopping forward movement!). Time after time, Los Angeles Police officers are reminded, he says, that the only way to stop a suspect is to aim for the body mass. Officers are not trained *to kill,* says Kroeker, but they are trained to *shoot to stop.* Thus, the rate of fatalities is high, but necessarily so. He remarks that a woman, should she miss, risks being disarmed, losing the advantage, and becoming totally subject to his wishes, whether his intent was to brutalize or kill or not.

Similarly, if the rapist does shoot her, neither is she likely to be killed, but will suffer a recovery time in the hospital and attendant costs. If the rapist is shot, he not only faces the same possibility of serious wounds and hospitalization with its costs, but a probable attempted murder charge added to the felony rape conviction and an added charge for use of a gun during a crime. However, in serious felonies prosecutors often use the illegal gun-carrying charge (when it brings mandatory imprisonment) to plea bargain for a longer jail sentence instead of a trial.

Today a woman can live in relative safety with adequate means to protect herself. If she wishes, she can choose to secure her safety with the very thing rapists fear most: a personal firearm! To a lesser degree of safety, she has available other self-protective means that need not involve owning a firearm. Here Lipman's book contains many fine suggestions.

Surely, most women are not desirous of killing anyone ever, be it a stranger, much less ex-husband, ex-boyfriend, or other male acquaintance. The object in brandishing a gun is to deter if possible, or at worst to immobilize. Hopefully, just brandishing a weapon with apparent resolve would be enough to turn away many threatening situations.

But should it be found necessary to fire her handgun, a woman at least knows that the chance of the assailant's recovery is 90 to 95 percent (shotgun, 75 percent, rifle only 35 percent). But use of a rifle or shotgun is a more remote possibility, unless the victim has it in readiness and also time to take careful aim. Handguns are recommended for self-defense, inasmuch as they are far easier both to keep secreted and to use. Semi-automatics, where they can be afforded, give the defender more than a single chance.

For anyone, of course, there are dangers in keeping any loaded gun at home. It is folly to do so without following instructions as to safety. But risk-taking is always a trade-off. The risk is especially high for the woman who is hesitant or emotionally unprepared to use a gun. In her planning, there must be a firm mental resolve and the willingness to familiarize herself with a gun and to learn how to use it safely and surely. It implies taking time to get lessons at a shooting range, letting the instructor advise her as to the type of gun to own, and then to practice using her gun under professional instruction. Cost for this should be her least concern (recognizing, of course, that the poor cannot do this). Another advantage is that practice can also reduce a woman's loathing or fear of guns sufficiently to give her emotional freedom to use the weapon if she has to.

Interestingly, as Kates observes, in the abstract the risks involved in a woman's having a gun are less than a man's. He is more likely to play around with it as an object of admiration or symbol of the macho man. He thinks of his boyhood movie or TV heroes who were gun-toting he-men. He is more likely to assume that he is master of his weapon without training or practice. Shooting range trainers agree, too, that women are easier to train and often more conscious of the need for taking safety measures.

Of course, rape is not the only form of assault upon women. Today we know how great the problem is of women being assaulted by ex-husbands or ex-boyfriends who are out to get revenge for having been rejected. In a study made for St. Louis Legal Aid some years ago, police reports of aggravated assault where women were the victims indicated over thirty-eight percent were perpetrated by ex-husbands or ex-boyfriends. The typical threat: *If I can't have you, no one else can either, and when I get through with you no one else will want you.*

SELF-PROTECTIVE STRATEGY

An interesting fact is reported by Lorraine Copeland, former director of the Queen's Bench Foundation Rape Victimization Project.[9] In sum, in not one rape case did a woman have her gun taken away and used against her. But even assuming that a rapist should wrest a woman's gun from her after considerable struggle, testimony is consistent that most likely he will not be inclined to kill or injure her with it. Having taken her gun, he is unlikely to be enraged to the point of using it against her. He takes it simply to remove it from her use.

Sometimes the rapist will brutalize his victim initially in order to provoke her to resist, so he can gain the satisfaction of suppressing her resistance, in this way adding to the excitement and sense of accomplishment. It all helps explain why only a small minority of rapists carry guns; self-satisfaction comes with physically overpowering another, providing as it does a sense of total personal domination—a veritable symbol of the fear of defeat.

To the woman who chooses to submit, Joyce Mallman has a word of counsel; she suggests the victim throw a psychological protection around herself. Let me formulate her suggestion a bit differently for the Christian woman.

During the attack, a woman might think to herself along some positive lines:

> I'm actually in control; it is my choice to allow this violence, hopefully in order to save my own life. I'm not really participating in a sex act; this isn't an act of sex but of hostility, of power-assuming. This poor man is acting out his brooding rage; he happened to select me as his victim. I mean nothing to him personally. All he has going for him is physical strength and a pitiful need to dominate some woman, whether me or another. If I let him dominate me now, I have really dominated him by my allowance. Nor am I giving him anything really, and hopefully there's nothing he can really take from me. Sure, it would be natural to give in to emotional distress, but I needn't. What I'm doing is for my own good. If I stay cool I may get out of this without too much damage. It may even be possible to feel pity for this man and receive grace from the Lord to pray for him and forgive him. I cling to this assurance, Lord, that You are with me even in this ordeal. You know there's the possibility of pregnancy, venereal disease, even AIDS. But I trust You to protect me, to see me through. And Your will for me is my deepest desire, even in suffering this.

It is this positive take-charge attitude that can bring some women through with the least amount of psychological trauma and physical harm as well. But she must discipline herself with this thinking in advance if it is to be present at the occasion. And least of all must she let him sense that she knows herself to be in control! For the woman committed to submission, this is the best word we can offer. It stands, however, that she has no guarantee of getting off with her life or escaping his brutalizing proclivities.

Now, whether a woman chooses to keep a gun for self-protection or rely on her trust in God and the option of non-resistance, she owes it to herself to understand the realities and then choose an option for herself. Clearly, prudence suggests that she know how to lessen her risks, especially that she know the practical means for making her residence more secure and her habits less capable of being detected and turned against her. Beyond this, she must be very careful to weigh all possible consequences to whatever action she inclines to pursue.

Mark Kroeker makes the point that well-trained police officers repeatedly rehearse crisis situations and their decision-making. Mentally, they go through numerous scenarios and visualize their responses. His advice: Decide now and rehearse your decision; ultimately, this is the best you can do.

For the woman convinced that she should be armed, the comment of Massad Ayoob is significant: *One who is armed is not above fear, but experiences it to a lesser degree.* He points out that it's this difference that allows her the added clarity of mind and emotions to calmly concentrate her thoughts upon the options as they develop.

For the woman committed to armed self-protection, we advise the purchase and careful reading of *Armed and Female* by Paxton Quigley.[10] Carefully researched, this book covers every major aspect of armed defense from a woman's point of view—from a woman who's made it her business to know what she's writing about.

So long as the National Institute of Mental Health estimates that 1.5 to 2 million women annually are victims of rape in the U.S., and the Bureau of Justice Statistics concludes that 44 percent of all completed rapes occur in the woman's home, while chances of the rapists' getting caught and convicted are 1 in 500, and then only after he's assaulted, on an average, seventeen women along the way, there is reason at least to consider armed self-protection as a prime option. Whatever a woman's age, her chances of being raped are, to take a few same cities, one in eight in New York City, one in seven in Los Angeles, one in five in Atlanta, and one in four in Detroit. The risk can hardly be dramatized enough.

SCENARIOS TO CONSIDER

What might be the reaction of a single mother living in an all-white neighborhood terrorized by blacks from another area of the city? Say she is middle class, alone with one child, fearful because homes nearby have been entered and the occupants terrorized. For the most part, the intruders have been burglars but have included rapists. Also, there are the neighborhood teens into drugs. Violence is not uncommon.

Suddenly one night she realizes her worst fears when she hears someone in the house. She grabs a loaded gun, then ventures to a point where she can see the person downstairs from an advantaged position, one relatively safe for herself.

Partially hidden behind a door jamb, she presses the light switch which illuminates the downstairs. There she sees a large, muscular black man grimacing through broken teeth, a large scar visible across one cheek. Her fears are heightened; to her this man's appearance is altogether threatening.

When the intruder makes a move in her direction, without further thought she fires her weapon, aiming at midbody, intent upon stopping him even if it means taking his life to do so. The consequence is the death of a man who, from all later evidence, was intent only upon robbery. He has no record of prior violence. But how could she have known?

Take another scenario. The scene is the same, but the intruder is a white teenager, fair-haired, about the same age as her own son, looking like he belonged in the neighborhood. He is slender, looking nothing like a criminal type. He seems nervous and unsure of himself. It doesn't appear that he is armed. When he makes a move in her direction, she finds herself more curious than frightened. Almost intuitively she lowers her gun and speaks to him, asking what he wants. But he, frightened by such an unexpected response, sees his newly turned advantage, fires and seriously wounds her. In this scenario, her intuitions were incorrect. She allowed herself to become the victim.

One scene: a career burglar; the other: a frightened drug-dependent adolescent inexperienced in home entry. She did what her instincts told her to do. In both instances she was wrong.

The burglar only hoped to get away without a conflict. If apprehended, he would be charged with no more than attempted burglary. He could prove he was unarmed, his only possession his burglar tools. Her first attempt should probably have been deterrence, scaring him off. But should she merely wound him, then her life would have been endangered. Having killed him, she might find it difficult to prove in court that she shot in self-defense. Hopefully, the court would decide that potential danger to life was adequate reason, even though an implicit threat is not the same as an explicit one. At the time, of course, legal subtleties were irrelevant, and to the court his very presence would probably appear a real enough threat.

She will ever afterward ask herself, *Did I have sufficient reason to act as I did?* She must live with a once-in-a-lifetime decision for the rest of her life. The terrible burden is that a decision was required in a split second. She will have to live with the knowledge of having killed a man who did not deserve death at her hand. Fortunately, the courts take such complexities and uncertainties into compassionate consideration.

The teenager is a boy down the street, desperate for money for drugs, not fully rational, frightened because trapped, but with no intent of harming anyone. He does not know she doesn't intend to use her gun except for deterring him. Fear takes over and he fires first. His intuition proves as faulty as her's.

The general lesson is: Don't assume anything as necessarily favorable to yourself, the defending householder. An intruder's motivation can never be confidently appraised. Be prepared for any eventuality and be sure you have the advantage before you take action. These illustrations simply underscore the need for any homeowner (and especially a woman) to have training if a gun is to be kept in the home for self-defense. Then she must think through the possibilities, and especially her emotional preparation to use her weapon if necessary.[11]

It should be observed that self-defense experts, on both sides of the *guns for home defense* controversy, agree that, in all but the most dire circumstances, armed civilians have no business attempting to confront household intruders. They particularly ought not to attempt to *clear* a house—this is a task for professionals. Rather, whenever possible, a threatened householder should either flee the scene or barricade themselves in a safe room, prepared in advance, and call for assistance. Ideally, the householder's weapon would be fired only if the intruder was to force entry into the *safe room* where the victim was taking refuge.

It was H. L. Mencken who observed that for every complex problem there is *a simple solution—that almost invariably proves to be wrong!* Perhaps the same can be said about the advocacy of any one approach to self-protection against an intruder. Thus the disclaimer: we can only advise the reader to make a careful study of all the options. Personal temperament, family background, religious convictions—all are relevant factors. An individual's choice must be his (and in the case of a woman facing a would-be rapist, hers) alone.

NOTES

1. Model Penal Code 3.04 (2) (b).
2. *See* Don B. Kates, Jr. and Nancy Jean Engberg, "Deadly Force Self-Defense Against Rape." 15 *University of California Davis Law Review* (1982) pp. 94–903.

3. Gary Kleck, "Guns and Self-Defense: Crime Control Through the Use of Force in the Private Sector," 35 *Social Problems* 1 (1988).

4. Kleck, Gary, Ibid.; *See* Kleck, Gary, *Guns and Violence.* Hawthorne: Aldine De Gruyter, 1991.

5. *See* G., Howell, Hill, F., and E. Driver, "Gender, Fear, and Protective Handgun Ownership." 23 *Criminology* (1985) 541–542; James De Fronzo, "Fear of Crime and Handgun Ownership," 17 *Criminology* (Nov. 3, 1979) pp. 331–339; Thompson, Bankston, James W., Bankston, Thayer-Doyle, et al., "Single Female Headed Households, Handgun Possession and the Fear of Rape." (Unpublished paper available from the Department of Sociology, Louisiana State University.)

6. Cruit, Ronald L., *Intruder in Your Home: How to Defend Yourself Legally With a Firearm,* New York: Stein & Day, 1983, p. 21.

7. Kates, Don B., Jr., *Guns, Murder and the Constitution: A Realistic Assessment of Gun Control.* San Francisco: Pacific Research Institute for Public Policy, Feb. 1990, p. 15.

8. Lipman, Ira A., *How to Protect Yourself from Crime,* Chicago: Contemporary Books (3rd ed.), 1989.

9. Copeland, Lorraine, *Rape Victimization Study.* San Francisco: Queen's Bench Foundation, 1975.

10. Quigley, Paxton, *Armed and Female.* New York: Dutton, 1989. *See:* Garrison, William, Jr., *Women's View on Guns and Self-Defense,* Bellevue, WA: Second Amendment Foundation (Monograph Series) 1983; Flynn, George and Alan Gottlieb, *Guns for Women: The Complete Handgun Buying Guide for Women.* Bellevue, WA: Merril, 1988. For further reading: Stephanie Rigier, et al, "Coping With Urban Crime: Women's Use of Precautionary Behaviors," *American Journal of Community Psychology* 10, No. 4, (1982); Ayoob, Massad, *In the Gravest Extreme.* Concord, NH: Police Bookshelf, 1983; Steve Bigelow and Timm Gilkison, "Proactive Protection," *Law and Order* 34, no. 3 (1986) 40–3; Joseph A. Harpold, "Rape: The Dangers of Providing Confrontational Advice," *FBI Law Enforcement Bulletin,* July 1986, pp. 1–5.

Part II
MORAL AND RELIGIOUS GROUNDS FOR LETHAL SELF-DEFENSE

INTRODUCTION TO PART II

Our task requires that we wrestle with biblical interpretation. How do Scripture's norms provide guidance in determining whether, and how far, we may defend against dangerous intruders? Can it not be established that are there exceptions to such rules as *You shall not kill?* Are there not overriding principles which allow exceptions? Are not the so-called *absolutes* (the Sixth Commandment) qualified? How do we deal with genuine absolutes when there is the necessity of making a tragic moral choice involving the choice of a lesser evil in order to achieve a greater good?

Self-preservation through self-defense is one of the more disturbing ethical questions facing Christian men and women in our time. Crucial indeed is the different ways in which the issue is perceived by Christian pacifists and non-pacifists.

To put the problem in a workable context, suppose an armed intruder is confronted inside the home of a householder with a wife and two children under his care. The householder is a committed Christian who has no desire that violence of any nature take place inside his home. Still, he grew up in a home where guns were possessed not only for hunting and sport shooting but additionally with the assumption that a gun was proper to keep for home protection. Still, it has not occurred to this responsible husband and father to give much thought to the possibility that one night he might find himself confronting a violent intruder. Part II is aimed at providing the moral and theological basis for such decision-making.

Chapter 8

CONSCIENCE: CONSENT BY CONVICTION

Frequently, individuals who find ethical theorizing difficult, or who regard it of little importance, face moral decisions by appealing to conscience: *Well, I let my conscience be my guide. I just do what conscience tells me; it's usually pretty reliable. Wouldn't you suppose that's enough?*

By *conscience,* such individuals often mean nothing more or less than natural, innate moral intuition from within their natural reason. It is as though each of us is endowed by nature with a sense of what is right or wrong, of what is morally appropriate or inappropriate. And while the appeal to conscience is perhaps not all-important, it certainly is not unimportant.

Problem is, often intuition is partially formed or misinformed, hence misleading. This raises the question as to how reliable a guide conscience is in moral decision-making, raising the more fundamental question: How is conscience informed? What is the source—or sources—informing it? What invests conscience with moral authority? Should it in fact be invested with authority? Can conscience function autonomously? How can we know for sure we're being genuinely and correctly directed by conscience? How might we detect when conscience in and of itself is insufficient? In short, just what is conscience and how does it operate?

These and other questions give pause to the thoughtful Christian inasmuch as the Scriptures frequently employ the term, taking for granted that conscience is a human given, that there is a capacity within human personality for understanding and making moral judgments. Scripture also suggests that moral decision-making on the basis of *conscience* is not a simple, uncomplicated matter. To understand what biblical theology makes of conscience thus requires a degree of study.

John Howard Yoder writes discerningly, "The immediate conviction of conscience shortcircuits the logical linkage between general moral considerations and particular conclusions." There is, he indicates, a distinction to be made between general moral considerations cognitively embedded, and the particular moral decision one arrives at under given circumstances of the moment. Conscience is a mediator, providing an immediate, intuitive conviction that bridges between the general moral consideration and the present immediate, specific question.

For the Christian, the conviction of conscience is one of the ways in which God speaks to the receptive mind of His own redeemed people, individually and in community. But the question is then, *How may one be sure that what we consider conscience is the voice of God, or merely one of myriad voices entering one's thinking?*

Yoder cautions that to any insistence upon the need to obey the dictates of conscience as one's duty, even should conscience be wrongly informed, *has serious shortcomings*. The reason for this is that

> the autonomous conscience is subject to no theological or moral criteria outside itself, and is therefore just as likely to be idolatrous as obedient. It escapes every kind of moral accountability. In fact, it is quite possible to be utterly sincere and utterly wrong; it is also possible to be doing the right and somehow not feel right about it.[1]

Can conscience indeed escape all accountability except to itself? Is conscience indeed subject to the vulnerability of *feeling right while being wrong?* Can conscience be misinformed and hence a misdirecting guide?

Henry Stob addressed this problem when he wrote,

> Conscience, which is given in and with humanness, is a natural and inalienable property of man, and by it he both apprehends moral truth and is laid under obligation to fulfill it. Yet conscience which is open to divine influences, is open to other influences as well, and this compromises its witness.[2]

Conscience can indeed be misinformed and to that extent corrupted, and disabled as a moral guide.

The basic question Stob addresses is how conscience is informed, how it derives its content. Another careful student, Daniel Maquire, understands conscience as fundamentally the conscious Self attuned to moral values and disvalues. He posits conscience as the sum of all the moral influences which impact upon and are internalized by the Self. Thus, conscience involves a developmental process, a continual forming and re-forming of an individual's orientation to moral values, as he encounters those values in daily relationships. Thus formed, conscience becomes a mode of moral discernment, sometimes accurate, sometimes not.[3]

Today, many prefer not to use the term conscience, simply referring instead to the cognitive aspects of value formation. Indeed, however this human capability is described, it speaks of the socialization process and how morally discernible content is embedded in our awareness. At any given point in time, conscience is the present product of one's total moral history to that moment—a point in the continuum of an ever-developing awareness of right and wrong as one has come to perceive it through self-analysis of experience. What is distinctive about this cognitive process is its focus upon moral values.

Christians acknowledge the term *conscience* as biblically descriptive, not of a faculty as such, nor of an *intuitive voice within all persons,* but as *a God-given capability for moral understanding* which is the possession of all rational human beings. However, it is a capability that must be informed if it is to function as intended.

Thomas Aquinas classically defined conscience as *the mind of man making moral judgments.* To him, conscience is a judgment of practical reason at work on matters of right and wrong, deciding in particular cases what is to be done or not done in the light of general moral principles. Along with being a capability for making moral assessments, conscience engenders convictions concerning one's moral obligations. In this regard, Christians maintain that the Holy Spirit communicates moral convictions to the mind and spirit of regenerate Christian men and women, the content of these convictions being rooted in biblical norms. To Christian understanding, consciences, for the regenerate, is instrumentally the voice of God within.

Interestingly, the New Testament contains thirty references to conscience, none of which are in the Gospels, Jesus not having used the term (although the reality of conscience is everywhere presumed in His teaching). It is found twenty-seven times in the Epistles, chiefly employed by Paul, who uses the term in the sense of an interior judge of past actions, not only condemning but approving as well (cf. Romans 2:14ff).[4] He also thinks of conscience as guiding decisions in advance. This extended sense is found in the five occurrences in Hebrews (9:9,14; 10:2,22; 13:18). The Apostle holds that, although conscience may err, it is still to be obeyed (I Corinthians 8 and 10), and it was this view that became the historic position of the church.

Inasmuch as conscience is a matter of a person's social development, it isn't difficult to understand how that development differs widely from individual to individual. Thus in one person the content of conscience is highly developed, while in another person it is minimally developed. As cultural factors differ between one life and another, and as social matur-ing proceeds at different rates, so the content of conscience is diversely formed. What is evident is diversity of content and differing levels of developmental maturity. So the question reduces to that of content, to how moral values are engendered. This may or may not include Christian values. Basic to Christian education is the assumption that moral development spans one's growth from earliest childhood to the close of one's rational history. As for Christian living, it is urgent that there be a growing degree of certainty that conscience accurately represent God's moral values, that one's own moral concepts truly take on the commands and expressed will of God.

Also included in conscience formation is its inward monitoring of personal behavior, the manner in which all the sensitivities of the human persona approve or disapprove one's personal behavior. When mistakes are made, moral wrongs committed, conscience serves as a moral corrector —not simply an accuser, but an educator prompting right behavior.

Christian theology teaches that the content of conscience was originally the Creator's direct gift. Before the Fall, the content of conscience was mediated by God, communicated directly from God to man. The moral assessments of mankind were meant to be in perfect conformity with the requirements of God's moral perfection, reflective of the divine moral nature. The human family was divinely enabled to understand moral standards as given by the Moral Source and Arbiter of the Universe. This was an integral part of human development in the image of God. However, in humanity's willful alienation from God through sin, conscience itself was alienated, rendered unresponsive to its informing Source, impacted more by false, evil, selfish influences. Sinful mankind was then no longer inclined toward God for moral direction, a pervasive disinclination that remains dominant in unregenerate lives today.

Ever since mankind rebelled against God and His moral commands, the formation of an autonomous conscience represents man's distorted response to the accumulation of influences impacting both his conscious and subconscious mind. There is no longer a dominant inner divine monitor distinguishing good from evil as at the beginning. Instead, conscience is the internal witness to values that arise out of social interaction pure and simple. At any given time, our conscience largely reflects the moral consensus of the primary groups we participate in from day to day, be they family, peer group, school, business associations or other— and whether those influences are secular or religious. As we've seen, powerful impacting takes place through television viewing, movies, reading material, etc. A constant diet of morally degraded materials will most certainly have its negative effect. The result is a highly diverse set of inputs from every quarter—not only diverse but contradictory—a constant flow of mixed, undiscriminated signals. These inputs total out as utterly unreliable for establishing conscience as an autonomous guide.

Lewis Smedes graphically makes the point, writing that

> natural law assumes that conscience is an unshakable moral bloodhound, inerrantly sniffing out the rights and wrongs of life. Actually, conscience is easily led astray; it is like a computer that can be fed false data and print out elaborate tissues of lies. Conscience can make us feel horrible when we are as innocent as babes or splendid when we are as guilty as Beelzebub. Conscience is by no means worthless; but left to its own devices, it is likely to pull the wool over our moral eyes.[5]

We are surreptitiously able even to insert out desires and prejudiced as part of the available moral input.

Helmut Thielicke has an erudite explanation of the transformation of conscience when an unregenerate person becomes regenerate in Christ. He says, "Conscience itself is one of the most profound expressions of the cleavage within man."[6] While true, yet even redeemed persons experience disquieted consciences that remain a truly disturbing force in moral life. Because Christians are sinful and in constant need of God's forgiving grace, Thielicke speaks of their never having a *good* conscience but rather a conscience *consoled by God's mercy.*[7] Still, peace comes from depending upon God's unconditional mercy rather than from vain attempts at self-justification.

Curiously, conscience in the Christian's life is still the *Accuser,* siding with God's law against wrongful thoughts, motives, and actions. It is, however, at the same time the *Consoler* that keeps the Christian leaning on the grace of God. Says Thielicke, conscience *drives me into His arms... prods me to ever greater faith in His forgiveness.* He speaks of the Christian's conscience as always bleeding, but continually bound up afresh to be a joyful conscience, a means of constant renewal.

Thus it is that the New Testament holds out hope for a God-informed—not autonomous—Christian conscience, one that has a prominent role in the formation of Christian character. In a sin- and self-oriented world, conscience provides a much less ambiguous sense of God's moral direction. Those who are maturing spiritually, the New Testament refers to as people who study the scriptures diligently and *who by constant use have trained themselves to distinguish good from evil* (Hebrews 5:14). So Christian conscience is meant to be informed by regular attention to God's Word, by the direct influence of God's Spirit through inter-communication between man and God through prayer, listening for God's voice to the inner person, and by attending to the wisdom found in the fellowship of earnest believing men and women. Paul tells us that *we have the mind of Christ* (I Corinthians 2:16), admonishing us to allow the Spirit to form Christ's mind in us.

A word of counsel from Paul Ramsey needs qualification. He says that "to go against conscience is to violate one's moral integrity . . . to cut oneself off from life, from the appeal and claims of the good, from God . . . a fundamental violation of our being human."[8] Donald Bloesch is careful to make this qualification: "Evangelical theology allows for the role of conscience in guiding moral action, but this is not an autonomous conscience (as in Kant), but a conscience illuminated by the Word of God."[9]

Bloesch adds an important point to our larger discussion, noting that *once we spurn the voice of conscience, we begin to lose sight of the norms of justice.*[10] What he emphasizes, and what is congruent with the position taken in this book, is that the role of conscience has its deepest concern with what is right and just rather than what is good. Conscience does indeed have primary concern with doing that which is just. Certainly, then, we can expect conscience to question pacifism's propensity to devalue justice in its undue exaltation of love and non-violence as the be-all and end-all of ethics.

The Catholic scholar, Charles Curran, adds an important note:

> The Christian always possesses an uneasy conscience. Compromise and adaptation to present needs can only be accepted reluctantly. . . . The conscience of the Christian can never rest content with any type of accommodation, but always seeks new ways to pursue the direction and goal pointed out in the radical ethics of Jesus. The ethic of Jesus for the contemporary Christian involves a creative tension between the present and the final stage of the reign of God.[11]

This theme is a consistent thread in the thesis of this chapter.

Curran also cautions against the dangers involved in leaning too heavily upon the subjective judgments of conscience, noting that the voice of conscience can never be synonymous with objectivity because of two basic elements: human finitude and sinfulness. Limited by our finitude, we see only a partial aspect of reality. Neither can we achieve all possible goods or values for the reason that our sinfulness causes us to be less than authentic despite out acting the restored image of God, and acting as mature Christians whose minds and spirits are informed by the Gospel.[12]

As every person knows by experience, there is an emotional component to conscience. When moral reasoning suggests what we ought to do or not do, either we are emotionally drawn toward the decision we are inclined to make. What conscience does rather inerringly, it reminds us that in making moral decisions we are responsible persons who are accountable to that inner voice.

How may all this be put in balance? Curran, in the same passage, says that in our response to conscience, that which remains constant is the need for the individual to be true to self. Conscience also stands in need of continual inspection of those elements being admitted as content-forming. Here the mind plays a primary role, while for the Christian the influence of scriptural traditions is of greatest importance.

To give point to this examination of conscience, we ask how it all relates to the quandary of meeting a violent intruder with lethal force if necessary.

We should at least take note that the nature of conscience being what it is, it may be surmised that the conscience of a street criminal—a felon, an experienced assailant, say—is going to be a world apart from the conscience of the average householder under assault. The householder cannot assume that the convictions forming his own conscience are going to be those in effect in the intruder.

Take one householder's case. His conscience carries the conviction, *I shall never use lethal force against anyone for any purpose.* This, he believes, is a conscience based on unchangeable conviction. We recognize a typical pacifist conviction. In principle, conscience and acted-out conviction are one.

But, now, suppose the circumstances of a given situation alert this individual to his responsibility for the safety of innocent third-party lives—a stark reality not previously thought through? And this is the situation he now faces. Conviction is newly informed by this urgent information that innocent lives are at risk of death. Alarmed with the recognition of a whole different set of conditions, there may arise a compelling desire to so act as to save life even if having to take life.

Against what he would say is his conscience, he shoots to save life. But then a struggle ensues because of conscience long-conditioned not to act in this manner. There can only follow a period of time for all this to be sorted out. It may require counseling assistance to do so.

For conscience to be formed around newly raised convictions, expectedly means being cast into a state of ambiguity and distress, a state of uncertainty. The traumatic act of shooting brings about a deep upheaval. This upheaval and its emotional trauma is then confused with the voice of conscience.

In moments of crisis, this householder acted as responsibly as possible before God and his own conscience. In moments of sudden reformulation, conscience was unable to prevent the newly conceived impulse to action.

At best, we have, as Curran describes it, the *uneasy conscience* with which we are consigned to live our flawed lives, our finite ability to make moral judgments. Our sole recourse—a glorious one at that—is the forgiveness of the God who *tries the heart*. This is the position taken by Lewis Smedes and other contemporary ethicists.

Take another householder, a similar situation, but with this difference: The householder has studied the issue, wrestled with his convictions, and now has a firm belief that he has a moral right to use lethal means defensively, especially when lives other than his own are at risk from an intruding assailant. He is prepared to act confidently. His conscience has been formed over time into firm belief. Still, when he actually finds such action necessary, his compassionate Christian heart is filled with remorse for what has taken place. Everything he can bring to mind corroborates the action, but there is an inconsolable despair remaining.

Is such remorse and sorrow to be equated with an ineffective conscience? Does it speak of an accusing conscience? No, indeed not. But it speaks of the ultimate ambiguity with which such situations are fraught. Knowing one's own finite and sinful heart and mind, there remains the *uneasy conscience*. Not that forgiveness is needed, but there is the sense of having to reaffirm one's commitment to a gracious God who understands the tragic nature of such necessities in human conduct, and who deals with them in His grace.

Clearly, while conscience isn't the only player in the difficult decision, it plays a major role. Among other things, there must be informed convictions that override emotional influences. Perhaps no less important is an understanding of one's own diffident, overly sensitive and self-deprecating spirit that always tends against taking aggressive action when situations call for it.

We conclude with two final thoughts

First and foremost, for the Christian, moral decision ought not to be a matter of the moment. Rather, it should be the culminating act of a daily life lived by Christian input and impulse. This means, as the Apostle Paul said, to be *controlled by the Spirit* (Ephesians 5:18), *to walk in the Spirit* (Galatians 5:16), and to not *quench the Spirit* (I Thessalonians 5:19). The Spirit of God is given opportunity in this way to direct one's conscience. An incidental example is given by Paul when in Romans 9:1 he remarks, *my conscience bears me witness in the Holy Spirit.* The Christian ought to make it his life to develop his moral sense, to inform his conscience and to exercise it all along the way.

Whereas an autonomous conscience can be terribly misleading and oppressive, a God-informed and Spirit-controlled conscience can be an essential determinant in knowing the right. This applies both to consistent hour-by-hour decision-making and to the terrifying moment of a violent confrontation.

Secondly, and most important to Christian relationships, we conclude that if obedience to conscience is *to be one's true self,* that is, to act insofar as one understands truth, then great latitude must be granted other individuals inasmuch as conscience is, after all, individual. Each person is accountable to self and to God for the responsibility assumed in a conflict situation. And since no one can presume that all ambiguity has been removed by one's presently held convictions, there is room for charity—always![13]

So let conscience find its place in the totality of considerations entering into the ethical question before us. Let it be neither all-important or unimportant. When all is said and done, the essence is that we be true to ourselves.

NOTES

1. Yoder, John Howard, *Nevertheless: The Varieties and Shortcomings of Religious Pacifism.* Scottdale, PA: Herald, 1971, pp. 89–90.
2. Stob, Henry, *Ethical Reflections.* Grand Rapids, MI: Eerdmans, 1977, pp. 126–127.
3. *See* Daniel C. Maquire, *The Moral Choice.* New York: Doubleday, 1978.
4. D'Arcy, Eric, *Conscience and Its Right to Freedom.* New York: Sheed and Ward, 1962.
5. Smedes, Lewis B., *Mere Morality.* Grand Rapids: Eerdmans, 1983, p. 251.
6. Thielicke, Helmut, *Theological Ethics* (Vol. 1) William H. Lazareth (ed.), Philadelphia: Fortress, p. 301. (*See* chapters 15 and 17.)
7. Ibid., p. 308.
8. *Doing Evil to Achieve Good: Moral Choice in Conflict Situations.* Richard A. McCormick and Paul Ramsey (eds.), Chicago: Loyola University, 1978, p. 85.

9. Bloesch, Donald G., *Freedom for Obedience: Evangelical Ethics In Contemporary Times.* San Francisco: Harper & Row, 1987, p. 30.

10. Ibid., p. 89.

11. Curran, Charles E., *Themes in Fundamental Moral Theology.* Notre Dame: University of Notre Dame, 1977, p. 20.

12. Ibid., pp. 23ff.

13. *See: Conscience: Its Freedom and Limitions.* William C. Bier (ed.), New York: Fordham University, 1971, pp. 20–28 (*see* especially David Little, "A View of Conscience Within Protestant Tradition"); Nelson, Carl E., *Don't Let Your Conscience Be Your Guide!* New York: Paulist Press, 1978; Long, Edward L. *Conscience and Compromise.* Philadelphia: Westminster, 1954.

Chapter 9

THOU SHALT NOT KILL, EXCEPT . . .

What biblical rights accord protection of human life—one's own or those under one's protective care? If stopping a would-be killer requires lethal force, is there biblical justification for using such force, or is non-violent resistance the only option? Should a Christian give up his own life rather than take that of another? Are preemptive actions ever justifiable? Can decision be grounded in biblical law (or principle)? Does theological ethics point the way toward making right judgments in advance?

We have the difficult task of balancing countermanding biblical imperatives and finding points of accommodation. Whenever absolute norms are in tension with one another, the conflict of values cannot remain unresolved.

For Protestant and Catholic Christians alike, the logical place to start is the Old Testament, moving on to the New Testament, all the while seeking to establish a comprehensive biblical ethic from which to make specific applications for different scenarios.

THE SIXTH COMMANDMENT AND ITS INTERPRETATION

God's law embodied in the Ten Commandments is unambiguously definitive. But the question arises, Are moral proscriptions absolute in the sense that they're to be universally enforced (in every situation, under every set of conditions, whatever the consequences)? Do they preclude any and all exceptions?

Actually, the Sixth Commandment is not an unqualified absolute, but rather serves as a pervasive, fundamental ethical norm from which specific applications can be made appropriate to cases at hand.

If the Sixth Commandment, *You shall not kill,* were an absolute proscription, no exceptions whatever, then quite simply human life might never be terminated justifiably—not for any reason, not under any conceivable circumstances, not because of a life-threatening provocation, not for any possible outcome of good or defeat of evil.

If this is indeed the case, unequivocally it must be granted that even defense of innocent third parties is utterly impermissible. The death penalty, too, is ruled out. No killing ever!

But are life-and-death choices subject to an arbitrary moral absolute? Can no other moral considerations alter the nature of a particular case? Are we to say that *no killing* is the only moral value having weight? Are there not counter-values that also carry weight?

To the committed Christian, biblical morality is not utilitarian — weighing good consequences against bad; it is normative. Not that consequences are without weight. Nor that since biblical morality is built upon absolute norms, these norms demand unqualified applications. Precisely at this point we get into trouble with the Sixth Commandment.

Scripture indicates that life's moral choices are not restricted to obeying arbitrary, unqualified moral absolutes. The commandment not to take life is one supreme value, but it does not stand in isolation from all other values. Certainly not when it is in conflict with other values equally important. This is the reason the commandment is considered not only proscriptive but prescriptive, pro- and pre- having equal weight. Arguably, the proscriptive (*Don't take life*) is meant to be supportive of the prescriptive (*Preserve life*).

OLD TESTAMENT BACKGROUND

In Old Testament times, whenever Israel assembled to worship, the people recalled the covenant made with God at Sinai. The commandments were recited to remind the people that they set forth basic moral principles upon which all laws were grounded. Along with the commandments, there were specific offenses with commensurate penalties accompanying their violation. As for the commandments themselves, they were given to establish God-given norms for living in God's chosen community. To this end they were stated in isolation from case law with its specific interpretations and applications.[1]

What is meant by case law is that judgments must be rendered on case-by-case assessment, not arbitrarily according to an absolute rule. All facts, all extenuating circumstances, must be determined. This gives case law a comprehensiveness not possible to general, all-embracing commandments.

Karl Barth emphasizes that the Sixth Commandment enables the community to test actions that result in the loss of human life.[2] Walter Harrelson puts it succinctly: "The Sixth Commandment stakes out the claim of God over all life and serves notice to all human beings ... that God's claim upon life is to be given priority in the decisions taken by a community or its individual members."[3]

The commandments depicted more than fundamental law; they revealed God's own righteous character. Thus, it is God's own righteousness which informs the commandments, endowing them with the absolute character of God's immutable nature. How these righteous absolutes are to be worked out within sinful human relationships is given us through case law interpretation.

It is in overall normative ways that the commandments bring personal life under moral obligation to God. Alongside each commandment, case law identifies offenses which carry the death penalty—the ultimate of retributive justice—death at the hands of judicial authorities. Case law also designates when someone other than an authority may execute lethal judgment.

The two equally important sides to the Sixth Commandment call for different responses: the proscriptive (don't take life) is tantamount to an *inaction decision;* the prescriptive (preserve and protect life) is tantamount to an *action-taking decision.* The requirements of the commandment differ according to which objective is in view.

To further clarify, the Sixth Commandment in its prescriptive sense could read: "Under certain strictly defined conditions, when for just cause life must be protected, and when lethal force is necessary to serve this end, killing is justified."

Paradoxically, since killing is sometimes the offense for which killing is also the punishment, there is killing that does not serve life, and killing that does serve life (as in lethal defense of innocent persons). Thus, killing per se is not intrinsically wrong.

Interestingly, in view of the major issue under consideration in this book, Mosaic law actually addresses the case of the dangerous intruder. In Exodus 22:2 we read, "If a thief is found breaking in, and is struck so that he dies, there shall be no bloodguilt for him."

From this passage, we assume that defending life by lethal means was justified on the same basis then as it is today: a thief was regarded as a life-threatening adversary against whom it was legitimate to use whatever means necessary to thwart his attack and preserve innocent life.

We cannot say to the contrary, however, that killing an assailant in order to save lives is an intrinsic good. Rather, a qualified good (saving lives of innocent persons at the cost of killing another human being) is inextricably entwined with a qualified evil (killing a fellow human being in the process of saving innocent lives). It is in this qualified sense that saving innocent life has been universally regarded the greater good, death of the assailant the lesser evil. The greater evil is what results from inaction.

The act of life preservation may at times prevent an additional evil: allowing an escaped killer freedom to later menace, brutalize, even kill others. Multiple good is achieved, multiple evil prevented, by the employment of what without a dominant good end would be an intrinsic evil.

To kill any human being, even an evil-doer who is threatening innocent life, is an act no victim would choose if it were at all avoidable. In itself, such an act is morally abhorrent. But it loses some of its abhorrence when a compelling necessity requires it in the rescue of innocent lives.

Of course, a non-lethal alternative would be preferable were it certain that endangered lives could thereby be rescued, the attacker stopped, hopefully apprehended and brought to justice. Of course, this is not always a live option. The assailant's death may be the inadvertent consequence of the rescue attempt that seems achievable only through lethal means.

THE KEY VERB

The Hebrew verb *rasah,* used in the Sixth Commandment to express the general notion of killing, is somewhat rare, far fewer occurrences that *harag hemit* — verbs commonly employed to express murder in general, killing a personal enemy, killing a political enemy in battle, killing someone who is punishable according to the law, and killing as a result of God's judgment.

The verb *rasah* nearly always occurs when descriptive of killing a personal enemy, never an enemy in battle. Or when used of God's destroying a person who has fallen under His judgment. Only once (Numbers 35:30) does it designate the killing of one legally judged guilty of death. To infer murder only, according to Stamm and Andrews, is only partially accurate.[4]

Sometimes *rasah* does mean *murder* — intentional, non-justifiable killing.

But at other times it refers to unintentional killing (Deuteronomy 4:41–43; 19:1–13; Numbers 35; Joshua, chapters 20 and 21).

Murder differs from manslaughter inasmuch as it carries the notion of intentionality — killing with deliberation. But *rasah* fits a much broader concept of homicide where intentionality is not the main issue.

In contrast with the other two verbs, *rasah* refers to illegal killing, killing inimical to the community, an idea that has its locus in the concept of manslaughter, although its scope is larger. *Rasah* forbids all killing not explicitly authorized, in brief, what the Old Testament specifies as *wrongful killing,* differentiated from *rightful killing.*

Old Testament scholar, Brevard Childs, provides the best contemporary commentary:

> In summary, the verb *rasah* at first had an objective meaning, and described a type of slaying which called forth blood vengeance. In order to protect innocent blood, an escape was provided in cities of refuge for the unintentional slayer, but this exception did not alter the objective context of the verb itself. However, at a somewhat later period . . . a change in meaning can be observed. The verb came to designate those acts of violence against a person which arose from personal feelings of hatred and malice. The command in its present form forbids such an act of violence and rejects the right of a person to take the law into his own hands out of a feeling of personal injury.[5]

To summarize, killing per se is not in question, but killing with evil intent, killing not lawfully authorized, killing inimical to the community.

While Old Testament references authorize killing in rightful defense of (1) self, (2) other individual persons, (3) the community, it forbids vengeful killing, non-defensive private punishment of criminals, and all killing where a non-lethal alternative would most likely prevent the intended crime and secure justice for the criminal. Nonetheless, these exceptions in no way countermand the fundamental duty to preserve and protect human life whenever possible.

LIVING OUT OUR CREATION IN GOD'S IMAGE

In biblical revelation, person-to-person relationships are what they are because of the relationship each person sustains with God. Related to Him, each individual is related to every other. Ultimately, what one person is to another person is the consequence of their both being in God's image.[6]

This relationship between God and His human community is the basis for His claim upon every living person expressed in the Decalogue. The relationship between community members is detailed in the second series of five commands. Thus, the relationship expressed in the Sixth Commandment is this: No person shall violate the sacredness of human life which is God's gift.

Along with both the proscriptive and prescriptive sides of the commandment are God's instructions with regard to retributive justice (capital punishment, rightful and wrongful killing, killing in warfare with enemies seeking to block Israel's taking the land which He had promised them, etc.). The presumption is that preemptive killing (in anticipation of attack) is, under certain conditions, a legitimate act.

In Psalm 149:6,7,9 this Old Testament teaching is summarized: "Let the high praises of God be in their throats, and two-edged swords in their hands . . . to wreak vengeance on the nations . . . to execute on them the judgment written." Whereas aggressive killing is forbidden save where God specifically commands it, defensive killing is allowed under certain stringent conditions.

Note carefully that the Sixth Commandment is fundamental inasmuch as it concerns the sacredness of persons from which is derived the sanctity of all human relationships. The commandment regards human life as it does God's life, since each living person reflects the image of God.

So, underlying every other human right, prerequisite to them all, is the right to life. Every human life without exception is sacred and inviolable in the sight of Him who gave it. In consequence, every human life is worthy of respect, preservation and protection.

Now, were there no conflict situations created by the violation of the proscriptive aspect of this commandment, there would not have arisen the dilemma of (a) how far one can proceed to stop a violator and so fulfill the prescriptive aspect and (b) to what degree retributive justice is permissible, especially neutralization of a threat through anticipation and preemptive action.

CLASSIC BIBLICAL ILLUSTRATION

A remarkable Old Testament story is that of Abraham and the test of that faith God laid upon him.

Abraham was commanded by God to slay his beloved son, Isaac. Born late in Abraham's life, Isaac was the *miracle son* of God's promise. He was the heir of God's covenant promise to bless all nations through Abraham. But when God called upon him to sacrifice Isaac, Abraham was led unto a classic conflict between two competing moral values. If Isaac dies, then how could God's promise be fulfilled? Abraham knew nothing of resurrection, but he believed God could even raise his son from the dead if this is what it took to fulfill the promise.

That Abraham intended to obey the command to kill Isaac is clear from the text itself and from the commentary in Hebrews chapter eleven. That Abraham ultimately was not required to go through with the act does not alter the moral nature of his decision to do so.

Quite correctly, Sören Kierkegaard considered this an example where one's duty to obey God's call transcended his duty to any known command of God not to kill. Kierkegaard did not consider Abraham's obedience a response to some moral law which supplanted or transcended a known command to not take life. His obedience was simply to the direct call of God.[7]

Remember, the Decalogue (the Ten Commandments) was not yet given; Abraham lived much earlier. Still, from earliest times God had made known to man that they were not to kill one another. Illustrations of His retributive justice went back as far as Cain's slaying of Abel, and to Genesis 9:6: "Whoever sheds the blood of man, by man shall his blood be shed."

The presupposition is this: a direct command of God takes precedence, even over laws which He has established for mankind. Within His sovereignty, God is both free and able to order whatever He pleases. Here, of course, the assumption is that whatever God wills is entirely compatible with His own righteous nature.

Abraham, knowing that God ordered an act that contravened the revelateion that man not kill brother man, how would he reply? Would he say, *But, Lord God, You commanded not to kill, therefore this is morally something I cannot do. You'll have to excuse me.* Not so. The command not to kill, given as primary law, is here superseded by the direct, precedence-taking word of God. This biblical example shows that the command not to take human life is not an absolute, killing not an intrinsic evil.

As Norman Geisler points out, this is not an ideal world but a real and fallen world, so for the Christian ethic to be adequate for this real world, we must not retreat into unqualified absolutes but find a way that preserves absolutes as norms while honestly and adequately providing answers for situations where two norms are in conflict and the requirement to fulfill them both is impossible.

A caution is in order. To see only *greater good* and *lesser evil* poses the danger of possibly losing sight of the tragic moral choices made necessary by an evil world. Where it is impossible to actualize the good apart from also actualizing evil in the process, the choice affords only the possibility of good maximized and evil minimized, no more. It is impossible to realize a moral ideal.

In the case of the violent intruder, where there is no possible ideal resolution of the confrontation from the victims' standpoint, there can hardly be culpability for failing to keep an obligation which is not possible without at the same time breaking a higher obligation. If one cannot protect innocent persons without killing the assailant, then fulfilling only one obligation does not incur culpability.

OLD TESTAMENT LAW TAKES TWO FORMS

From the time of Alt's definitive biblical studies in 1934, a fundamental distinction has been made between apodictic and casuistic law, between absolute norms and individual case applications which qualify the absolute. If we are to resolve our quandary biblically, it is crucial to understand the difference between apodictic and casuistic law.[8]

Apodictic Law

This is the form of law expressed by the Ten Commandments, characterized by terse, unconditional commands. The commands are expressed as absolute fundamental imperatives, formulated negatively as proscriptions. These are general norms in that they do not explicitly stipulate how to treat various cases, each in the same broad category yet different. Neither do the commandments stipulate specific violations or the penalties which compensate those violations. This is left for casuistic law.

Casuistic Law

Casuistic law differentiates the circumstantial makeup of each particular case, the severity of the violation, together with the penalties God Himself appoints. It is not possible for case law to be directly incorporated into the corpus of the Ten Commandments, but is divided off and enunciated separately.

In this light, many pacifist appeals to *You shall not kill* are outside the proper biblical context. They lack a grasp of the difference between apodictic and casuistic law, hence are invalid. What is meant as a general norm is confused with particular application.

RIGHTFUL KILLING VS. WRONGFUL KILLING

The Sixth Commandment is apodictic law at its tersest—only two words in Hebrew—as blunt as our saying *No killing!* As we now understand, the verb *rasah* cannot by itself determine just what the Sixth Commandment means by *not kill* except as a general fundamental moral norm governing the most sacred relationship between human beings. But in case law, in some instances killing is seen to be right and proper. Under certain circumstances killing is more serious (intentional or premeditated murder, requiring the death penalty), in other circumstances less serious (manslaughter, which under the Mosaic covenant allowed killers to escape to a city of refuge). Thus some killing is legitimate, even ordered. What case law does is to remove the non-specificity attaching to the more general apodictic law, legitimizing certain exceptions which in the eyes of God are right and just.

The general commandment *You shall not kill* does not provide a definitive sense of whether lethal force may be employed or whether preemptive action may be taken in defense of one's own life or third parties under one's protective care. Inasmuch as the Old Testament permits retributive killing for certain offenses, the presumption is supportive of the view that killing is legitimate if necessary to protect innocent lives. Further on we'll ask whether the New Testament affirms or overturns this presumption.

WITH EVERY RIGHT, A COMMENSURATE DUTY

Because every human person is created in God's image, the one universal human right upon which all other rights are contingent is the right to life itself. But every right has a commensurate duty. Corresponding to the right to life is the duty to preserve and protect life insofar as it lies within our power to do so. In some instances, even lethally coercive means will be necessary against anyone intending to take life without just cause.

So the answer is *Yes* to the question *Are there conceivable circumstances in which this universal right to life can be rescinded? Is it possible for one person, by threatening the life of another person, to forfeit his own right to life?*

Again, this brings us back to those cases in which conditions are present which abridge this otherwise inherent right to life, behavior that renders an individual no longer a legitimate claimant to this right. Might this not include instances where one person's right to life conflicts with another person's, and where a forced choice must be made as to which life shall be preserved, which sacrificed? The next question is: In determining which life is to be preserved and which is not, what values and what order of precedence governs the choice?

WHEN IS AN ABSOLUTE NOT AN ABSOLUTE?

To start with a standard definition: *By an "absolute" value (or good) is meant one that maintains its validity for all persons at all times and under all circumstances.* Technically, essential to an ethical absolute is its unexceptional nature; it is universally binding. *Webster's Dictionary* speaks of law as absolute when it is without conditions. In itself it is perfect, complete, pure. In philosophy the characteristics are "that which is thought of as existing in and by itself, without relation to anything else, that is, without qualification, without condition. It is law in perfection, in completion, en toto."[9]

Traditionally, the term *absolute* has been used with reference to the Ten Commandments in the attempt to ward off relativizing God's law. While commendable this is faulty, for the definition *absolute* holds with some commandments, not with others. Indeed, it cannot be said that *the Sixth Commandment is without relation to anything else, that is, without qualification.*

The fallacy lies in a traditional mind-set: the assumption that what is true of one commandment is true of all, then assigning the attribute *absolute* to, say, the Sixth Commandment, before examining how it is applied in Scripture and noting the exceptions. So the place to begin is to ask, Is the commandment universally binding for all persons, at all times, under all circumstances?

Whatever God decrees is absolute simply because He declares it so. It has divine finality and is universally binding. The problem is in declaring a commandment absolute in every case when God has not done so.

We can understand Paul Ramsey's frustration: "Perhaps the term absolute should be banned forever from the discussion of moral questions."[10] But this goes too far. We are somewhat more comfortable with Donald Evans' *virtually exceptionless absolute.*[11] There seems good reason to adapt his point of view that God has (a) pure absolutes, (b) *near* absolutes, and (c) general principles, norms not categorized as absolutes. Still, we may be playing on the fringes of contradiction when we say *virtually exceptionless absolute.*

It seems better that we begin with no presupposition which makes the Sixth Commandment absolute. We are then free to explore Scripture's obviously conditioned applications, noting the circumstances under which exceptions are permissible.

Theologian Walter Harrelson frames the basic question: "If life belongs to God, what are the circumstances under which any human community can understand itself to be invited by God to act in his place to take the life of another human being?" Partially in answer to this he says that "...the commandment was probably never understood by the ancient Israelites as ruling out in principle the taking of the life of the murder... or others who did deeds of such violence or horror that the community could not endure letting the perpetrator live." He concludes that the Sixth Commandment does not require a pacifist rigor.[12]

Suffice it to conclude: The Sixth Commandment is subject to casuistic application; it is not an unqualified, universally binding absolute under all circumstances. This is the clear indication of Scripture itself, and contributes helpfully toward understanding what we believe to be the proper place of casuistry and contextualism in Christian ethics. It also enables us to appreciate with clarity the Sixth Commandment's two sides, especially as the prescriptive side inclines us toward granting legitimate defensive action of a lethal nature in the preservation of life.

CONSISTENT POSITION OF THE OLD TESTAMENT

What can we say of the rest of the Old Testament? We find a clear presupposition that warfare is a legitimate endeavor under certain conditions. Abraham is cited as an example of faith by New Testament writers (Romans 4:11,12; Hebrews 11:8–10). He led a military expedition to rescue his nephew Lot (Genesis 14:13–16). Joshua, the Judges, and

King David (*the man after God's own heart*, Acts 13:22) all engaged in warfare approved, even commanded by God. In Hebrews 11:33,24 they are said to have *enforced justice* among other things. Faith itself was exhibited through their military valor, their trust that God would bring them through victorious. Here the enforcement of justice had higher priority on the divine scale of values than non-violence when these two were in conflict.[13]

Sometimes it is objected that any appeal to the Old Testament must give way to New Testament teaching. But there is instruction in learning from all of Scripture. Paul wrote, *For whatever was written in former days was written for our instruction* (Romans 15:4). Instruction includes example.

God commanded Nehemiah to lead His people in the rebuilding of the walls of Jerusalem. It was a treacherous task inasmuch as they were opposed by Sanballat and his armies. How did God intend for them to be successful?

First we read, *And we prayed to our God and set a guard as a protection against them day and night* (vs. 9). They first sought God's will through prayer. Then, under His instruction, Nehemiah *stationed the people according to their families, with their swords and their bows* (vs. 13). Addressing the people, Nehemiah inspired and instructed them:

> "Do not be afraid of them. Remember the Lord, who is great and terrible, and fight for your brethren, your sons, your daughters, your wives, and your homes" (vs. 14).

Clearly, here is biblical tradition, nowhere rescinded, for legitimate defensive action in the face of violent enemies who would destroy life and liberty.

The pacifist theologian, Stanley Hauerwas, rejects as legitimately Christian the depiction of war and violence in the Old Testament.[14] He refers to the work of Millard Lind, who argues that Yahweh the warrior fought by means of miracle, not through the armies of his people.[15] But the notion of separating God's ultimate means of victory from the instrumentality of His people, and the actions He Himself commanded of them, is not credible and need not be argued here.[15] Quite the opposite, Richard J. Mouw, provost of Fuller Theological Seminary, reflects our view when he states his conviction that God's sanction of violence in the Old Testament is indeed a convincing line of argument.

Had the commandment not been cast according to its proscriptive aspect, there would not have arisen the dilemma of (a) how far one can proceed to stop a violator and so fulfill the prescriptive aspect or (b) to what degree is retributive justice permissible, especially neutralization of a threat through anticipation and then through taking preemptive action. How necessary it is that we understand the commandment as having both its proscriptive and prescriptive sides.

NOTES

1. *See* Clements, R. E., *Exodus.* Cambridge: Cambridge University, 1972, p. 121.
2. Barth, Karl, *Studies in Religion.* 6 (1976–77) pp. 229–240.
3. Harrelson, Walter, *The Ten Commandments and Human Rights.* Philadelphia: Fortress, 1980, pp. 121–122.
4. Stamm, Johann J., "The Ten Commandments in Recent Research," *Biblical Theology* (Second Series 2), London: SCM Press, 1967, pp. 98–99.
5. Childs, Brevard S., *The Book of Exodus.* Philadelphia: Westminster, 1974, p. 421.
6. Rylaarsdam, J. Coert, *The Interpreter's Bible,* vol. 1, Nashville: Abingdon, 1952, p. 986.
7. Kierkegaard, Soren, *Fear and Trembling,* trans. Walter Lowrie, New York: Doubleday, 1954, pp. 47, 64–77.
8. Cole, Alan., *Exodus.* London: Tyndale, 1973, pp. 159–160.
9. Smith, John E., *Dictionary of Christian Ethics.* Macquarrie, John (ed), Philadelphia: Westminster, 1967, pp. 1–3.
10. Ramsey, Paul, "Paul Ramsey on Exceptionless Moral Rules," *The American Journal of Jurisprudence.* 16 (1971) p. 183.
11. Evans, Donald, "The Virtually Exceptionless Absolute." Ibid., pp. 184–214; Curran, Charles E. (ed) *Absolutes in Moral Theology?* Washington, DC: Corpus Books, 1968.
12. Harrelson, op. cit., pp. 111–119.
13. Kaiser, Walter J., Jr., *Toward Old Testament Ethics.* Grand Rapids: Zondervan, 1983; Phillips, Anthony, *Ancient Israel's Criminal Law.* New York: Schocken Books, 1970.
14. Hauerwas, Stanley, *The Peaceable Kingdom: A Primer in Christian Ethics.* Notre Dame: Notre Dame Press, 1983, p. 163 (*see* note 11).
15. Lind, Millard, *Yahweh is a Warrior: The Theology of Warfare in Ancient Israel.* Scottdale, PA: Herald, 1980.

Chapter 10

NON-VIOLENCE: NEW TESTAMENT ABSOLUTE?

For Christians, the foremost concern is to understand what the New Testament has to say. A division of thought has traditionally caused some interpreters to be pacifists, the majority not. So our initial task is to let the Word of God inform our thinking directly.

THE SWORD—LUKE 22:35-36

Critical is Jesus' admonition to the disciples shortly before His arrest and crucifixion:

> When I sent you out with no purse or bag or sandals, did you lack anything? They said, *Nothing* (see Luke 9:3-5 for the background). He said to them, *But now, let him who has a purse take it, and likewise a bag. And let him who has no sword sell his mantle and buy one.*

Following a short word about His coming trial, their response was, *Look, Lord, here are two swords.* To this He replied, *It is enough.*

The problem here has to do with the sword. Later on when Jesus was arrested, Peter drew his sword in a defensive tactic, managing to cut off the ear of the High Priest's servant before Jesus intervened: "Put your sword into its sheath; shall I not drink the cup which the Father has given me?" (John 18:11). At first glance, the two passages seem contradictory. Does this suggest that Jesus did not mean to be taken literally, that the disciples misunderstood Him? Crucial is His accompanying word: ... *shall I not drink the cup which the Father has given me.* Here Jesus indirectly gives the clue to His meaning.

If we take Luke 22:35-36 at face value, evidently Jesus did not forbid the disciples from carrying weapons on their journey from Galilee to Jerusalem. In fact, this is exactly what he instructed them to do. So far, this is unequivocal. And why this admonition? G. C. G. MacGregor, a pacifist, quotes Principle W. A. Curtis as saying that the obvious reason would be that these weapons were the customary means of protection which travellers always used when travelling beyond the armed protection of the law. So it may be inferred that Jesus took no exception to their bearing the ordinary means of self-defense when travelling in bandit-infested country beyond the protection of armed authorities. It seems a well-founded conclusion that swords, while inadmissible in the defense of Jesus (for reasons we shall see), were a legitimate means of personal self-defense. MacGregor affirms that we cannot cite Jesus as discountenancing the recognized habit of carrying arms for self-defense.[1] That certainly seems the case.

In the parallel account in Matthew 26:51–53, Jesus is recorded as adding, "for all who take the sword will perish by the sword. Do you think that I cannot appeal to my Father, and he will at once send me more than twelve legions of angels? But how then should the scriptures be fulfilled?" Again, His own explanation is the key.

Note the several elements to this statement. First, Jesus didn't say, *Get rid of your swords; this is what I was trying to tell you before but you didn't understand.* No, He simply had Peter put his sword back *in its sheath.* In terms of His fulfilling the Father's will, He was to be arrested, then give His life a sacrifice. This He had told them, although they had difficulty comprehending. Later, when Peter sought to defend him, it seems He is saying, *Peter, see the problem it causes Me when you attempt to defend Me. Had I intended to be defended, I would not have requested your help with the two swords. I would have called upon legions of angels available to Me. You see, defending Me is not what I have in mind. Furthermore, when you undertake to defend Me, you risk perishing by the sword.*

Jesus emphasizes that in the very employment of the sword there is the risk of perishing by the sword. He implies there is indeed a legitimate defensive use of the sword (today a gun), but offers no comfort to those who *live by* the sword (gun)! Obviously, the disciples who wore swords for self-defense did not *live* by them (nor do armed householders *live* by their guns!).

Staying within the context, the valid question is *Why, then, did Jesus tell His disciples to sheath their swords on this occasion?* Was it because the sword was a means of violence? Was it because Jesus was teaching them the lesson not to use lethal force for defense—even in a life-threatening situation?

Rather, it was because of the special circumstances—Jesus' supreme purpose for laying down His life. This had nothing in common with their defending themselves or others, say, against bandits encountered along the way.

This is God's appointed time for Jesus to be taken and crucified, even as He told them it would happen. He called it *my hour.* His purpose was to die for man's sin, and the time had arrived. Sure, it was the disciples' natural inclination to defend Him. But any attempt to prevent His arrest would be to oppose Jesus' own declared purpose. Is this not exactly the reason He Himself gave? Thus, clearly, to misconstrue this unique event to teach that defensive use of the sword is impermissible is patently unwarranted.

Charles Raven, in an important study, puts the matter in fair balance:

> Of course, we can only say that this was the case with Jesus the Son of God, the Redeemer; we cannot directly infer for sure that this is laid upon His followers as a universal obligation to do likewise. May it be that we shall best serve the cause of righteousness by realizing that attainment is an age-long process involving us in an inevitable measure of compromise with what is, affording only a gradual step-by-step fulfillment of His will? May it be our best wisdom that resistance, sometimes lethal, is still necessary to ongoing life? It seems plain that some degree of accommodation is necessary if we are to live in a sinful world. May it be that for some, not all, a life of total non-resistance is possible, but that for many the ideal has attached to it a *not yet.*[2]

As for the incident at Gethsemane upon which hinged Jesus' progress toward His sacrifice on Calvary, here is Stephen Mott's summary:

> The Gospels indeed portray Jesus as dying without using violence, but do they see his death resulting from an intentional rejection of violence? The mere absence of the use of force by Jesus does not necessarily mean that force is disapproved of in principle. The hermeneutical principle that whatever is not made normative is therefore wrong is not satisfactory. The silence may only indicate that the question was not present in the minds of the authors.[3]

John Jefferson Davis adds a similar word: "His death was not intended to be the sole and comprehensive model for dealing with questions of civil justice in the temporal order."[4]

Jesus' death is to be interpreted as sacrifice. It did not come about as the result of choosing non-violence; rather, He chose death. He gave no admonition whatever to His disciples that the use of defensive violence was prohibited. And we would add, had He this in mind, then was the perfect time to instruct them. It was wrong at this time for one reason appropriate to the occasion, one particular end it would preclude.

In pursuit of the meaning of the Christians' right to bear swords for defensive use (in our nation a defensive weapon at home is allowed, whereas carrying such a weapon is only granted by permit to certain persons), we note that commentators stand on opposite sides, with many formidable scholars on each side.

First, a sampling of two prominent pacifist writers who believe Jesus did not mean to be taken literally.

Richard McSorley[5] believes a literal understanding conflicts with Jesus' follow-up statement *It is enough.* This, he says, conflicts with the whole context of the gospel and with Jesus' refusal to be defended. Rather, Jesus was using figurative language to speak, not of literal battles, but of spiritual ones. When He realized the disciples were childishly presenting Him with two swords, he says, frustrated with their lack of understanding, *Enough,* as though to say *You don't know what I'm talking about. This is pitiful. Forget it. The Holy Spirit will have to take care of this later. Go ahead and carry your little swords for awhile and you will see what I mean. Enough of this for now.* Sarcasm? We think not.

McSorley believes that the text, being obscure, can only be interpreted in accord with clearer texts, something he believes the spiritualizing interpretation makes probable. Or, he suggests, perhaps Jesus was testing how well the disciples had learned the lesson of the non-violent, suffering nature of his servanthood. If this were such a test, they failed, having an erroneous idea that the sword did have a place in the establishment of his kingdom.

Prominent pacifist, Jean Lasserre, claims that the disciples never bore arms except at Gethsemane where this conversation was recorded, a fact he finds exceptional. (Of course, *never bore arms except. . .* is his assumption). But how often must something be mentioned for it to be authentic? Further, he asserts the passage is obscure inasmuch as it is difficult to reconcile with other texts. (Is Jesus' plain word really *obscure,* or do we make it obscure by not believing Jesus meant what He said?).[6]

Lasserre also thinks the sword refers to their knowing how seriously they must prepare for coming spiritual battles:

> Jesus was using the word "sword" not literally but figuratively. . . . He was trying to give them moral stiffening. . . . By solemnly commanding them to take a purse, scrip, and a sword, He wanted to make them understand through striking imagery that the hour had come for them to prepare themselves for a tragic spiritual battle. They would need a supply of moral forces and a spiritual pugnacity to help them overcome the ordeal of their dispersion and the despair in which He would leave them by His death.[7]

Lasserre also points to the fact that *sword* is used in the Gospels figuratively nine times, over against five times to designate a literal sword (as if that determined anything!). Enumerated usage such as this has no relevance to the situation at hand, certainly not to Jesus' unambiguous word to the disciples.

Curiously, when Lasserre refers to Jesus' statement *It is enough* as meaning, *that's enough, don't say anymore* (perfectly possible interpretation) he adds,

> . . . let us imagine Jesus tired, anxious, discouraged by his disciples' incomprehension, simply wishing to cut short, perhaps with some irony in His voice, their stupid and untimely search for material arms, perhaps feeling there was no time to explain how they had misunderstood Him.[8]

I'm rather amazed at Lasserre's own imagination and incomprehension! Does he really think Jesus was displaying anxiety and discouragement? Did Jesus really wish to cut them short, or feel he had no time to correct a misunderstanding? I find this an incredible appraisal of Jesus' temperament!

No, Jesus spoke seriously, unambiguously, with no hint that He had anything in mind other than a literal understanding (as with purse and bag). Are we warranted, then, imputing anything other? Biblical interpretation requires statements be taken at face value unless there is sufficient warrant for taking them figuratively!

Take one clear instance where Jesus did say something the disciples failed to understand. Note how He treated their misunderstanding. In Mark 8:14–21 Jesus was speaking of the leaven of the Pharisees. The disciples, who had forgotten to bring bread with them on this occasion, thought it was bread He was talking about. Did Jesus get frustrated, impatient, or answer in a sarcastic way, insensitively showing up their ignorance, then leaving them in the dark? Not at all! Dispassionately, He explained what He meant. This is the true model of Jesus' response to the disciples' lack of understanding. Jesus never manifested frustration or impatience. Nor did He turn them off. Occasionally, He let them grow into fuller understanding. But here He is dealing with possibly dire consequences in the near future. It required more than a spiritual point. What they understood about the sword was critical to life as they might soon experience it. Equally decisive is this to be with taking purse and scrip.

As for Peter's defending Jesus, the authors find unacceptable the explanation of pacifist John Howard Yoder:

> His disavowal of Peter's well-intentioned effort to defend him . . . was because God's will for God's man in this world is that he should renounce legitimate defense. . . . God's man in this world was facing, and rejecting, the claim that the exercise of social responsibility through the use of self-evidently necessary means is a moral duty. It is not.[9]

Yoder generalizes what is particular—and with no warrant for doing this. Nor can he say, *because God's will for man is . . .* , since Yoder doesn't know what God's will for man is. He errs in his speculation.

To say, as do some pacifist writers, that a literal understanding of Jesus' admonition to buy a sword *contradicts the entire New Testament,* is to forget that the disciples did not have a New Testament to guide their understanding; their guidance was the direct word of Jesus (nor was it modern comparative studies of New Testament texts!). Absent such advanced instruction, what would incline them to need any further explanation, really, than this straightforward, imminently practical statement?

Foremost New Testament scholar, Robert Gundry, points out that in this period in Jesus' progress toward the cross, the expectancy of apocalyptic now yields, to a significant degree though not completely, to the normalcy of ongoing life in this world. In particular, as in this passage, the restrictions imposed during the critical period of Jesus' ministry are for the future lifted. Among other things, a sword can legitimately be owned and carried again. The instruction is to be taken literally. In terms of being physically together with them, Jesus' ministry is coming to an end; no longer will they have him by their side. The former conditions are changing.[10]

How biased interpreters can be is illustrated by a comment of Richard Cassidy:[11] *A more accurate rendering . . . would be "Enough of this." It was Jesus' way of breaking off the discussion* (so far, an acceptable exegesis), but then he adds *frustrated with the disciples' lack of comprehension.* Sheer unwarranted speculation!

Note that while Jesus was undoubtedly *breaking off the discussion,* there is no reason whatever to impute *frustration* or the implication of impatience, leading to a negative connotation. Jesus may very well have been simply closing discussion with a statement that for now this was sufficient instruction (*enough of all this for the present*).

We find the conclusion of S. Maclean Gilmour far more congenial:

The disciples took Jesus literally, and any hypothesis that they were mistaken is too subtle to be probable.[12] Exactly!

The contrast of conditions is perfectly clear: formerly, when the popularity of Jesus was shared by the disciples, they could travel without purse, scrip, or sword. As His disciples, they were well-known and revered by the populace. He was their protection. But soon they'll be on their own, their Master crucified, His cause and theirs in disrepute. Everything will have changed following His death, and they're to be prepared for the new life. Even travel in dangerous areas resumes as a threatening part of daily existence.

MATTHEW 5:38-48

Now we turn to the non-resistance, love-your-enemy sections in the Gospel. Here the disciples are instructed not to resist the evil person. Primarily, this is a reference to the treatment of one's personal enemy. It says nothing about retributive justice, certainly nothing about defensively preserving life itself against a violent assailant. Rather, it teaches the power of forbearance, even suffering, in cases of personal hostility. This would be especially important in their response to persecution for the gospel's sake. Neither revenge nor hostile response is in the Christian's spiritual interest nor witness.[13]

There is a custom involved here that needs to be understood. Stephen Mott refers affirmingly to Stuart D. Currie's persuasive argument that the expression *resist not the evil person* speaks concretely of a Jewish citizen not protesting wrong in court; it does not refer to the enemy as an outsider. Rather, it forbids speaking against someone in court in one's own defense. The word for evil person does not refer to a foreigner, and has its background in the law of talio. Knowing the custom of the day is an aid to interpretation.[14]

Among recent commentators on Matthew's Gospel, Robert Gundry affirms that this verse speaks of an *evil person,* commenting that "Matthew draws . . . from Isaiah 50:8 (cf. esp. the LXX), where the expression has to do with verbal resistance in a court of law; the Lord himself will vindicate his Servant; thus the vindication will not be the Servant's own doing."[15]

William Barclay is also helpful:

Jesus begins by citing the oldest law in the world—an eye for an eye, and a tooth for a tooth. That law is known as the Lex Talionis, and it may be described as the law of tit for tat. . . . In the Old Testament we find it laid down no fewer than three times. . . . So far from being a savage and bloodthirsty law, it is in fact the beginning of mercy. Its original aim was definitely the limitation of vengeance . . . punishment must be no more than the equivalent of the injury inflicted and the damage done. . . . Further, this was never a law which gave a private individual the right to extract vengeance; it was always a law which laid down how a judge in the law court must assess punishment and penalty (Comp. Exodus 19:18).[16] Note how this translates into the modern legal notion of *proportional reason* in the exercise of appropriate degrees of defensive response.

So, on scholarly authority, we understand that the law never intended to give to the individual the right to indulge more than tit for tat when the purpose was retribution; retribution itself was permissible but in a proportional manner. But now the remarkable thing is that Jesus abolishes even the law of equitable retaliation in cases of personal abuse, and introduces the new spirit of non-retaliation. We might conclude, as does Norman Geisler, that the Sermon is not pacifist, simply non-retaliatory.

Now, of course, nothing about personal retaliation or revenge can so much as intimate what may or may not be done in defensive action against a violent outsider intent upon taking life. The passage cannot be construed to argue against necessary life-preserving defensive measures. We must be vigilant not to equate life-preserving defensive action with the prohibition of retaliation or vengeance-taking. Again, our best scriptural support of self-defensive is Jesus' admonition to bear a sword (admonition, not mere permission!).

We need care not to overemphasize the antitheses in the Sermon on the Mount. R. V. G. Tasker comments that, in His teaching,

> Jesus insists that He is in no way contradicting the Mosaic Law, though He is opposed to the legalistic type of religion that the scribes had built upon it. That He regards the Old Testament as possessing permanent validity as the Word of God is clear from the uncompromising sayings in verses 17–19. At the same time, it is also clear that He regards His own teaching as equally binding; and His emphasis upon this truth has sometimes given readers of this section of the Gospel of Matthew the impression that in some instances the abiding nature of the old law seems to be denied. . . . If, however, there was in fact any real antithesis between what the law stated and the fuller implications of it unfolded by Jesus, the statements in verses 17–19 would be unintelligible.[17]

With this, Gundry is in full agreement.[18] Tasker further points out that Jesus is obviously not in the least degree impinging upon the permanent validity of the Sixth Commandment.

Now, it must not be denied that Jesus' sayings in the Sermon on the Mount were meant to have universal and present application. This is indicated by their not being restricted to a specific narrative framework. Nor it is suggested anywhere in the Gospels that the disciples were to postpone their obedience until such time as obedience could be universalized in the fully realized eschatological Kingdom. The Kingdom rule which Jesus introduced at His first coming is the Christian's pattern for a personal life-style, the ideal to be approximated as closely as possible, even in the midst of an evil society. This despite our understanding that the ideal shall not be fully attained until Jesus' return, nor will human conditions always allow it to be possible. By the enabling power of the Holy Spirit, this ideal is to be embraced.[19]

In contrast with this present evil world, the Kingdom of our Lord is to be a peaceable kingdom where violence shall be no more. Whether physical violence, psychological violence, economic, social or political violence—every kind of violence shall be removed forever. Justice, righteousness and peace shall ultimately prevail when the Kingdom comes. No longer will defensive self-protection be required, no lethal force ever again need be employed against one's fellows. The full manifestation of the eschatological Kingdom awaits Christ's return in power and glory—the righteous rule of the risen, transformed Christ of God in the fulness of His Deity. Then all things shall be brought under His rule. But until then we live fragile and sinful lives amid the world's continuing evil. Nor can we expect a just social order free from human violence and the need to restrain it. Those who commit crimes against persons are to be punished in ways proportionate with their crimes. There must be just compensation for unacceptable and evil behavior. To maintain a just order, one with minimal crime, protective measures must be in place. Often this requires coercive (and not infrequently, lethally coercive) means. And where protective forces are unable to provide safety, the individual is sometimes compelled to provide his own protection. Still, as His disciples, we are to live apart from unnecessary violence as may be possible. We are, after all, living in an evil world as members of His Kingdom now!

MacGregor says that Jesus' word, "*My kingdom is not of this world* cannot be read as if Jesus meant, *My kingdom is not for this world.* For the disciple this is part of what it means to be *in the world but not of it.*" We have a dual citizenship, earthly and heavenly, but presently we must live as peaceably as we can as citizens of this evil world. So we approximate the ideal as far as it is possible to do so. Where it is impossible, we look to the grace and forgiveness of God.

MacGregor points out that, measured against the absolute perfection of the Kingdom ethic, lethal defense may never be *right* in the sense of *ultimately right*, or *ideally right*. But measured against a fallen, disordered human society in which innocent people must be protected against criminal violence, it may, in God's sight, be *relatively right* under certain conditions.[20] Lethal defense, it seems, is a legitimate, necessary expression of divinely ordained governance for living in this world at this time, during this interim period when the Kingdom both *is*, but still *is not yet*.

Pacifists hold to a more literal interpretation of the Sermon, something most difficult to maintain. It overlooks the hyperbole that Jesus frequently employed to arrest attention (plucking out the lustful eye, cutting off the sinning hand).

Quite differently, selectivists hold the teachings of the Sermon as principles to be approximated as nearly as possible, not as literal commands on every occasion possible of fulfillment. In the particular quandary of defending against a violent intruder, the principles of the Sermon are primarily those of non-revenge and non-retaliation for personal offenses. That these principles are applicable to protective defense of self or third parties must remain questionable at least. As selectivists, we have reason to look beyond the Sermon in search of a resolution to our quandary.

ROMANS 12:17, 21 AND 13:10

Once again, pacifists appeal to the Apostle's words, *Repay no one with evil . . . but overcome evil with good, and Love does no wrong to a neighbor.* These passages they cite as prohibiting violence (there being no repayment of any kind for evil, and the incapacity of love to do violence).

Note, however, that neither passage is directed to life-threatening situations, so neither passage has to do with the issue of life preservation. Nor does facing a violent intruder inspire an *evil* response, only a life-preserving defensive response (hardly *evil*). It has nothing to do with doing *wrong* to a neighbor. Thus we conclude that the admonitions here simply do not apply to our quandary.

FIRST PETER 2:18-21

This final New Testament scripture, considered by pacifists important to the issue, is directed specifically to servants serving their masters. The servants' personal conduct is under review. Peter says to them, *For to this you have been called, because Christ also suffered for you, leaving you an example, that you should follow in his steps* (verse 11). And how are they to follow Him? In this respect: *when he suffered, he did not threaten, but he trusted to him who judges justly.*

The application is personal between two people in relationship, not lifted to the social plane where it speaks to life-threatening acts of an outsider. Most importantly, there is nothing directly prohibiting force, even preemptive lethal force in the protection of innocent life. Rather, it is an admonition found within the context of the relationship of servants to their masters and has to do with their Christian response to a master's mistreatment, and the application may be broadened to include mistreatment within any personal relationship. It does not go beyond that.

Again, it appears that the reference is to non-retaliation against personal abuse, especially as it concerns the witness of the Christian in a provoking personal relational circumstance. It cannot be said to provide a definitive word about either retributive justice in general or the preemptive use of lethal force to protect life.

ACTS 10:47

There are additional indications in the New Testament, in themselves at least suggestive. These include the scene depicted in Acts 10:47. There the Apostle Peter baptized the Centurion, Cornelius, apparently without requiring him to renounce and leave his military profession. This is congruent with the episode in Luke 3:14 where John the Baptist was baptizing the people with the baptism of repentance. As he instructed them what repentance required, we read that *the multitudes asked him, "What then shall we do?"* Further along, *Soldiers also asked him, "And we, what shall we do?"* John did not require that they forsake the military. Augustine, in his sermon on the healing of the centurion's son, wrote:

> If Christian teaching forbade war altogether, those looking for the salutary advice of the gospel would have been told to get rid of their arms and give up soldiering. But instead they were told, "Rob no one by violence or by false

accusation, and be content with your wages" (Luke 3:14). If the gospel ordered them to be satisfied with their pay, then it did not forbid a military career.

He merely told them to avoid the abuse of weapons.

Another intimation of this comes before us in Hebrews 11:33, 34. Here is explicit reference to the military exploits of the judges and of David. Their actions are characterized in the New Testament as demonstrations of active, positive examples of faith. Here is the association of faith and works to which James gave such strong emphasis (James 2:14–26). James demonstrates repeatedly how faith is made real by works—the consistent relationship between living faith and active obedience. The New Testament clearly approves their *putting foreign armies to flight* as well as the use of arms in the enforcement of justice.

We've long been told that leaving the military was required in the early centuries of the church, but Edward A. Ryan shows that pacifism was never the dominant position in the early church.[21] At any rate, this requirement was not part of the church we read about in the New Testament.

NOTES

1. MacGregor, G. H. C., *The New Testament Basis of Pacifism and the Relevance of an Impossible Ideal.* (rev. ed.) Nyack, NY: Fellowship, 1984.
2. Raven, Charles. *War and the Christian.* New York: Macmillan, 1938, pp. 95–97.
3. Mott, Stephen, *Biblical Ethics and Social Concerns.* London: Oxford University, 1982, p. 179.
4. Davis, John Jefferson, *Evangelical Ethics: Issues Facing the Church Today.* Phillipsburg, PA: Presbyterian and Reformed, 1985, p. 233.
5. McSorley, op. cit., pp. 441–443.
6. Lasserre, op. cit., pp. 37–41.
7. Ibid., pp. 42–43.
8. Ibid., p. 44.
9. Yoder, op. cit., p. 100.
10. Personal memo dated Feb. 4, 1991.
11. Cassidy, op. cit.
12. Gilmour, S. Maclean, *Luke* (*The Interpreter's Bible,* Vol. VIII), New York: Abingdon, 1952, p. 387.
13. "Non-resistance to evil, for example, is not a universal principle that holds true for all situations, but is an ethical ideal that pertains to some, but not all, situations." Bloesch, Donald G., *Freedom for Obedience: Evangelical Ethics in Contemporary Times.* San Francisco: Harper & Row, 1987, p. 65.
14. Mott, op. cit.

15. Gundry, Robert H. *Matthew: A Commentary on His Literary and Theological Art.* Grand Rapids: Eerdmans, 1982, p. 94.
16. Barclay, William, *The Gospel of Matthew* (VOL. 1) Philadelphia: Westminster, 1956, pp. 160–163.
17. Tasker, R.V.G., *The Gospel According to St. Matthew.* Grand Rapids: Eerdmans, 1961, pp. 64–65.
18. Gundry, op. cit., p. 83.
19. Ladd, George Eldon, *Theology of the New Testament.* Grand Rapids: Eerdmans, (*see* chaps. 4–9); *See* A.M. Hunter, *A Pattern for Life* (1953); R. Schnackenburg, *The Moral Teaching of the New Testament* (1965); Martin Dibelius, *The Sermon on the Mount* (1940); S. Maclean Gilmour, "How Relevant is the Ethic of Jesus," *Journal of Religion* XXI (1941) p. 263.
20. MacGregor, op. cit., p. 145.
21. Ryan, Edward A., "The Rejection of Military Service by the Early Christians," *Theological Studies* 13 (1952) pp. 1–32.

Chapter 11

MANDATE FOR DOING WHAT IS *JUST*

No biblical appeal to the validity of self-defense is complete without noting the pervasive theme of justice which runs through both Old and New Testaments. No attribute is more fundamental to the moral nature of God, not even that of love. No quality of life more relevant to our theme.

In the Scriptures, justice and righteousness are scarcely distinguished from each other. The same word in the original becomes in English either *justice* or *righteousness,* in terms of the context where it is found almost a translator's choice.

When God announced the destruction of Sodom, Abraham interceded with God for the righteous living within the city, reminding God that he, Abraham, knew God would act in conformity with His own nature, saying,

> Will you indeed destroy the righteous with the wicked? . . . Far be it from you to do such a thing, to slay the righteous with the wicked, so that the righteous fare as the wicked! Far be that from you! Shall not the Judge of all the earth do right? (Genesis 18:23, 25).

Two ideas stand out. First, God is the one and only ultimate Judge of mankind. Second, His judgment is just, a righteous apportioning of reward or punishment according to divine justice.

It is sometimes said, *Justice requires God to do thus and so.* But this postulates justice as a principle outside of God which compels Him to act in conformity with a principle existing independently of Himself. It puts justice outside His sovereign will and hence superior to His will. In truth, all that moves God comes from within His uncreated being. When He acts justly, that action conforms to His nature and will. Human actions are unjust which fail to conform to His will.[1]

In a full-orbed view of justice, theology joins philosophy in distinguishing distributive justice from retributive justice. Hear John Macquarrie:

> One of the commonest distinctions is between retributive justice which aims at punishing the infringement of a right, or at restoring the enjoyment of a right,

and distributive justice, which attempts to ensure the fair distribution of rights and privileges on the maxim "to every man his due."[2]

To get at the essential meaning of justice, we locate two core concepts: First, all persons are to be treated equally and fairly on the basis of inalienable human rights. Second, every person is to receive his due. These two concepts, however, are too general; they require further definition. To do this, we shall proceed along four avenues until eventually a complete working definition is formulated.[3]

(1) Justice Concerns *What is Due*

Emil Brunner correctly observed that from time immemorial the principle of justice has been defined as *rendering to each person his or her due.* As members of the human family, created in the image of God and hence equal before Him, every person has claim to what is rightfully due in the distribution of life's essential benefits. The ground is God-given inherent rights.

There are also *acquired* rights which encompass what each person earns in consequence of his or her treatment of other persons. This notion goes as far back as Aristotle's assertion that justice means distribution in accordance with merit earned.

Justice discriminates rewards earned from sanctions or punishments earned. The concept of acquired rights shifts away from *equal rights* to *unequally distributed rewards or sanctions.* As Nicholas Rescher sums it, "Distributive justice consists in the treatment of people according to their legitimate claims."[4] One way of expressing this is the formula, *To each according to....* For example, if a person's treatment of others is judged to be good, certain rewards are earned. If, on the contrary, treatment of others is judged to be bad, certain sanctions or punishments are earned.

The formula *To each according to...,* is variously filled according to specific behavior. For instance, in the conflict between an assailant and his victims, justice is allocated (a) *according to the intruder's treatment of his victims* or (b) *according to the innocent parties' treatment of the intruder.* Compensatory justice is ultimately assessed on the basis of each participant receiving his or her rightful *due* in terms of *good to whomever good is due, ill to whomever ill is due.*

Biblically, for example, God is referred to as *him who judges justly* (I

Peter 2:23). In the Book of Revelation John sees the vision of the bowls of wrath which God is to pour out upon an unrepentant earth at the end of history. John hears an angel say, *Just art thou in thy judgments. . . . It is their due* (16:4.6).

For distribution to be just, it must be fair. It is generally agreed that nothing is stronger to native moral sensibility than the sense of fairness, or equity. The major contention of John Rawls is that fairness lies at the heart of justice.[5]

Distributive justice operates without partiality, a feature notable in all God's acts toward His human family, explicitly declared in Ephesians 6:9, *there is no partiality with him* [God], and in Colossians 3:25, "For the wrongdoer will be paid back for the wrong he has done, and there is no partiality."

The objective of justice is: (1) that treatment of others mirror God's just treatment of us (retributive as well as distributive), (2) that God-given human rights be preserved and protected (including those of victims of injustice), and (3) that injustices be justly rectified.

Wherever a householder, responsible for third parties within his or her care, confronts an intruder who intends violence, it must be decided what is rightfully *due* each participant—victim himself, innocent third parties, victimizing assailant—what is neither more nor less than is justly due.

The intruder evokes just retribution for wrongful treatment of others. But assuming the householder could intervene, suppose he stands aside, leaving third parties to suffer harmful treatment. His action (in this case, inaction) is in complicity *with harmful treatment,* hence unjust.

Further, it must be asked, "What is justly due the community to which both assailant and victims belong? What of a just future for all who participate in the community social order?"

It has been correctly said, "In a social order that is just, everything matters; in a social order that is unjust, nothing matters." This has as much to do with retributive as with distributive justice. What loss, hence injustice, does the community suffer if the assailant kills his victims?

(2) Justice Concerns *Personal Rights*

Whenever anyone can claim something *my due*, personal rights are to be respected, for claims are made on the basis of those rights. John Stuart Mill correctly asserted, "Justice implies something which it is not only right to do, and wrong not to do, but which an individual person can claim from us as his moral right."

Incidentally, Mill also suggested that "the most intense feelings are raised around certain types of injustice, to wit, "acts of wrongful aggression or wrongful exercised power over someone. . . . "[7]

Since God is the source of inalienable human rights, every personal relationship stands before the requirements of divine justice. To this point, Lewis Smedes adds that the powerful reason a Christian affirms human rights is that we are all created in the image of God, thus the task of justice is the preservation of the human rights given us of God.[8] Thus, while Scripture does not use the term *rights,* the implication is clear. Smedes' point seems incontestable.

Since our concern is with what is merited in consequence of one's personal treatment of others, treatment that proves *harmful* may merit what could range from simple sanctions to severest punishment. In other terms, it is *the acquisition of the right to be held accountable, to be sanctioned, perhaps to be punished.* When there is a moral wrong, what is merited may amount to simple reward deprivation, minor sanctions, or possibly severe punishment.

(3) Justice Concerns *Just-Desserts*

Curiously, the importance of just-desserts is generally downplayed by pacifists. It is fair to observe that those who espouse *love* or *non-violence* as the be-all and end-all of ethics tend away from proper allocation of just-desserts, allowing justice to be subsumed under some amorphous notion labeled *love, compassion, mercy, forgiveness,* or whatever. This is nothing less than reluctance to acknowledge the reality of justice as God's darker face. Just-desserts rightly rewards individual social behavior —not with what an individual is but does.

Under the principle of proportionality—responding to threats of violence with *neither more nor less than is justly due* —punishment may never be greater than the crime it compensates, but it may be equal to it. Incidentally, the Old Testament *eye for an eye,* properly understood, was simply a way of stating this very principle—giving back no more than is due.

In the situation where one is face-to-face with an intruder evidently bent upon violence, the broader concerns of equal justice yield to the narrower concerns of retributive justice. In some cases wisdom may dictate preemptive action (innocent victims are awaiting rescue, their lives on the line). The defender must seek to accurately determine the just-desserts due the initiator of this evil behavior.

Within this whole process, we expect of course that the aims of love will be present. Surely, conscientious Christians with concern for other human beings will earnestly seek the possibility of any redemptive ministry, also whether the consequences can be compassionately mitigated. If no such possibility arises, of necessity the householder's response may be dictated by the principle of just-desserts.

Thus far our analysis has led to a complex, multifaceted concept, having to do with rights, claims, desserts, and more. At times, compensatory justice means retributive justice. All this leads to a very important fourth element.

(4) Justice Concerns *Obligation*

Whenever a person legitimately presents a claim based on either inherent or acquired rights, there falls upon some other person or persons the obligation to satisfy that claim. Stated axiomatically, *With every legitimate right there is a corresponding claim, and with every legitimate claim there is a corresponding obligation to satisfy it.*

This axiom respects the fact that obligation has a negative as well as positive side to it. Where there is the threat of harm, there is the corresponding obligation to stop it.

Among modern theologians with a strong central understanding, Reinhold Niebuhr stands out. His *Christian realism* takes seriously the limits of social possibilities. He says: "If selfishness were a simple possibility in history, there would be no need for justice, since all would coexist in a perfect harmony of love."[9] But, he adds, unfortunately there is no such possibility. Love remains an *impossible possibility,* for *the love command stands in juxtaposition to the fact of sin* (not a micro view of persons and individual possibilities, but the macro view of society). This leads to his conclusion that *the moral dimension of sin, therefore, is injustice — an unwillingness to value the claims of the other....* [10] The root injustice is exploitation, taking advantage of another's life.[11]

Justice is seen by Niebuhr as an absolute, but not in isolation from at least one other absolute. *Justice that is only justice is less than justice.*[12] Inseparably related to justice is love. We recall Lewis Smedes's statement,

For God nothing is enough without justice, but for God justice is not enough by itself.[13]

Donald Bloesch says, *Like him* [Niebuhr], "I hold that there are norms of justice that have a universal import, but I believe that only in the light of biblical revelation do we have an adequate understanding of the nature of these norms."[14]

Niebuhr says, "It is because men are sinners that justice can be achieved only by a certain degree of coercion on the one hand, and by a resistance to coercion and tyranny on the other hand."[15] He finds no absolute arguments against violence in principle; what is morally relevant is the use to which violence is put.

What Niebuhr does for us is to lift to its rightful place the divine attribute of justice, placing it alongside love as one of two scriptural absolutes, affirming twin norms, neither of which is sufficient in itself. Interestingly, his different-leaning brother H. Richard Niebuhr also claimed that no single human virtue such as love can adequately explain the ethical teaching of Jesus. Would that love ethicists might understand this!

MAJESTIC DIVINE ATTRIBUTE

Justice as a divine attribute reflects an even more basic quality in God—His moral purity, or as it is called, **holiness**—His moral perfection. Because He is holy, all God's acts manifest themselves morally as *rightness* (scriptural term: *righteousness*). Whatever God does is in perfect conformity with what He is; to act righteously is to act justly. In any given instance God may choose to transcend the demands of justice by acts of love or mercy, but never does His love compromise justice. Note some sample passages from Scripture:

> Isaiah 61:8: *For I the Lord love justice.*
> Deuteronomy 32:4: *all his [God's] ways are justice.*
> Proverbs 28:5: *Evil men do not understand justice, but those who seek the Lord understand it completely.*

RETRIBUTIVE JUSTICE: ITS BIBLICAL ROOTS

Defending against a violent intruder is a form of compensatory justice retributive in nature. Retribution is basically considered re-active, not pro-active. It is compensatory justice coming on the heels of a criminal offense. In contrast, preemptive defensive action is pro-active against violence presumably about to take place.

Retribution is a biblical theme running through both Old and New Testaments. The meaning of the Greek word apodidomai, often translated *recompense,* is *to render or give back what is due.* The major lexicons agree that *what is due* is reward or punishment for either good or bad behavior.

Among the major philosophers, Plato, an early example, developed a concept of retribution, found at the end of *The Republic.*[16] Immanuel Kant affirmed that along with the dignity or worth of each person is associated the principle of retributive justice—punishment given not because it serves any utility but solely because it is right, just, deserved. Kant also observed, "No one undergoes punishment because he has willed to be punished, but because he has willed a punishable action."[17] The same theme is later developed by Georg Hegel and other so-called retributionists.[18]

H. L. A. Hart, Oxford professor of jurisprudence, in his essay, *Retribution,*[19] discusses the strict usage of the term as we are using it. A person may be punished only if he has voluntarily done something morally wrong. The justification for punishing persons under such conditions is that the return of suffering for his moral evil is both just and considered morally good.

Hart points out that modern retributivists have generally shifted toward weakened utilitarian versions, away from justice or intrinsic moral goodness. Hence we have a substitute value: reprobation rather than retribution. Reprobation doesn't require justice, only an offender's personal reclamation.

To strict retributionists, punishment should be proportionate to the gravity of the crime. To reprobationists, it suffices merely to express moral condemnation, hoping to reclaim the offender. The retributionist has the greater concern for justice. The reprobationist claims greater concern for love, mercy and compassion, but it is improper to accuse retributionists of being without love, compassion, or mercy. As for biblical theology, it stands with retribution, not merely with reprobation.

Now, if defensive shooting of an intruder is to be legitimated as preemptive retribution, Christians must find its justification on two grounds: first, historically, in the biblical story of God's people, and secondly, in God's command.

A JUST SOCIAL ORDER

God is depicted in Scripture as ordaining human government (1) to stabilize and maintain order in the social structure, (2) to protect citizens from harm, and (3) to secure a peaceful existence. A just social order is made possible through the establishment of just laws which in turn are enforced by necessary, sometimes coercive means.

Governments are given the prerogative to punish criminal offenders, including capital punishment for crimes of great gravity against persons. As recorded in Genesis 9:5–6, capital punishment was established early in human history. God destroyed Noah's generation because or prevailing corruption and unrestricted violence. Retributively, God employed violence to recompense violence. He made a covenant with Noah including the words, *Whoever sheds the blood of man, by man shall his blood be shed.* This is retributive justice authorized by God to be carried out by the hand of man.

As the penalty for willfully, unjustly taking the life of another, the offender's life is forfeited. Mosaic Law specified what shall be judged willful, unjustified taking of life. Theologian Walter Harrelson speaks of "the distinction between killing that serves the cause of life and the killing that does not serve the cause of life—an exceedingly important distinction indeed!"[20]

Retributive justice, requiring the just taking of life in compensation for unjust taking of life, is built into the social order by God's own directive. Historically, Catholic doctrine also affirms that to be what determines the just and the unjust is God's intentions for human life. Protestant doctrine likewise locates the standard of justice in the revelation of God's intent for His human family. Throughout the military actions God commanded of His people Israel, and on to descriptions of the yet-future earthly return of our conquering Lord and His victory over His enemies, retribution is executed upon God's intractable enemies. Retributive justice corresponds to the realities of a sinful humanity alienated from God, hostile to Him and to one another, and violent in their ways.

In Hebrews 2:2, the exact terminology is *just retribution.* Divine retribution, while future, predates that future time when God shall bring about *the new heavens and the new earth* in His final restoration of all things in Christ (cf. Ephesians 1:9–10; Revelation 21:22). Paradoxically, the biblical depiction is of One who hates human violence yet employs and commands it in human situations. Furthermore, He Himself will ultimately exercise violent retribution. A word of caution: Retribution is not to be confused with a vengeful spirit, but recognized objectively as what is justly due for offenses against His law.

JESUS AND RETRIBUTION

Since commands to love and the example of non-violence are attributable to Jesus, some have a serious problem with associating retribution with Him. Yet to suggest that the retributive God of the Old Testament has been replaced by a non-retributive God of the New, is a monumental mistake, for it negates the consistent revelation in both testaments. The same Jesus who taught unconditional love, forgiveness, and non-retaliation— including *enemy love*—used parables to illustrate the moral balance which retributive justice secures both in this life and in the life to come.

In Matthew 21:33–43, Jesus replies to a rhetorical question He Himself raised. The situation He describes is one of treachery by servants against their master. The wicked servants are put to death. Jesus does not so much as hint that this fearful retributive consummation to wickedness is wrong, mistaken, or even of transient validity. Furthermore, Jesus is recorded as saying, *And he who falls on this stone will be broken to pieces; but when it falls on any one, it will crush him.*

However we view Jesus' vivid imagery, the meaning of violent destruction at the hand of the Lord is beyond question. He is indeed the Lord of retributive justice who brings His enemies to a violent end. Jesus depicts Himself as the Master whom the servants hate and maltreat, then gives a warning about the destruction awaiting those who persistently reject Him.

The parable is calculated to bring its hearers to the logical conclusion that as the absent owner will one day wreak destruction upon the wicked tenants, so the Lord Himself will, upon His return to earth, wreak destruction upon those who rejected God's plan of redemption through His beloved Son.

What more could this master have done? Shall there not be moral compensation in the scales of His righteous purposes? This has nothing to do with personal reaction to having been hated and slain; it has to do with justice and the moral order of all things.

The climax of the parable is, surprisingly, not a redemptive event. Representing none other than the Father of love, Jesus announces the reality of retributive judgment. Thus, in His teaching, redemption and retribution are compatible, of a single piece.

One further illustration from Jesus' teaching should suffice to make the point. Luke 12:42–48 records His parable about a master who leaves his household in charge of a steward while he is away. Although knowing his master will return, the steward takes advantage of his absence to indulge his every whim. In the process he severely beats both male and female servants. Unexpectedly, the master returns to find all this going on. Then Jesus describes the retribution that follows: "And that servant who knew his master's will, but did not make ready or act according to his will, shall receive a severe beating. But he who did not know, and did what deserved a beating, shall receive a light beating." Here is the use of proportionate recompense as just retribution. This is New Testament teaching! The Lord of Life and Love is none other than the Retributive Judge!

Strikingly, Jesus ends the parable abruptly, in full recognition of the place of just-desserts. Not that God always carries out retributive justice in fulfillment of His purposes, only that there are occasions when He does so. There is no questioning His divine prerogative as the Moral Sovereign of the Universe which He Himself created and rules! And His rule presently admits the reality of sinfulness and its consequences. But God is not prudent; He is just! He executes His will, according to justice or according to grace; it is His to do as He wishes. And what He wishes is not arbitrary.

Several additional texts enhance this truth. Jeremiah 51:56 reads, *for the Lord is a God of recompense.* The Apostle Paul, for whom retributive justice is a theological mainstay, wrote:

> ...Since indeed God deems it just to repay with affliction those who afflict you...when the Lord Jesus is revealed from heaven with his mighty angels in flaming fire, inflicting vengeance upon those who do not know God and upon those who do not obey the gospel of our Lord Jesus. They shall suffer the punishment of eternal destruction and exclusion from the presence of the Lord and from the glory of his might (2 Thessalonians 1:6ff).

A dreadful picture indeed—but just!

The Apostle Paul, speaking of the coming Antichrist, writes, *and the Lord Jesus will slay him with the breath of his mouth and destroy him by his appearing...* (2 Thessalonians 2:8). Retributive justice is an unmistakable thread woven throughout the very fabric of redemption theology. The core truth here is that Christ suffered the just retribution of God in our stead. Only the Just One could take the place of the unjust in suffering the penalty which God the Father's retributive justice demanded.

In the revelation of the end-time, the Apostle Paul writes, "Then comes the end, when he [Christ] delivers the kingdom to God the Father after destroying every rule and every authority and every power. For He must reign until he has put all his enemies under his feet" (I Corinthians 15:24, 25). The earthly reign of Christ is to establish peace, but in preparation for peace He destroys all wickedness, every intruding evil that would undo that peace.

On the last page of the Bible, John's final word is of the risen Christ saying, "Behold, I am coming soon, bringing my recompense, to repay every one for what he has done" (Revelation 22:12).

What is significant about these references is that retributive justice is seen as perfectly compatible with unconditional, redemptive love. For those who reject the Savior, the startling fact is that retributive justice shall then prevail. For salvation is contingent upon the all-important condition of receptive faith. It is either one of two fates: eternal life through faith in His justifying atonement, or retribution at the hand of a just God.

Of course, we must be careful not to confuse retributive justice with revenge or personal retaliation, both of which are plainly disavowed in Scripture (Romans 12:19; 13:4; I Peter 2:13–14). Retributive justice is a far cry from what critics label *sanitized revenge.*

But, it might be asked, is not the prerogative of executing retributive justice that of God alone? Ultimately, yes. But He shares His prerogatives with us in numerous ways. He delegates action. Consider the statement in 2 Peter 1:4 that we have *become partakers of the divine nature.* Are we to say that in our participation in His nature the one quality exempted is that of exercising retributive justice in the world of injustice in human affairs? The presumption is otherwise.

Lewis Smedes sums this well:

> God's unique authority to determine the ending of human life is a strong theological reason for our duty to respect and not to destroy it. But for the most part God shares his authority with us when he makes us caretakers for one another. He lets us decide whether a human being shall appear on earth by giving us direction over contraception. He gives us the right to stave off death, if we can, with medicines and machines. At both ends of life's line, he lets us collaborate. . . . Divine authority over human life is a powerful reason

not to kill. But his magnanimous way of sharing authority indicates that we may sometimes be responsible to act in ways that determine death itself.[21]

Does this shared authority extend to taking a criminal's life when necessary to repel an attack aimed at taking innocent life? Smedes's comment: "In a broken world, it is necessary sometimes to break a commandment. . . . It may be necessary to kill a person to save a cause."[22] Donald Bloesch phrases it: "Since it is a gift from God, life must be respected and may be taken only for the sake of life."[23]

Having established the biblical ground for (a) retributive justice and (b) forfeiture of life through willful, unjust killing, we conclude that preemptively stopping a dangerous intruder is an application of these principles, yet with a difference: retributive compensation takes place in advance, by anticipation, based upon a reasonable presumption that it is necessary to act first in order to prevent a lethal-force attack.

A COSMIC ILLUSTRATION

If ever Christians, Protestant and Catholic alike, had a core illustration of how love functions inseparably with justice, it is the Gospel of redemption. For, indisputably, redemption is the work of love, conceived in the compassionate, merciful heart of God. Redemption is not a creation of justice, but of love. Yet to achieve redemption, God neither abrogated nor circumvented the requirements of justice. Nothing in the nature of God could permit His acting in love at the expense of justice, pitting one divine attribute against another. Instead, with full regard for the claims of justice, He condemned our sin as worthy of death inasmuch as sin stands against the Person and holiness of God. He then took our judgment upon Himself, assuming responsibility for our penalty, enduring the weight of every charge which divine righteousness could level. The incredible story is summed in Romans 3:26. God is *just and the Justifier of him that believeth in Jesus* (KJV).

How could God at the same time be both just and the Justifier of the ungodly? Jesus, second Person of the Trinity, paid our penalty. As Son of God incarnate in human flesh, He was worthy to stand in our stead, worthy to act as Mediator between God and man—the Substitute Sin-Bearer.

Were there no just claims against us, His suffering would be unnecessary. For God to allow, let alone appoint, such suffering would be tantamount to wronging His innocent Son! But in one act at the cross, both the immeasurableness of divine love and the uncompromised fulfillment of divine justice were forever joined. In Jesus' sacrifice, both love and justice acted conjointly to achieve what neither could have accomplished alone.

Well, couldn't a God of love simply have forgiven us if He wished? Isn't a declaration of mercy enough? Mercy is not enough, nor is forgiveness possible without justice being satisfied. It was not merely that humanity had sinned, but had sinned against God and His righteousness. In the substitutionary sacrifice of God incarnate, every moral attribute is honored. Redemption was justly won.

The cross of Christ is at once a declaration of judgment and of triumphant mercy and grace! Mercy because our redemption is undeserved and cannot be earned, grace because God Himself freely initiated the gift of forgiveness and life. Both love and justice were honored in that single act. As Henry Stob remarked, "It tells us that grace is not cheap. Before God dispenses pardons He purchases them, thus preserving the moral order."

THE LARGER PICTURE

Our concern ranges farther than the welfare of individuals. The community's welfare is also at stake. In moral communities, human life is regulated and common values sustained only if those values are predictable and enforceable. This also assumes the fundamental requisite of personal accountability for all members of the community.

Think again of the home intruder, the possibility of violence, and of the victim's responsibility to stop him if possible, to assist in his arrest, conviction, and removal from further violent crime. If the assailant gets away with his crime, the ultimate victim is the community itself. The quality of community life is diminished. All persons are then under continual threat, without peace, and the community is rendered less just. The violent intruder continues without proper accountability for present or future actions.

Andrew Oldenquist addresses this question, pointing out that moral integrity and accountability require retributive justice: "Serious crimes, when they go unpunished, diminish the value we place on our social identities, and hence the valuation of ourselves." More pointedly, he adds: "Personal accountability does not make sense unless it implies that transgressors deserve punishment, that is, they are owed retribution."[24] Retribution is *owed and payable* in a just and ordered society whenever one or more members suffer injustice at the hands of another.

In a moral community, members hold one another accountable for maintaining community values, chief of which is freedom to live their lives in security and personal autonomy. This is the minimum for achieving the common good. Yet for accountability to be all-embracing (being the sinful humans that we are), it must be enforced. Thus retributive justice is institutionalized in the police establishment and in the criminal court process. But where the police are unable to fulfill this function, the householder acquires a primary responsibility.

The practical side of accountability for crime, its prevention and punishment, is taken up by Reuben M. Greenberg, chief of police in Charleston, South Carolina, in his book *Let's Take Back Our Streets.*[25] Greenberg calls accountability the greatest need in society today if we are to successfully solve the crime problem. As a police officer daily in the trenches, Greenberg reminds us that accountability conceives of every individual person as being (1) responsible for his or her own actions, (2) liable for the consequences of those actions, and (3) answerable to someone if those actions harm others, and not only to the person or persons harmed but to the community as a whole. Either we exercise accountability or, as Greenberg puts it, we have *a society of endless excuses.* In one way or another, the criminal must be held accountable to all who are members of the community.

Violent intruders are accountable for their actions, and so are victims who take action against them. Moreover, victims who choose to do nothing in the face of violent intruders are no less accountable to the community for the consequences of the injustice they perpetuate. They are accountable whether they choose action or inaction.

Thus we must question the assertion of pacifist Stanley Hauerwas: "We must be a people who have learned to be patient in the face of injustice."[26] He disallows any possibility that we "legitimize the use of force to overcome injustice."[27] Rather, we "must often endure injustice that might appear to be quickly eliminated through violence."[28] He cannot acknowledge the place of relative values which permit the valid use of violence to achieve the greater benefits of a just order, a secure community.

Hauerwas further argues,

Once *justice* is made a criterion of Christian social strategy, it can too easily take on a meaning and life of its own that is not informed by the Christian's fundamental convictions. It can, for example, be used to justify the Christian's resort to violence to secure a more *relative justice.*[29]

Granted, violence must not be allowed to take on a life of its own apart from other values it may serve—a point we too are making. But it does not follow that we are not to seek relative justice, or that violence per se is never a just means to correct injustice.

Once again, Hauerwas declares: "Moreover, when violence is justified in principle as a necessary strategy for securing justice, it stills the imaginative search for nonviolent ways of resistance to injustice."[30] Not always. In some conceivable instances, yes, but not as an overriding probability, not as determinative of all use of violence.

What we have labored to establish in this chapter is the inescapable role of justice in determining the use of lethal force in confronting a violent intruder when one's life and that of others is on the line. Now the task is to take an in-depth look at that other biblical absolute—love, seeing that while love is at the heart of ethical conduct in its highest forms, by itself love is not enough. We need a strand of two threads—justice and love woven together.

NOTES

1. *See* Charnock, Stephen, *Discourses upon the Existence and Attributes of God* (Vol. 2), Grand Rapids, MI: Baker Book House, 1979.
2. Macquarrie, John, ed., *Dictionary of Christian Ethics.* Philadelphia: Westminster, 1967, p. 183.
3. Stob, Henry. *Ethical Reflections.* Grand Rapids: Eerdmans, 1978, pp. 123–133.
4. Rescher, Nicholas, *Distributive Justice: A Constructive Critique of the Utilitarian Theory of Distribution.* Indianapolis: Bobbs-Merrill, 1966, p. 81.
5. Rawls, John, *A Theory of Justice.* Cambridge, MA: Harvard University, 1971.
6. Mill, John Stuart, *Utilitarianism.* New York: Bobbs-Merrill, 1957, p. 62.
7. Ibid., p. 74.
8. Smedes, Lewis B., *Mere Morality.* Grand Rapids: Eerdmans, pp. 33–36.
9. Robertson, D. B. (ed), *Love and Justice: Selections From the Shorter Writings of Reinhold Niebuhr.* Gloucester: Peter Smith, 1976, p. 27.
10. Niebuhr, Reinhold, *An Interpretation of Christian Ethics.* New York: Seabury, 1979, p. 39.
11. Robertson, op. cit., p. 282.
12. Ibid., p. 32.

13. Smedes, op. cit., p. 31.
14. Bloesch, Donald G., *Freedom for Obedience: Evangelical Ethics in Contemporary Times.* San Francisco: Harper & Row, 1987, p. 102.
15. Niebuhr, Reinhold, *Christianity and Power Politics.* New York: Scribner, 1946, 14; see *Moral Man and Immoral Society.* New York: Scribner, 1960; *The Nature and Destiny of Man.* 2 Vols.. New York: Scribner's, 1964; Harland, Gordon, *The Thought of Reinhold Niebuhr.* New York: Oxford University, 1960. Merle Longwood, "Niebuhr and a Theory of Justice," *Dialog* 14 (1985) pp. 253–262; Kegley Charles W. and Robert W. Bretall (eds.), *Reinhold Niebuhr: His Religious, Social, and Political Thought,* New York: Macmillan, 1956.
16. Plato, *The Republic,* VI, pp. 508b–510b.
17. Kant, Immanuel, *Kant's Philosophy of Law.* (W. Hastie, trans. & ed.), Edinburgh: T. & T. Clark, 1887, p. 198.
18. Hegel, Georg, *Philosophy of Right.* (T.M. Knox, trans.), New York: Oxford University, 1969, Sec. 100, p. 91.
19. Hart, H. L. A., *Punishment and Responsibility: Essays in the Philosophy of Law.* New York: Oxford University, 1968, pp. 230–237.
20. Harrelson, Walter, *The Ten Commandments and Human Rights.* Philadelphia: Fortress, 1980, p. 121.
21. Smedes, op. cit., pp. 108, p. 242.
22. Ibid., p. 108.
23. Bloesch, op. cit., p. 207.
24. Andrew Oldenquist, "An Explanation of Retribution," *The Journal of Philosophy.* vol. LXXXV, no. 9 (Sept. 1988) pp. 464–478.
25. Reuben M. Greenberg, *"Let's Take Back the Streets."* Quoted in "Crime and Punishment (USA)," *The Wall Street Journal* (Feb. 1, 1991), Boston: Dow Jones.
26. Hauerwas, Stanley, *The Peaceable Kingdom: A Primer In Christian Ethics.* Notre Dame: University of Notre Dame, 1983, p. 104.
27. Ibid., p. 104.
28. Ibid., p. 114.
29. Ibid., pp. 112–113.
30. Ibid., p. 114.

Chapter 12

DUAL MANDATE FOR *JUST-LOVE*

If justice were our only consideration, we would not even touch the core of New Testament ethics. Beyond dispute, the dominant theme of the Gospels and Epistles alike is God's love given through Jesus Christ. But love and justice are on a convergent path, ultimately standing together and inseparably.

The New Testament demands unconditional love for others—even enemies—making Christian love for all persons an obligation. But how does this obligation apply, for example, where the other person is an intruder menacing mine and other's lives? How do I express love toward the intruder? Does my love obligation to him mean risking my own life or the lives of others *in loving deference* to him? What does love *owe* him?

Strange as it may seem, love is inclusive of justice, justice subservient to love. To love justly is love's minimum demand. As Lewis Smedes, following Henry Stob, puts it, *Nothing is enough without love, but love alone is not enough.*[1] The *not enough* refers directly to justice. Smedes adds:

> Justice and love are absolute, unconditional, unequivocal. They are global, universal, all-embracing commands . . . no qualifications or evasions. They are the be-all and end-all of the moral life. . . . Justice and love must function together to represent God's relation to man. The two are inseparable.[2]

Reinhold Niebuhr, too, saw that the demands of justice are, in the end, the demands of love.[3]

Consider this: Since love cares about everything that concerns fellow human beings, it necessarily cares deeply that every person be treated fairly, that each receive what each has coming. Thus love can be nothing less than just—more perhaps, but never less.

Stanley Hauerwas writes that while it is true that God is love, love is not to be regarded an end in itself; loving is not the end point of God's purpose, nor does Jesus urge love as though it were an end itself.[4]

Hauerwas rightly notes that the problem with a love ethic is that it places love at our disposal to do with as we wish; then it is we who decide

149

what love deems right and good! But Christians are not directed by an abstraction called love, nor by a love ethic as such; we are directed by the Author of love, Jesus Christ.[5] Jesus Christ cannot be placed at our disposal.

Smedes summarizes succinctly:

> The law of love is too general to tell us when we ought to do what a commandment tells us not to do. We need more than love, say, to tell us when we "ought" to shoot a human being. We need solid evidence that it is necessary to break a commandment in order to respect both the rights and needs of someone for whom we are responsible. We need a reasonable indication that breaking a commandment will serve the cause of justice as well as the law of love—and to serve over the long run at that.[6]

Precisely!

Much to the point of our study, Hauerwas writes, "We exist as social creatures, and as such we confront social problems that require not love but justice."[7] He argues forcefully that a mere love ethic makes the question truth irrelevant and is merely an attempt to respond to the breakdown of moral consensus in our society by substituting the language of love for the language of the right, the good, and the true—the primary determinants of moral life.[8]

In a powerful conclusion, he writes,

> When love, forgiveness, and kindness become an end in themselves, it simply indicates people who no longer believe in anything. Being unwilling to make others and ourselves suffer for our principles is but to admit that nothing in this life is worth ourselves or others making a sacrifice for. What becomes crucial when this is admitted is not that we suffer, but that we suffer for the truth. That is, that the principles we hold are not arbitrary, but are prerequisites for any attempt to live a morally worthy life.[9]

This is another way of saying that there are relative values, that some things in life are of greater value than the preservation of particular human life. In his later writings Hauerwas backs off from giving place to relative values.

Justice is solidly in the camp of truth, and thus in position to point love to serve proper ends. In this sense justice is a necessary adjunct to love. Nor is it too much to say that every social dilemma has the possibility of being resolved when love and justice work concurrently.

In conflict situation, Paul Ramsey writes that "love is always the primary notion, justice derivative, since justice may be defined as what Christian love does when confronted by two or more neighbors."[10] But although it is primary, love still looks to justice. As Donald Bloesch points out (other ethicists such as John C. Bennett and Richard Neuhaus also hold this position), *the ethic of pure love needs to be united with the rational norm of justice in order to be relevant to the situation,* adding that he is convinced of the need to recover the dualistic motif of love and justice.[11] In other words, neither love nor justice can claim primacy. Henry Stob wrote, "You cannot live responsibly by a love which is abstracted and divorced from justice, and from the rational and structural elements which constitute justice . . . but must be held together in the unity of their polar tensions."[12]

Admittedly, love possesses a transcendent quality which justice does not. Rising above the requirements of justice is love's freedom to seek redemptive ends. The implication is that love is never satisfied with merely fulfilling the canons of justice. Here again, justice without love is less than justice. Love insists that some caring ministry be part of every just decision. Wherever possible it strives for a selfless love-oriented outcome. *Let no one seek his own good, but the good of his neighbor* (I Corinthians 10:24).

Quite evidently, love is different from justice—seemingly its opposite. Love entertains no concern for rights, claims, obligations, just-desserts and the like; these are strictly the domain of justice. Nor does love have expertise in allocating *what is due* different individuals in different situations. Love needs a standard for differentiating. Neither does love concern itself with merits or demerits, but is motivated to give freely and uncalculating in order to unconditionally benefit whomever it can. In other words, love operates disinterestedly, seeking only the good of other persons. It is non-discriminatory; this is love's glory, also its limitation.

As for encountering a dangerous intruder, the first requirement of love is compassionate regard for every person present. Love asks *What are the most likely consequences to come from love's action on behalf of innocent victims? On behalf of the assailant himself? What constitutes love's priority* (scale of relative values)? Will not love require something outside itself to help make these decisions?

LOVE YOUR NEIGHBOR AS YOURSELF

Jesus' ethic is *You shall love your neighbor as yourself* (Matthew 22:39). Here Jesus is not teaching the importance of self-love, but simply, *Love your neighbor with the same consuming concern you already have for yourself.* The tenacity of self-love is the model for loving others.

Another common supposition can be dispatched: Jesus doesn't mean we are to love our neighbor unconditionally at the expense of justice, as though justice placed no conditions whatever upon love's action. This is not what is meant by *unconditional love.* Love is granted no prerogative to violate or displace justice as a substitute value.

Love makes allowance for the necessity of punishment for wrongdoing. So make no mistake, when one is awakened in the dead of night to face a dangerous intruder, love is no substitute for tough choices! At such a moment of decision, love is ancillary to justice. The decision is *how to incorporate what we believe love and justice together dictate.*

NEIGHBORS CLOSEST TO US

Furthermore, it may be asked, *If love of neighbor is my duty, must I not first take into account my commitments to those special "neighbors" placed within my intimate family circle? Don't those relationships have clear priority? Is there not a precedence-taking obligation to express loving care to them first of all, and then turn to acts of love to others?*

In the event I may sometime face a violent intruder, I shall want to know as best possible what the rights of each person present are, for each one is my *neighbor* — even the intruder himself! As objectively as possible, I must ask, *How can "neighbor love" best reach out to each one present?*

Even though this dangerous intruder is also my *neighbor,* what he has justly coming to him is obviously not the same as what his victims have coming to them. We agree with Smedes: *Criminals do not have the same rights as law-abiding citizens.* [13] Nor is it likely that love would be forthcoming as unqualified beneficence. What he has coming may well turn out to be no more than the consequence of love's protecting ministry first given on behalf of these other *neighbors* — my beloved family. Love to the assailant would include stopping his self-recriminating act. Despite my attempt to treat him with Christian love, the end result may be his harm or even death. Yes, I might feel pitying love for him, yet still have to take a harmful action against him.

In the very nature of a conflict situation, love is not in position to extend its protective care in equal shares to both victims and assailant alike. The choice will favor the individuals for whom the householder has the most direct responsibility — and that includes himself. Is there not also value in his own life which God has appointed, a value not to be surrendered apart from an overriding conviction that God has directed it so?

Of course, love will desire whatever might prove a promising alternative to defensive violence. But absent such an alternative, if lethal force must be called upon, love will seek to minimize the hurt and loss while making sure the assailant is stopped and hopefully brought to justice.

FREEDOM TO RISK

In all truth, love might direct the Christian to place himself at the assailant's mercy, in hopes of avoiding all violence. Such decisions have historically been among the amazing qualities of Christian love—its freedom to choose self-risk for the potential good of a less-than-worthy individual. For the Christian who is assured of eternal life in Christ (the life far better), altruistic decisions of even a radical sort are not unreasonable.

Placing myself at the assailant's mercy is my option. However, in the defense of third parties, freedom to risk my own life is rendered questionable by my responsibility to them as co-victims. It is not so easy to say that freedom to risk my own life includes the freedom to risk theirs along with mine.

It might still be asked, *How can love conceivably have any part in a stopping action that is likely to bring about the intruder's harm or death? Won't love opt for mercy and a chance for the assailant to change his criminal life-style? Isn't this the nature of forgiving love—what love is all about?*

This is indeed what love is all about, but not all that love is about. Nor is it what justice is all about, and we are talking about just-love. Neither are we talking about taking retributive justice into our own hands for unloving purposes, but rather to lovingly preserve life. Love, of course, has no bent to see punishment inflicted, especially lethal punishment. Instead, love searches every opportunity to forgive, redeem and restore. Love wishes no harm or death to anyone—even to violent intruders. But what love wishes and what is mandated by the sheer necessities of the situation may well be two different things. Love and justice must work together to determine priorities.

We repeat, love has a freedom to act which justice does not have, freedom at times to seek higher ends, freedom to take risks, even to sacrificing self for the sake of other persons. Nonetheless, in a conflict-of-interests situation, where justice has the clearer vision of who is most worthy of love's prior ministry (hence also who will suffer loss), love wisely defers to the dictates of justice: the decision of just-love.

WHO PAYS THE PRICE?

Love always pays a price; this is the very heart of love. To effect redemptive ends, love is willing to pay even an ultimate price. But when love must stand aside and let justice bring about just-desserts, it also pays a price. In those instances, love vicariously suffers along with the one who pays the penalty which justice exacts.

Scripture makes it clear that God suffers as He grieves over those upon whom He inflicts just judgment for sin. just-love is not influence by who it is that suffers most, who pays the greatest cost, but solely by who suffers justly.

Justice exacts a price; it never pays the price. But where justice and love work together as just-love, justice helps love determine where there can be a loving ministry in accordance with what is both just and beneficent—whatever is possible. Just-love demands more difficult decisions than those made in accordance with justice alone or love alone. Just-love helps determine both who benefits and who pays, thus achieving the most loving and just of all possible outcomes.

Ever part of the equation, love seeks to temper the stringent effects of justice wherever and however possible. Realistically, however, love rarely succeeds in finding a way to save an assailant from harm when its first priority is the safety of innocent, defenseless victims.

There is no debating that justice devoid of love is inhumane and non-Christian. Still, in the most loving approach to a conflict situation, there are occasions when the ends of justice must be served *love notwithstanding*. At times it is appropriate that punishment be meted out, that guilty people suffer justly, that would-be killers meet their end. Often the vision of justice lends strength, courage, and moral focus to keep love from degenerating into mere sentiment, into ill-considered, wrongly directed benevolence. In instances where it is proper that the ends of justice be served, love's task is that of mitigating the hurt and loss however possible.

We conclude: love alone is not the way to responsible personhood, anymore than justice alone is that way; just-love leads the way to responsible personhood! And just-love must make the most difficult of human choices.

LOVE'S FORESIGHT

Fuller seminary's Lewis Smedes introduces a beautiful thought: *Imagination is love's foresight.*[14] Creative imagination adapts itself to the notion of love, for love is free to explore every possibility for doing good to others. By contrast, *creative imagination* is hardly attributable to the inflexible canons of justice. Not justice, but love, looks for positive alternatives to save an evil day. Love searches all possible ways to mitigate the harsh effects of justice—as Smedes suggests, *by courageous use of the imagination when by all appearances there is no other way.*[15]

The problem arises when Christian pacifists place absolute trust in the creative possibilities of unconditional, sacrificial love, to the neglect of a more principled solution—that which just-love requires.

What we've established can be put into four words: *Love never acts unjustly* (or: *Love always acts justly*). Justice is love's minimal demand. On occasion, an impossible situation may be retrievable by an imaginative, innovative love. On other occasions, tough love allows the unjust to suffer their just-desserts.

In a dangerous home confrontation, love would wish to deter, dissuade, possibly even attempt to win over the evildoer in a redemptive offer of forgiveness and goodwill. However commendable, this approach is fraught with great risks. Sometimes love must let justice be served through a preemptive act which accomplishes its intended goal (rescue of victims) but unavoidably ends with the unintended (harm or death of the criminal). In the end, the less-than-ideal-yet-necessary action may prove to be the more loving way.

LOVE LOOKS TO CONSEQUENCES ONLY

An unqualified love ethic expresses itself as a morality of consequences. Allegedly, the best consequences follow from taking the most loving way. This is the motif of *situation ethics,* whose one moral absolute is love. Whatever results in the highest possible good in social terms love seeks to do. Love seeks the greatest good for the greatest number, hence the most loving outcome. But how do we determine what is the most loving-thing outcome for the greatest number? Consult just-love. Or in the words of William Frankena, "I have contended that we should recognize a principle of justice to guide our distribution of good and evil that is independent of any principle about maximizing the balance of good over evil."[16] The most loving outcome is exceedingly important, but not apart from what is just.[17]

Love simply cannot be all things to all people in all instances. Nor is loving in itself the whole of moral behavior. Neither can love by itself supply a complete rationale for social action. Love anticipates some but not all the consequences that follow from its action. Especially deficient is love's ability to fulfill its objectives of general beneficence where a choice must be made between the claims of more than one recipient, say, victim and victimizer.

So, while to many the terms *love* and *justice* appear incongruent—all but opposed—we see them functioning inseparably with no incongruity at all. So much so that we merge the two terms into the singular *just-love*—a truly unified concept, what is called an *oxymoron*, a figure of speech in which seemingly contradictory ideas are combined (like *sweet sorrow*).

It was F. Scott Fitzgerald who suggested that *the test of a first-rate intelligence is the ability to hold two opposed ideas in the mind at the same time.* In biblical theology, to think *love* also means thinking *justice;* to think *justice* also means thinking *love.*

There is a technical way to look at this combining of justice and love. The term is *synergism,* from two roots meaning *to work together.* It refers to a working together where the combined effect exceeds the sum of its separate constituent effects. Buckminster Fuller, in his book *Synergetics,* defines synergy as *the behavior of whole systems unpredicted by the behavior of their parts taken separately.* The key word is *unpredicted.*[18]

Theologically, it is not enough to inventory God's attributes separably, for this is not to see the *whole system.* Justice and love are better integrated than differentiated, forming a *whole system.* What is achieved thereby is comprehensiveness.

If love and justice were mutually exclusive, some important and overreaching effects would be precluded. But when justice and love function in combination *the effect of the whole is unpredicted by the effect of either taken separately* (because the effect lies within their conjoint action).[19] Each transforms the other into something more than each is separately.

Incidentally, this principle is illustrated in a wonderful promise God makes to His people. He says, "All things work together for good to those who love God, to those who are called according to his purpose" (Romans 8:28). Even evil works together with what is not evil to accomplish an overall good which God purposes. In our study, the things that work together synergetically are love and justice. Proper response to a dangerous intruder must combine the elements of just-love.

STRAND OF TWO THREADS

Shall we not expect a divine model for this combining of justice and love? Rightly so! Note two Scriptural examples. First, Psalm 89:14: *He loves righteousness and justice; the earth is full of the steadfast love of the Lord.* Justice and love are intertwined in God's action. Secondly, note the occasion Jesus condemned the Pharisees because they *neglect justice and the love of God* (Luke 11:42). The Catholic Ethicist, Richard McCormick suggests that "we need to understand the polarity between love and justice, to become aware of their inseparability and also their logical discontinuity."[20] What could make for the greater sum of human goodness and rightness, if not this co-functioning—*just-love?*

No better summary is available than that of Reinhold Niebuhr, as quoted by Pacific School of Religion Professor Karen Lebacqz:

> Because justice is always relative, it is always capable of improvement. Any historical manifestation of justice could conceivably approximate more closely the ideal of love. Justice is the best possible harmony within the conditions created by sin, but it is not the best imaginable harmony. Hence all historical enactments of justice stand under the judgment of love. Love requires justice for the complex realities of the sinful social world. Yet, love also transcends, fulfills, negates, and judges justice. It transcends justice by going beyond it, exceeding the demands of justice. It fulfills justice because it never implies less than justice; where life affirms life, justice is done. It negates and judges justice because every historical justice is imperfect and stands under the judgment of more perfect possibilities of human community. Every relative justice is a relative injustice as well. One can never rest satisfied that justice has been done simply because "the greatest good" has been done. Each instance of historical justice has within it a perversion of justice. Each awaits the closer approximation of the harmony of love that is perfect justice. Love ever stands as a reminder of the need to keep seeking a more perfect resolution to the conflict.[21]

This point is also made by John Macquarrie:

> It is a false disjunction that suggests an opposition between justice and love. In an imperfect world, justice must be maintained and enforced in face of the

constant threats of injustice, and the Christian has the duty to uphold justice as well as to exercise love.[22]

Theologian Millard Erickson puts it succinctly: "If we begin with the assumption that God is an integrated being and the divine attributes are harmonious, we will define the attributes in the light of one another. Thus justice is loving justice and love is just love."[23]

Never has it been said better. This simply affirms the theologian's perception that both justice and love are necessary norms, neither of which is sufficient in itself. With God the demands of justice are, in the end, the demands of love; the demands of love are the demands of justice. Love and justice are in dialectical relationship—the interplay of seeming opposites.

Our challenge is to emulate the divine model. Ultimately every decision, while sharpened by concerns of both justice and love, lies in choosing obedience to Jesus Christ, who Himself is always loving, always just. To know His mind in an emergency situation is always the more difficult to achieve.

TRAGIC MORAL CHOICE

Should any of us ever confront a dangerous intruder, we will face making what Edward John Carnell termed the *tragic moral choice.* Tragically, that choice may be to shoot. It only reinforces Herbert McCabe's tough words: "Every moral problem of the slightest interest is a problem about who is to get hurt; an injunction to love everyone concerned does not help to decide that question." McCabe goes on to say that the question is not *to hurt or not to hurt,* but *whom to hurt with justice.*[24]

Are these Christian words? The authors dare to believe so. A supportive word comes from the Catholic Pastoral Letter on War and Peace by the National Conference of Bishops in 1983: "Faced with the fact of attack on the innocent, the presumption that we do no harm, even to our enemy, yields to the command of love understood as the need to restrain an enemy who would injure the innocent."[25] Donald G. Bloesch gives this opinion:

> Jesus Christ may call us into a situation where armed conflict and lethal violence are inevitable, but we must be obedient to the divine imperative even where sin is unavoidable. . . . In some very exceptional circumstances, it may even involve taking up the sword in defense of the rights of others.[26]

NOTES

1. Smedes, Lewis B., *Choices.* San Francisco: Harper & Row, 1986, p. 55.
2. Smedes, Lewis B., *Mere Morality.* Grand Rapids: Eerdmans, 1983, p. 15.
3. *See* Harland, Gordon, *The Thought of Reinhold Niebuhr.* New York: Oxford University, 1960, p. 35.
4. Stanley Hauerwas, "Love's Not All You Need," *Cross Currents* (Summer–Fall 1972), pp. 227–228.
5. Ibid., pp. 228–229.
6. Smedes, *Mere Morality,* op. cit., p. 6.
7. Hauerwas, op. cit., p. 230.
8. Ibid., pp. 228–230.
9. Ibid., pp. 232–233.
10. Ramsey, Paul, *Basic Christianity.* New York: Scribner's, 1950, p. 243.
11. Bloesch, Donald G., *Freedom for Obedience: Evangelical Ethics for Contemporary Times.* San Francisco: Harper & Row, 1981, p. 188.
12. Stob, Henry, *Ethical Reflections.* Grand Rapids: Eerdmans, 1978, pp. 134–143.
13. Smedes, Mere Morality. cit., p. 36.
14. Smedes, *Choices.* op. cit., p. 111.
15. Ibid., p. 111.
16. Frankena, William K., *Ethics* (2nd ed.). Englewood Cliffs, NJ: Prentice-Hall, 1973, p. 43.
17. On the weakness of Situation Ethic's absolute rule of love: *see* Germain Grisez and Russell Shaw, *Beyond the New Morality: The Responsibilities of Freedom.* Notre Dame: University of Notre Dame, 1974 (esp. chapter 9); Paul Ramsey, *Deeds and Rules in Christian Ethics.* New York: Scribner's, 1967.
18. Fuller, Buckminster R., *Synergetics: Explorations In The Geometry of Thinking.* New York: Macmillan, 1975, p. 3.
19. Ibid., p. 10.
20. McCormick, Richard A. and Paul Ramsey (eds.), *Doing Evil to Achieve Good: Moral Choice in Conflict Situations.* Chicago: Loyola, 1978, p. 88.
21. Lebacqz, Karen, *Six Theories of Justice: Perspectives from Philosophical and Theological Ethics.* Minneapolis: Augsburg, 1986, p. 86.
22. Macquarrie, John, ed., *Dictionary of Christian Ethics.* Philadelphia: Westminster, 1967, p. 184.
23. Erickson, Millard J., *Christian Theology* (Vol. 1). Grand Rapids: Baker, 1983, p. 298.
24. McCabe, Herbert. *What Ethics is All About.* Washington: Corpus, 1969, p. 33.
25. *The Challenge of Peace: God's Promise and Our Response.* A Pastoral Letter on War and Peace by the National Conference of Catholic Bishops. May 3, 1983. pp. 40–41.
26. Bloesch, op. cit., p. 218.
27. Ibid., p. 63.

Chapter 13

TRADITIONAL RELIGIOUS PACIFISM

Today there are three positions relating to the use of necessary violence in defensive situations. Pacifism is one classic Christian position, as is non-pacifism. More recently, the third position has been termed selectivism.

NON-PACIFISM

Pragmatists generally tend to be non-pacifists, their responses usually quite spontaneous, little thought through what might be termed a common sense view that *simple justice* ought always to prevail. To this end they advocate using whatever defensive means necessary to stop potentially violent intruders. If in the course of saving innocent lives a criminal's life must be forfeited, so be it. It's all a matter of comparative worth—victim's against victimizer's.

Little moral theory is required to reach this conclusion. For non-pacifists this theory poses no real issue; the matter is settled in advance without apparent need for serious reflection. Since protection of innocent life is all that matters, this view can be classified as utilitarian. Everything focuses on the outcome—in this case, whatever consequences square with innocent victims' best interests.

For non-pacifists, the one viable objective becomes *the best possible outcome* for *persons most deserving*—assuming that *persons most deserving* refers to victims, not assailants, to the innocent not the guilty. Other considerations count for little or nothing. The focus is altogether upon self and anyone for whom one has protective care.

So the end result is everything. And to accomplish this, our pragmatist friends see a deadly weapon as the best, perhaps only, means. Of course, with this approach many relevant considerations are left unexamined. For example, no thought is given to what might be the best interests of the assailant—also a human being with life-preserving claims. It is unlikely the life value accorded the victims will be accorded him, a reasonable assumption being that killing a guilty assailant is justified to stop a killing of innocent lives.

By virtue of his criminal action, the violent intruder has lost *value parity* with the innocent party or parties. So it all comes down to this: for non-pacifists the means employed is *whatever is necessary for achieving the most desirable consequences.* The sole consideration: What is the most competent way to get the job done with minimum human suffering, with least amount of human loss?

Reason and law dictate that the means employed be proportional to the end attained, never more. One implication is that extreme cases may turn out nothing less than shooting the intruder. Regardless, the householder's primary intention—only intention—remains the preservation of lives he's defending. The death of the assailant is an inadvertent consequence of necessary actions taken to stop violence.

PACIFISM

While the non-pacifist position described above is unquestionably that of the majority of Christians, a minority of equally thoughtful Christian men and women believe differently, and for deeply studied biblical and ethical reasons.

For Christian pacifists, violence is intrinsically wrong, hence wrong in every circumstance, no exceptions. Pacifists understand the New Testament love ethic as demanding of Jesus' disciples that they emulate the non-violent course He exemplified, leaving God their sole Protector. God will order their life chances according to His good will. Jesus' command to love one's enemies is seen as nothing less than non-violent, benevolent response to whatever evil is received. It implies non-retaliation and forgiveness. At the very most, non-lethal deterrence might be attempted, but never so as to bring harm.

For the pacifist, should life itself be laid down in commitment to non-violence—even with no discernible good resulting from such sacrifice —the deciding principle is uncompromised commitment to non-violence regardless of mitigating factors. What is required is the shield of faith and unwavering trust that God's way is the way of the cross, that in His wisdom, goodness, and power, He will bring about the consequences of His own choosing. Whatever He chooses is guaranteed right in principle and good in what it achieves. Pacifists cast themselves upon the providential care of a wise God Who makes no mistakes.

To the pacifist, the question is never utilitarian: *What will work?* Even less *What will work best?* It is solely *What way would Jesus take?* Jesus' rule of love and His non-violent example, not utilitarian ends, are determinative. To pacifists, it is inconceivable that Jesus would take violent action even in a life-threatening situation such as we are describing.

Now, if one is fully convinced that it may never be right to take another person's life under any circumstance nor to achieve any end however superior, then the only recourse is resignation to whatever outcome God sovereignly chooses. Trust in God's perfect will and power and complete acceptance of whatever consequences He ordains—these considerations alone dictate the Christian pacifist conviction.

For some pacifists, their stance goes so far as to mandate non-resistance of any kind—even non-violent resistance. By not making allowance for mitigating circumstances or other ethical considerations, discounting relative values, the pacifist totally disallows the use of force to counter force. His options are closed off.

SELECTIVISM (QUALIFIED NON-PACIFISM)

Inasmuch as neither absolute pacifism nor absolute non-pacifism appears satisfactory in terms of biblical requirements or the desideratum of reasoned theory, a third way appears.

Between pacifism and non-pacifism lies selectivism (qualified non-pacifism). For growing numbers of thoughtful Christians this is the position of choice. When it comes to the particular quandary we are now examining, selectivism places us close to non-pacifism. It finds acceptable a reasonable biblical permissive use of lethal defensive means. This position does not derive from a predetermined, inflexible rule, yet is grounded on scriptural norms. The selectivist positions himself or herself to make a discerning, God-instructed choice between two conflicting, equally compelling duties.

Selectivism leaves room for a variation of circumstances which mitigate specific cases, applying biblical principles and *sanctified reason,* making for a well-thought-out, prayed-through decision. Each case is decided on its own merits, taking the normative moral principles of Scripture as the primary reference point, but giving full consideration to those consequences that might best fulfill biblical values and ends.

The authors themselves are selectivists, a mediating view which appears both biblical and the best manner in which protective love is distributed between victims and victimizer. Selectivism generally allows for full defensive measures on behalf of self or innocent third-party victims as primary objects of Christian love in action, leaving the assailant a secondary object of love's action.

What is difficult for pacifists to understand is that Scripture presents two sides to death and killing. While God declares that He is not desirous that anyone should perish (2 Peter 3:9), He nevertheless allows people to make that choice. While He offers salvation to all, He lets the decision be theirs individually. Similarly, while He says, *I have no pleasure in the death of anyone* (Ezekiel 18:32), He nevertheless does not prevent it. Sometimes He even commands that individuals be slain for just cause. Moreover, He declares that He Himself one day shall wreak vengeance upon the earth—nothing short of death to the unrepentant.

In a world where evil dominates the hearts of humankind and where men and women continue to alienate themselves from Him, God's holiness is not mocked. Scripture teaches that vengeance belongs to God, not man (see Psalm 94:1; Isaiah 61:2; I Thessalonians 1:5–8; Hebrews 10::30–31). But make no mistake, it does belong to Him!

The Book of Revelation tells of the end of the history of evil in this world. It depicts the warring Lord and His armies returning to conquer. God is more than a God of retribution but indeed is that too. The unrepentant wicked shall not go unpunished. While God is patient with sinful humankind, neither His patience nor His mercy are infinite. Nor is there moral complacency with Him. That He is a God of just retribution is foundational doctrine.

There are outstanding biblical scholars who hold pacifism as a biblical imperative, who find no place whatever for violence, regardless of what good end violence may at times achieve. So we dare not proceed without first coming to terms with the claims of Christian pacifism. For such a study to be complete would require an extensive review of the literature not possible here.[1]

The Christian pacifist looks to a single model of non-violence provided by Scripture—Jesus, His arrest and cross. Jesus' sacrificial death is their mandate for a completely non-violent life-style. So if ever in a situation in which it is impossible to preserve the values of both justice and non-violence, the pacifist chooses non-violence, even at the cost of allowing great injustices to be perpetrated against oneself and upon third parties under one's care. Inaction is imperative even if it costs the life of innocent victims. To the ruling principle of non-violence there are no exceptions, no justifiable exemptions.

IS JESUS' CROSS A MODEL FOR NON-VIOLENCE?

Neither non-pacifists nor selectivists interpret Jesus' cross as being a model for universal non-violence. Rather, His cross is a unique, unrepeatable demonstration of God's punishment of sin and the accomplishment of His redemptive work. Jesus, sinless in His own Person, willingly took upon Himself the guilt of the world's sin as though it were His own, and God the Father punished that sin as He laid our penalty upon His Son. Not that Jesus was an unwilling or passive victim of the Father's plan of atonement—plainly that would be immoral on the Father's part. Prior to His earthly incarnation, Jesus willingly committed Himself to this end. His own Self-sacrifice accomplished an efficacious atonement, providing divine justification for sinners who have no means of justifying themselves. That sacrifice was efficacious by virtue of Who it was who made it—the eternal, infinitely holy and meritorious Son of God—Deity in human flesh! He alone could represent both God in His Deity, Man in his Humanity—Mediator between God and man. This atoning work at the cross was forever unique, unrepeatable, once for all—a divine work not meant as a pattern for individual emulation.

I like Stephen Mott's summary:

> The Gospels portray Jesus as dying without using violence, but do they see his death resulting from an intentional rejection of violence? The mere absence of the use of force by Jesus does not necessarily mean that force is disapproved of in principle. The hermeneutical principle that whatever is not made normative is therefore wrong is not satisfactory. The silence may only indicate that the question was not present in the minds of the authors.[2]

John Jefferson Davis makes the same point: "His death was not intended to be the sole and comprehensive model of dealing with questions of civil justice in the temporal world."[3]

UNUSUAL PERSPECTIVE

Some pacifists argue that whenever a Christian is menaced by an assailant, his or her certainty of eternal life in Christ should bring willingness to lay down one's own life if need be. The life of the intruder is entitled to prior consideration inasmuch as his eternal destiny is most likely in doubt. Shouldn't he be the one allowed to live, in hopes that he might have future opportunity to experience God's redemptive grace? In fact, might he not be actually moved toward God by the Christian's sacrifice on his behalf?

Let's be quick to concede that there are occasions when a Christian should be willing to risk having his life taken, willing to lay it down for others—even the least deserving. But is this one of those occasions?

John Jefferson Davis provides the rejoinder:

> The imbalance of responsibility in favor of the assailant unfairly prejudices the case to the assailant's advantage. Not only does this tend toward a miscarriage of justice, but may even exacerbate a more widespread compromising of the community's moral structure. To favor the assailant surely does compromise the safety of others both present and in the future. Thus there are compounded reasons for favoring the victim's right to prior protection.[4]

Is it really so simple a matter as presuming the Christian victim's life is eternally secure, hence dispensable now? He or she may be a parent responsible for a household, a brother or sister responsible for an invalid sibling, a pastor responsible for a congregation. Aren't these values also worthy of consideration?

Realistically, how genuine is the hope the assailant may come to know the Savior such as to make this the overriding determination? If not, is the victim's sacrifice not ill-conceived? Has God called upon us to make such sacrifices? We think not.

An unarmed, non-resisting householder is unable to exercise deterrence of any kind other than dissuasion. Nor is he or she in any position to capture and bring the intruder to justice. Much risked, little achieved.

The Christian pacifist may counter that he or she trusts God for the outcome, that if life is to be taken, this too is in God's providential purpose. Conceivably, this may be what God requires on special occasion. He alone knows the end from the beginning, has His own purposes, and He is in full control. He is sovereign over all circumstances and perfectly capable of protecting His own.

No Christian can deny the moral validity of this position. Indeed, God can and does do the unexpected. Can He not strike sudden fear into the heart of the intruder, causing him to flee? Or cause his weapon to malfunction? Or bring an unexpected conviction of wrongdoing that paralyzes his intended action? Could not his heart be opened to a message of forgiveness and acceptance, and an invitation to come to

Christ? What limits God—Circumstances? People? Guns? Maybe only our own less-than-robust faith!

Who are we to say what God can or cannot do on behalf of those who trust Him? No Christian who truly believes God to be Who He has revealed Himself to be dare denigrate the pacifist's faith solution! Not that we have less trust in God; rather, ours is trust based upon a different perspective on God and His purposes.

When all is added up, it is our conviction that the pacifist principle of non-violence is weak, that it overrides the whole issue of relative values at stake in the balance of life and death in conflict situations. It is difficult to understand why pacifists do not question whether values other than physical life apply, and in what order these values might be protected or at what price and to whom. They subordinate all values to an absolute of non-violence. But if valuing consequences isn't allowed in the equation, if inaction is preferred to protective action, if compassionate love is first extended to the assailant—then it's possible for non-violence to be responsible for extinguishing not only innocent lives but also the God-given values which make living those lives worthwhile.

This was the criticism of Reinhold Niebuhr, even that of Jan Narveson who writes from a consequentialist point of view:

> The pacifist must show that nothing else has weight comparable to violence. In other words, violence is wrong in every situation regardless of what else is true about that situation. The perplexity arises when, for example, the harm done by an act of violence is relatively small in comparison with the evils averted.[5]

Both Niebiuhr and Narveson appeal to the greater good, the lesser evil.

Richard Mouw accurately expresses the author's opinion, saying "there are occasions in which Christians are permitted, perhaps even obligated, to take up the sword in pursuit of just and righteous goals."[6] It is the question of a relatively just cause.

Curiously, some pacifists tend to place the life of a violent, life-threatening assailant on a par with the lives of his victims, at least implicitly. Their basis is that every life is created in the image of God, infinitely precious to Him, and the object of Christ's atoning death. Inasmuch as God alone has the prerogative to take life, under no circumstances has fellow man this prerogative. From this, the inference is often drawn that every human being maintains equal standing before his human fellows without qualification.

To the contrary, as James Gustafson points out: "Individual persons are not of absolute value, and thus continuation of physical life is not an ultimate value. Physical life, while the indispensable condition for all human values, is not an end in itself."[7]

No blanket appeal can thus be made to an amorphous *sanctity of life,* for this in itself provides no guidance for resolving conflict situations in which either one person's life or another's will likely be forfeited.

Were there not relative values based on quality of life (and here we think especially of biblically ordered values), then physical life does become an end in itself, in fact the highest of all values, the highest end of action. But the selectivist argues that it is not continuance but quality of human life that is paramount. Sustaining life also has to do with the role an individual is called to fulfill, the measure of life in God's purpose.

DISTRIBUTION OF RESPONSIBILITY

Davis comments on the role of civil government as God has appointed it: "The Apostle Paul stated that the magistrate does not bear the sword in vain; he is the servant of God to execute his wrath on the wrongdoer" (Romans 13:4). The sword in question (Greek: *machaira*) is not a ceremonial instrument; in the Septuagint (the Greek translation of the Old Testament), the same word is used of a deadly weapon (Genesis 34:26; Judges 3:16), a connotation that carries forward into New Testament times. *So here we have,* says Davis, *a proper expression of authority delegated from God Himself.*[8] Nor does this authority merely rely upon the deterrent use of the sword; it holds out more than an empty threat. Indeed, provision is made for its overt use where necessary to carry out the authority.

For the selectivist, the principle's affirmed: God ordains the violent use of the sword in the hands of civil protectors; this must not be so construed as to limit the use of the sword to authorities under circumstances where those authorities are unable to protect threatened life, as in response to instances of violent assault.

Note, too, that the Apostle does not touch on the question of self-protection when civil protection is not available. The question is left open as to what means may be taken should we find ourselves unprotected by security forces. We've noted that the custom of the day was to carry a small sword (dagger) concealed under the tunic as protection against marauding bandits who not only robbed but killed to cover their tracks.

While no argument from silence is ever determinative, the suggestion is nonetheless strong that the self-protective use of the *sword* is biblically affirmed.

The fundamental issue is whether or not God delegates the prerogative of defensive action to individuals in instances where civil measures of protection are not immediately available, so often exactly the case.

There is a passage in pacifist John Yoder's writings that we find unacceptable:

> The triumph of the right is assured not by the might that comes to the aid of the right, which is of course the justification of the use of violence and other kinds of power in every human conflict; the triumph of the right, although it is assured, is sure because of the power of the resurrection and not because of any calculation of causes and effects, not because of the inherently greater strength of the good guys. The relationship between the obedience of God's people and the triumph of God's cause is not a relationship between cause and effect but one of cross and resurrection.[9]

Had Yoder said that the triumph of the right is sure *in the end,* because of the power of the resurrection we could agree. Ultimately it will be so. And Christians do live spiritually in the power of the cross and resurrection. However, in this interim church age we live in a real world of violent crime and the necessity of defense against it. We cannot escape the realities of the world which God has designed for us to live out our years and from which He has not yet chosen to remove us (see John 17:15).

Although we the authors have fundamental disagreement with the theological orientation of Reinhold Niebuhr, we do share significant points of agreement with his non-pacifist position and theology of the Kingdom. Niebuhr and Yoder are diametrically opposed to each other, having basically different views of the Kingdom.

Niebuhr considers the realization of the radicalized love which Jesus taught in the Sermon on the Mount a simple impossibility in the ongoing history we experience. In Niebuhr's view, to think that national states can refuse to use violence is to underestimate the dominant presence of sin in the world. For a pacifist strategy, appealing to love and good will while letting a tyrant win without resistance is in reality to surrender too easily to evil. To refuse to go to war against a tyrant is complicity in his tyranny, something worse than war because it marks a refusal to assume responsibility for correcting the situation in its present and future consequences. Yoder then quotes Niebuhr's statement: "Tyranny is not war; it is peace, but it is a peace which has nothing to do with the peace of the kingdom of God."[10]

Yoder protests Niebuhr's claim that responsible action not only requires the struggle against injustice, but that the nature of the struggle is such that the methods of love are ineffective, an ineffectiveness shown by the cross itself, which is *the symbol of love triumphant in its own integrity, but not triumphant in the world and in society.*[11] Yoder cannot accept Niebuhr's assertion that love is the *impossible possibility,* countering: *The existence of a moral imperative is meaningless if its accomplishment is excluded by definition.*[12] But not so, as we shall see.

Yoder charges Niebuhr with making an absolute out of necessity, rather than permitting necessity nothing more than instrumental value. Yoder asserts that so far as ethics is concerned, nothing in itself is a necessity, only so far as one seeks to obtain a certain end (interestingly, Yoder considers love an absolute necessity, bypassing justice as part of the total equation). He argues his point by saying that

> it is not necessary to defend myself unless I desire survival; it is not necessary to defend the social order unless I prefer it to that which would replace it. Thus there is no absolute necessity, only the instrumental necessity defined by what stands to be gained or lost. There is no necessity of abandoning love as an ethical absolute unless something more important than love stands to be lost. This is in turn possible only if there is a moral absolute higher than love, and for a Christian such an absolute is difficult to imagine.[13]

He adds:

> Of course, according to pacifist belief, there exists a real Christian responsibility for the social order, but that responsibility is a derivative of Christian love, not a contradictory and self-defining ethical norm.[14]

In contrast to Niebuhr's pessimism, Yoder's optimism is expressed in the words,

> Sin is vanquished every time a Christian in the power of God chooses... obedience instead of necessity, love instead of compromise. No insistence upon "maintaining the tension" between the good and the possible...can change this reality.[15]

THE NON-PACIFIST THOUGHT OF HELMUT THIELICKE

Contrary to Yoder, the German theologian Helmut Thielicke also makes much of the notion of necessity. In a chapter *God's "Compromises"*

With The World,[16] he discusses the necessity for Christians having to make compromises:

> The confession that this world "demands" compromises implies the fact that this world, and my own action within it, stands in need of forgiveness. . . . On the other hand, compromise is imposed upon us as a task. For without it we fall victim to a fanatical radicalism.

(He refers specifically to a radicalized view of the Sermon on the Mount, making its demands absolute for our time.)[17]

Thielicke's thesis is expressed in these words:

> First, the making of a compromise is in a certain limited sense a reflection and reenactment of what God himself has done in patiently bearing with us. In condescension he "accommodates" himself to the nature of the world and sustains it in the sphere of its remaining possibilities until the last day.[18]

Saying that man is forced to compromise by the structure of the world around him, Thielicke continues that "the will of God which is at work is not his original will but a will which is altered for the sake of man, which is relevant to man, and has regard to man's possibilities."[19]

Whereas pacifists Ellul, Yoder, Hauerwas and others dismiss the reality of necessity in daily Christian life (and with it any true place for compromise), we cannot do so. In this sense we are closer to Niebuhr and Thielike.

Another confused notion appears in MacGregor. He writes:

> Neither Jesus' teaching or Paul's means that justice has been dethroned by love; it does mean that all human relationships must ultimately be based on the Gospel of love; that justice "fulfilled" is an outcome of love, rather than love a mere by-product of justice; that if we aim at love we shall establish justice by the way; that we can in fact secure justice only when we aim primarily not at it, but at love out of which it springs.[20]

We concur with Niebuhr in his allegation that pacifists hold to a false optimism, a naive faith in simple solutions, of having adopted the simple expedient of denying the persistent reality of entrenched evil in this world in order to maintain a vain hope of the triumph of the ideal of love in this present world. He locates the issue between pacifists *who have a confidence in human nature which human nature cannot support,* and non-pacifists *who have looked too deeply into life and their own souls to place their trust in so broken a reed.* So it has ever been and will continue to be until the Kingdom is truly manifest and consummated with the King's return. Idealism will not change the basic structure of this world.

Niebuhr views pacifism as *an absolute perfectionist ethic—an impossible dream*. With this Niebuhrian *realism* the authors agree (including an eschatological view which is not identical but similar to our own). It is a view of Jesus' Kingdom ideal as partially realizable in the present evil world, but fully realizable only in the second advent yet to come. In the interim age of the church, we live in far less than Kingdom-fulfilling ways, ways made impossible by the pervasive sin of the world.

According to Niebuhr, the ideal transcends every possible historical achievement, so that in the interim before the Kingdom's historical realization the world of sin must be held in check. Nonetheless, the Kingdom ethic does give us norms for guidance. Moreover, it holds up a perspective from which to critically evaluate every human action, also a standard against which we can measure every failure. This of course does not mean that Christ's disciples are not called to approximate the Kingdom ethic as best they can under the enabling power of God.

We have no disagreement with Yoder's declaration:

> Sin is vanquished every time a Christian in the power of God chooses... obedience instead of necessity, love instead of compromise.... No insistence upon "maintaining the tension" between the good and the possible... can change this reality.

Our point of departure is simply that not always is there an ideal set of options that does not contain some undeniable tension where necessity and compromise dictate the choice.

It is the necessity of coercion in the achievement of justice which pacifists reject; a necessity which Niebuhr affirms: "It is because men are sinners that justice can be achieved only by a certain degree of coercion on the one hand, and by resistance to coercion and tyranny on the other hand."[21]

Whereas Niebuhr sees the pacifist as refusing to discriminate between relative values in the real world, he also cautions the non-pacifist that the relativity of moral ideals cannot absolve us of the duty of choosing between relative values; and the choice is sometimes so clear as to become an imperative one. As to how we respond defensively to a violent intruder, it seems indeed the choice is clear enough as to become an imperative one. And with the choice comes responsibility and accountability.

To adopt Niebuhr's point of reference is not, as sometimes alleged, to adopt an ethic of prudence or expediency. There are biblical norms which must always be weighed, especially just-love. Apart from pragmatic and utilitarian considerations, the Christian's ethical responsibility is first and foremost to perceive what commandments or admonitions may be relevant, then what God's Will appears to be in the present situation.

As Christians, we are called to be peacemakers; therefore aggressive use of weapons against persons cannot be justified except on those rare occasions when, necessarily, preemptive force is justified as a defensive act. Incidentally, to be a peacemaker is not identical with being a pacifist, as many non-pacifists are actively involved in the ranks of today's peacemakers.

J. B. Phillips, noted translator of *The New Testament in Modern English,* makes this acute observation:

> It always seems to me the weakness of the pacifist position that while they are prepared to be Good Samaritans after the event they are not prepared to protect, forcibly if need be, the life and the liberty of the weak. In others words, Peace is their God, and not the real God.[23]

Thus, to be either an absolute pacifist or an absolute non-pacifist can only disable one's capacity for biblically and morally assessing given situations within their context. The selectivist takes a middle ground, seeking to discriminate relative values and thus to retain an openness to alternative options.

An excellent summary of the authors' position is given by John Jefferson Davis. Having discussed the pacifist's confusion of private and public duties, he says,

> As a private individual, considering only my own interests and standing before God, I may choose to literally turn the other cheek in the face of unjust aggression. However, when I stand in a relation of guardianship to third parties, as a civil magistrate, a parent, or a husband, then the responsibilities of Christian love have a different application. Because of my love for those under my care, and out of concern for their lives and welfare, I must resist unjust aggression against them. Love of my neighbor does not mean standing idly by when my wife is being brutally raped; it means using whatever force is necessary to protect her life and safety. My divine obligation to provide for the needs of my own family (I Tim. 5:8) certainly includes, as an irreducible minimum, protecting them from deadly assault. . . . [The] demands of divine justice and love of the neighbor sometimes require the use of force in the legitimate defense of innocent human life.[24]

Before closing the chapter, a brief historical note is in order. The so-called *just war* concept (an option open to *selectivism*) represents the dominant view within historic Christianity. This includes Protestantism in nearly all of its branches, official Roman Catholic theology, and Eastern Orthodoxy. During the reformation period, pacifism was most staunchly promoted by the Anabaptists and is principally represented in our time by the Mennonite Brethren.

Augustine was the first major theologian and early biblical commentator to develop criteria for distinguishing justifiable from unjustifiable wars, notably in his classic work *The City of God*. The greatest of Roman Catholic scholars, Thomas Aquinas, reiterated Augustine's teachings in his monumental *Summa Theologica*. Aquinas placed his emphasis upon the advancement of the good, avoidance of evil, restoration of peace, and establishment of a just social order as making armed force necessary. The German Reformer, Martin Luther, said that without armaments peace could not be kept. Swiss Reformer John Calvin's theology also builds upon that of Augustine. Calvin accented the necessity of arms not only for defending domains under attack but also for restraining the misdeeds of private individuals. The great Scottish Reformer John Knox held the same position.[25]

Without going further into traditional pacifism we conclude there is little biblical support for an absolute pacifism or an absolute non-pacifism. Preference, we believe, falls to selectivism as making the best biblical case.

NOTES

1. Books called the "Peace Shelf," available through Herald, Scottdale, PA.
   Yoder, John H., *Nevertheless: the Varieties of Christian Pacifism.* 1977; *What Would You Do?*, 1983; *The Politics of Jesus*, 1972; *The Original Revolution*, 1971;
   Lasserre, Jean, *War and the Gospel.* 1962.
   Hershberger, G. F., *The Way of the Cross in Human Relations.* 1958.
   McSorley, Richard, *New Testament Basis of Peacemaking.* 1985.
   Sider, Ronald J., *Christ and Violence.* 1979.
   Trocme, Andre, *Jesus and the Nonviolent Revolution*, 1974.
   Aukerman, Dale, *Darkening Valley.* 1981.
   On pacifism generally: Ferguson, John, *The Politics of Love: The New Testament and Non-Violent Revolution.* Greenwood: Attic, n.d.; Grannis, Chris, Laflin, Arthur, and Elin Schade, *The Risk of the Cross.* New York: Seabury, 1981; Merton, Thomas, *Faith and Violence.* Notre Dame: University of Notre Dame, 1968.
2. Mott, Stephen. *Biblical Ethics and Social Concerns.* Oxford, 1982, pp. 178–180.
3. Davis, John Jefferson, *Evangelical Ethics: Issues Facing the Church Today.* Phillipsburg, PA: Presbyterian and Reformed, 1985, p. 233.

4. Ibid., pp. 239ff.

5. Jan Narveson, in Wasserstrom, Richard A. (ed.), *War and Morality.* Belmont: Wadsworth, 1970, pp. 68–69.

6. Bernbaum, John A. (ed.) *Perspectives on Peacemaking: Biblical Options in the Nuclear Age.* Ventura: Regal, 1984, p. 193.

7. Gustafson, James M., *Ethics From a Theological Perspective* (Vol. 2, *Ethics and Theology*), Chicago: University of Chicago, 1984, pp. 213, 275–276.

8. Davis, op. cit., pp. 201–202.

9. Yoder, John Howard, *The Politics of Jesus.* Grand Rapids: Eerdmans, p. 238.

10. Yoder, John Howard, "Reinhold Niebuhr and Christian Pacifism." *Mennonite Quarterly Review,* Vol XXIX, (April, 1955), pp. 101ff.

11. Ibid., p. 11.

12. Ibid., p. 11.

13. Ibid., p. 15.

14. Ibid., p. 15.

15. Ibid., p. 18.

16. Thielicke, Helmut, *Theological Ethics* (Vol. I: Foundations), ed. William H. Lazareth. Philadelphia: Fortress, 1966.

17. Ibid., p. 567.

18. Ibid., p. 568.

19. Ibid., pp. 570–573.

20. MacGregor, G. H. C., *The New Testament Basis of Pacifism* and *The Relevance of an Impossible Ideal.* Nyack: Fellowship, (rev. ed.) 1954.

21. Reinhold Niebuhr, "Why The Church Is Not Pacifist," *Christianity and Power Politics.* New York: Scribner's, 1940, p. 30.

22. Niebuhr, Reinhold, *An Interpretation of Christian Ethics.* New York: Seabury, 1979, p. 38; *See* Harries, Richard (ed.), *Reinhold Niebuhr and the Issues of Our Time.* Grand Rapids: Eerdmans, 1976.

23. Phillips, Vera, and Robertson, Edwin, *The Wounded Healer,* Grand Rapids: Eerdmans, 1984, p. 63.

24. Davis, John Jefferson., *Evangelical Ethics: Issues Facing The Church Today.* Phillipsburg, PA: Presbyterian and Reformed, 1985, p. 233.

25. Paolucci, Henry (ed.), *The Political Writings of St. Augustine.* South Bend: Henry Regnery, 1962, pp. 162–183; *Summa Theologica,* Pt. II–II, 40, art. 1, (trans. Fathers of the English Dominican Province), New York: Benziger Brothers, 1947; Richard McCormick, "Morality of War," *New Catholic Encyclopedia.* New York: McGraw-Hill, 1967, p. 803.

Chapter 14

CONTEMPORARY PACIFIST APPROACHES

THE PACIFISM OF JACQUES ELLUL

The noted French theologian and social critic Jacques Ellul builds his case for pacifism upon a false assumption and a false principle.

First, the assumption. Ellul claims there is an unbreakable link between violence and hatred, that hatred is the motivator of violence. He contends that violence has its source in hatred, that violence expresses hatred.[1] This means, of course, that Ellul rejects biblical violence on all counts, even divine retribution (God cannot be accused of hatred). Moreover, Ellul is led to say that violence cannot be legitimized when put to the service of man, for *violence always breaks and corrupts the relation of men to each other.*[2]

Illustrations abound to refute this untenable assumption. In our recent history, United Nation coalition forces under General Norman Schwartz-kopf defeated the Iraqi armies. General Schwartzkopf is known as a man of compassion who has repeatedly said that he hates war because it kills people. His compassionate treatment of enemy soldiers is legendary. Would anyone say that violent suppression of the ravaging forces of the Iraqis by Schwartzkopf was motivated by hatred?

Another illustration is found in an address given by Richard Mouw during a conference held in 1983 under the topic *The Church and Peacemaking in the Nuclear Age.* Mouw formulates a hypothetical scene:

> A terrorist is holding a large group of school children hostage. He refuses to release them unless certain demands are met—demands which are morally repugnant and practically impossible. He has begun to execute two of these children each hour; six of them are already dead, and many more will die if the terrorist is not stopped. I have a high-powered rifle with telescopic lens at my disposal, and suddenly I see the terrorist standing with his back to the window. Should I pull the trigger? Would doing so be a violation of the demands of discipleship? As a Christian who has attempted to allow the Gospel to shape my moral sensitivities, I must report that I would pull the trigger in such a situation. I see nothing in the Scriptures that would prevent me from doing so.[3]

Decision translates to responsibility. Addressing this aspect, Richard Neuhaus stated,

> At its heart is whether we are responsible before God for the probable consequences of the position we take or whether we are simply to say No to war and Yes to peace and leave whatever may be the policy implications and their consequences up to God? . . . Are those who take the latter position *fools for Christ,* or as Reinhold Niebuhr would have it, *just plain fools?*

Then Neuhaus adds that morality is "accepting responsibility for probable outcomes, while knowing that on the far side of our uncertainties it is really up to God."[4]

As selectivists, we find congenial the statement of Francis Schaeffer quoted by Senator John Armstrong of Colorado in his address to the Pasadena conference: "I am not a pacifist because pacifism in this fallen world in which we live means that we desert the people who need our greatest help."[5]

This was the essence of the 1983 pastoral letter of the Roman Catholic Bishops. It quotes Pope John Paul II:

> [I]*n the name of an elementary requirement of justice, peoples have a right and even a duty to protect their existence and freedom by proportionate means against an unjust aggressor.*
>
> Also, *Faced with the fact of attack on the innocent, the presumption that we do no harm, even to our enemy, yields to the command of love understood as the need to restrain an enemy who would injure the innocent.*[6]

As far back as Cicero this argument can be found: "There are two kinds of injustice: the first is found in those who do an injury, the second in those who fail to protect another from injury." To this might be added the contemporary word of Norman Geisler, who says,

> it can be argued that a truly benevolent person will protect the innocent against an evil aggressor. . . . To let the aggressor do his evil work is an inconsistent application of benevolence to the aggressor but not to the victim. . . . Pacifists, by attempting to avoid an error of commission, are guilty of an error of omission.

And on the question of responding to the violent intruder, Geisler concludes: "Any man who refuses to protect his wife and children against a violent intruder fails them morally."[7]

How very different is the thinking of Ellul, who asserts,

> The Christian can never entertain this idea of "last resort." He understands that for others this may be so, because they place all their hopes in this world

and the meaning of this world.... The Christian knows only one last resort, and that is prayer, resort to God.[8]

He says that to choose otherwise is infidelity, absence of faith. But isn't this rather an unreal notion of what it means to live in the real world, a notion wholly unsupported by Scripture? To regard prayer as the one last resort is both naive and unbiblical. Think back upon Mouw's illustration.

Ellul's conclusion:

> Thus violence can never be justified or acceptable before God. The Christian can only admit humbly that he could not do otherwise, that he took the easy way and yielded to necessity and the pressures of the world. That is why the Christian, even when he permits himself to use violence in what he considers the best of causes, cannot either feel or say that he is justified; he can only confess that he is a sinner, submit to God's judgment, and hope for God's grace and forgiveness.[9]

Contrary to Ellul, defensive violence when necessary for life preservation of the innocent has no *unbreakable link* with hatred. Instead, it is often accompanied by genuine compassion for the one who has initiated the crisis in which he himself stands the chance of being harmed, possibly killed. Necessity is not related to attitude!

PACIFISM AS VIRTUE

Stanley Hauerwas, currently teaching at Duke University and formerly at Notre Dame, is a Christian pacifist whose contemporary approach can be called *the art of narrative,* a method of biblical interpretation which emphasizes Christian virtues rather than rules or principles. Christian life is interpreted in terms of the narrative of our lives as an assimilation of the narrative of Jesus' life. It stresses emulation of Jesus. While there is much to commend, there is also a fundamental flaw. As with any single emphasis, the approach is reductionist, not correlated with other approaches.

Hauerwas, in *The Peaceable Kingdom,* [10] begins by stressing the centrality of non-violence as the hallmark of the Christian moral life, no mere option for those who seek to live faithfully in Jesus' Kingdom: "Indeed, non-violence is not just one implication among others that can be drawn from our Christian beliefs; it is at the very heart of our understanding of God."[11]

His initial presupposition is that non-violence is a given for it is rooted in the character of God. For all his objection to unqualified absolutes, he posits non-violence as an unqualified absolute: God's nature is non-violent, ours must be also.

Later on an equally fundamental presupposition appears: *A "truth" that must use violence to secure its existence cannot be truth.*[12] Crucial to his method is that *theological ethics might best focus on character and the virtues for displaying the nature of Christian moral existence.*[13] Theology is not the telling of God's story, only a critical reflection on that story; it is the story that must be elevated. Where he parts ways with traditional theological formulations is in giving primacy to narrative while according only secondary importance to doctrinal affirmations about the Christian life. But isn't Jesus' and the Apostles' teaching primary, narrative illustrative of doctrinal givens?

Strongly influenced by former colleague pacifist John Howard Yoder, Hauerwas's references allow us to also interact with Yoder, H. Richard Niebuhr and his brother, Reinhold.

Hauerwas objects to grounding ethics in unqualified absolutes. Curiously, he himself (as does Ellul) presupposes an absolute in his premise of invariable non-violence.

Developing an ethics of character and virtues (through the mode of narrative), Hauerwas subordinates the question *What ought we to do?* to the question *What ought we to be?* He contends that *the kind of convictions Christians hold are better exhibited by an analysis of the virtues.*[14] But isn't this one-sided?

It is these presuppositions we dispute, for clearly Scripture is replete with laws and principles as God's authoritative word binding upon Christian behavior. Quite different is Hauerwas's approach: [T]o be a Christian is not principally to obey certain commandments or rules, but to learn to grow into the story of Jesus as the form of God's kingdom.[15] Or: "[T]he content of the kingdom, the means of citizenship, turns out to be nothing more or less than learning to imitate Jesus' life through taking on the tasks of being his disciple.[16]

Citing Reinhold Niebuhr's locating our sinfulness in rebellion against God, in our effort to usurp God's place by making self-pride and will-to-power the center of existence, Hauerwas claims this a distortion of our existence, a short step *to the use of force in defense of what we think to be the truth, so our sin becomes the root and branch of violence.*[17] We concur with Niebuhr.

Unquestionably, sinfulness leads to a distortion of what we were created to be. Yes, the very essence of Man's Fall is self-pride and will-to-power as creatures seeking to be autonomous. Yes, violence is one of the fruits of sinfulness. But does it follow that every form of violence roots in that distortion of our nature? Certainly not every form of violence, and certainly not the necessary violence employed in defense of life itself.

Hauerwas writes, "Moreover our need to be in control is the basis for the violence of our lives. For since our *control* and *power* cannot help but be built on an insufficient basis, we must use force to maintain the illusion that we are in control.[18] He adds that "the more we seek to bring *under our control,* the more violent we have to become to protect what we have."[19]

In some cases perhaps, but not as a rule. Protecting what we have—our very life or that of others—this cannot be equated with an inordinate need for control.

Indeed, life is ultimately under God's sovereign control, lived within His providential rule, hence not under our own control. But in another sense, God calls us to responsibility and gives us means to control many aspects of life. Think, for example, of the Apostle Paul's admonition to exercise *self-control*—control over thoughts, passions, personal actions, etc. (Galatians 5:23). Scripture does not relieve us of responsibility for exercising many of life's controls. Surely, included is the attempt to control a situation where we might stop a violent crime from taking place.

Since Jesus calls us to be perfect as God is perfect (Matthew 5:38), a perfection that only comes by emulation of Jesus the perfect One, Hauerwas cites this as reason to attend primarily to the narratives which reveal what He is like. Then comes the crux of his pacifist views: *this*, he says,

> involves seeing in his cross the summary of his whole life. Thus to be like Jesus is to join him in the journey through which we are trained to be a people capable of claiming citizenship in God's kingdom of non-violent love—a love that would overcome the powers of this world, not through coercion and force, but through the power of this man's death.[20]

We've already rejected the notion that the cross is the summary of Jesus' whole life, but instead, the climactic event in His atoning work as the Messiah. To extrapolate from this that love can now overcome the powers of this world (not through coercion and force), through the power of this man's death, raises all manner of problems.

Interestingly, Hauerwas rejects the description of Satan as *god of this world,* saying, "The world is not, that is to say, given over to Satan, or to Caesar, until God will restore his rule over it by destroying the alien rulers. On the contrary, God is already present in this *evil age,* overcoming it by mercy."[21] This, too, runs contrary to Scripture and requires no further argument. Satan has not been removed nor his evil influence curtailed, despite the fact that he was defeated at the cross.

Where is it found in Scripture that God intends to rule the world presently solely through *the power of His people's humility and love?* Do we not recognize the difference between His present rule in absentia during this interim when sin and Satan have world-ruling power, and His future rule when He shall be present bodily and all-powerfully as King of Kings and Lord of Lords?

Take the story of the rich young ruler (Luke 18:18–30). Note how emulation could lead us astray. Jesus said to the rich young ruler, *Sell all that you have, and distribute to the poor....* Here His demand is made to a particular individual under particular circumstances to teach a particular lesson. To make emulation a condition of discipleship for all who follow Jesus is clearly incorrect.

The key to understanding discipleship is found in Jesus' words prior to His leaving: "I have yet many things to say to you, but you cannot bear them now. When the Spirit of truth comes, he will guide you into all the truth . . . " (John 16:12, 13). This extends to all New Testament teaching. Much of our behavioral guidance comes as the Holy Spirit speaks to the church, especially through the canon of Scripture.

Once again, Hauerwas states, "Because we have confidence that God has raised this crucified man, we believe that forgiveness and love are alternatives to the coercion the world thinks necessary for existence."[22] But in what contexts are forgiveness and love alternatives to coercion? Can forgiveness and love by themselves change this world? Can forgiveness and love stop a violent intruder?

Hauerwas declares: "We do not value life as an end in itself—there is much worth dying for—rather all life is valued, even the lives of our enemies, because God has valued them.[23] This point we ourselves made earlier. But while we value *even the lives of our enemies,* when it comes to a violent intruder about to take life, we come back to his statement *there is much worth dying for.* We're forced back to relative values, including values greater than the life of the intruder. One cannot have it both ways. One relevant Scripture would be Paul's admonition, *so far as it depends upon you, live peaceably with all* (Romans 12:18). It doesn't always depend upon us.

Another statement we find illogical: "For it is my contention that if we are genuinely nonviolent we can no more decide to use violence even if the situation seems to warrant it, than the courageous can decide, under certain conditions, to be cowardly."[24] This totally underestimates the nature of human response to life-threatening situations, and denigrates the character of genuinely non-violent people who nonetheless find themselves called upon to use violent means in saving life.

Our dispute with Hauerwas continues,

> Christians cannot seek justice from the barrel of a gun . . . for God does not rule creation through coercion, but through a cross. . . . We must be a people who have learned to be patient in the face of injustice . . . not . . . that we ought to legitimize the use of force to overcome injustice.[25]

This is sheer unreality. Under certain circumstances, patience and endurance are proper, but not in all. Nor do we agree that "when violence is justified in principle as a necessary strategy for securing justice, it stills the imaginative search for nonviolent ways of resistance to injustice."[26]

JOHN HOWARD YODER

Referring to the prominent pacifist John Howard Yoder, Hauerwas discusses Yoder's short book *What Would You Do If. . . .* He cites Yoder's statement: "Christianity relativizes the value of self and survival as it affirms the dignity of the enemy and offender."[27] Yet, is it not possible to relativize the value of self, even that of the violent offender, and still find the right course of action is shooting to stop him.

Yoder wisely takes up a number of options when faced with *What would you do if?. . .* We've attempted the same. However, his underpinning of those options is questionable. Take his second option, sacrificing life as a martyr. Yoder says, "The death of that Christian disciple makes a greater contribution to the cause of God and to the welfare of the world than his staying alive at the cost of killing would have done. For ever after it is looked on with respect. Why not accept suffering? Jesus did."[28]

Who determines that the Christian's voluntary sacrifice is the greater contribution? Under what circumstances? Can we really affirm it would be respected by everyone? Won't a majority think he sacrificed life unwisely, unnecessarily? In the same connection, Yoder finds justification for martyrdom as sharing *God's way with His world.* But can we be confident that this form of self-martyrdom is in fact *God's way with His world?*

Yoder insists that *it must be denied that death is the greatest evil which one can suffer.*[29] We agree. But this argument can be turned around: *It must also be denied that bringing death to a murderous intruder is the greatest evil,* especially in view of the evil he may bring about now and in the future.

Curiously, Hauerwas says, "For we know that by nature we are not violent, by nature we are not liars, by nature we seek not injustice. Christians therefore cannot be content with a morality that accepts sin as a given."[30]

This is startling! Do we not accept sin as a given? Are we not by nature violent, liars and much more? Even the converted Paul agonized in his new nature in Christ, troubled over his own plight in this very regard (see Romans 7:15–25). There is not a single member of God's Kingdom now on earth who does not sin (including Hauerwas and the authors of this book)!

NIEBUHR VERSUS NIEBUHR

Hauerwas refers to two brothers, two articles, two opposing positions, rightly stating that their debate is as relevant today as when written.

Soon after Japan's invasion of Manchuria in 1932 H. Richard Niebuhr wrote an article for *Christian Century* to which his brother Reinhold was asked to respond. At issue: *Is the ethic of non-violence out of step with the violent world in which we live if it requires that we sit on the sidelines doing nothing? Is this not irresponsible?* Does this not as a result breed callousness, and lead to a repetition of gross and brutal injustices, in the face of endless wars and human suffering at the hands of aggressors?

H. Richard Niebuhr's article was entitled *The Grace of Doing Nothing,* his brother Reinhold's *Must We Do Nothing?*[31] H. Richard argues that there is a force in history that will ultimately create a different kind of world than we presently experience. This assertion he justifies by belief in the inevitably good outcome of the mundane process. To do nothing is really assurance that something is being done, something which is divine in its promise.[32]

For H. Richard, the grace to do nothing rests upon faith in a God who has the power to use our faithfulness to make the kingdom of peace a reality in the world. This in turn requires the development of a special spiritual discipline.

Reinhold finds Richard's faith illusory, an error to think whatever happens derives from the counsels of God. He finds it an incoherent notion that God is at work in the midst of brutal forces, only finally to establish an ideal, peaceful society in which pure love will reign.

Reinhold concludes that "as long as the world of man remains a place where nature and God, the real and the ideal, meet, human progress will depend upon the judicious use of the forces of nature in the service of the ideal."[33]

He further asserts that

> those who make the attempt to bring society under the dominion of perfect love will die on the cross. And those who behold the cross are quite right in seeing it as a revelation of the divine, of what man ought to be and cannot be, at least not so long as he is enmeshed in the processes of history.[34]

Hauerwas is in agreement with H. Richard, we with Reinhold.

In *Christianity and Power Politics,* [35] Reinhold begins with a chapter, *Why the Christian Church is Not Pacifist.* His thesis is "that modern Christian . . . perfectionism, which places a premium upon non-participation in conflict, is a very sentimentalized version of the Christian faith and is at variance with the profoundest insights of the Christian religion."[36]

We regard the term *sentimentalized version* unfair. I much prefer Helmut Thielicke's respectful characterization of Christian Pacifism as absolutizing the radical demands of the Sermon on the Mount for the present era. It is this absolutizing that Reinhold finds in error. We agree with him that this *is at variance with the profoundest insights of the Christian religion.*[37]

Reinhold maintains that the church correctly "refuses simply to equate the Gospel with the *law of love.* Christianity is not simply a new law, namely, the law of love. . . . Christianity is a religion which measures the total dimension of human existence not only in terms of the final norm of human conduct, which is expressed in the law of love, but also in terms of the fact of sin."[38] This he sees as a permanent aspect of human history. He comments that the New Testament *pictures history as moving toward a climax in which both Christ and anti-Christ are revealed.* The New Testament does not, in other words, envisage a simple triumph of good over evil in history prior to the coming of Christ's Kingdom. It sees human history involved in the contradictions of sin to the end. That is why it sees no simple resolution of the problem of history. Reinhold believes that *the Kingdom of God will finally resolve the contradictions of history; but the Kingdom of God is no simple historical possibility.*[39] We concur that the radicalized fulfillment of the Sermon awaits the coming of the King with the establishment of His Kingdom in its full consummation.

Reinhold sees pacifism as "a version of Christian perfectionism . . . a genuine impulse in the heart of Christianity, the impulse to take the law of Christ seriously and not allow the political strategies, which the sinful character of man makes necessary, to become final norms.[40] He finds a positive asset in pacifism insofar as it serves as

> a reminder to the Christian community that the relative norms of social justice, which justify both coercion and resistance to coercion, are not final norms, and that Christians are in constant peril of forgetting their relative and tentative character and of making them too completely normative.[41]

Reinhold affirms that pacifists are little concerned with contradictions between the law of love and the persistent sin of man, hence do not appreciate the deeper complexity of the problem of justice and do not see the need for coercion, nor the values of achieving relative justice.

His positive affirmation: The Christian is freed by grace "to act in history; to give his devotion to the highest values he knows; to defend those citadels of civilization of which necessity and historic destiny have made him the defender. . . . "[42]

All things considered, we find ourselves closest to the position of Reinhold, not his brother, not Hauerwas, not Yoder, not Ellul. Neither pure pacifism nor pure non-pacifism meets the criteria for living responsibly in a sinful world. The position most comprehensively biblical and rational is that of selectivism.

NOTES

1. Ellul, Jacques, *Violence: Reflections From A Christian Perspective.* New York: Seabury, 1969, p. 109.
2. Ibid., p. 113.
3. Bernbaum, op. cit., p. 195.
4. Richard Neuhaus, "Consider the Ethics of Consequences," *Eternity.* Oct. 1982, p. 38

5. From a speech given in Washington, DC, June 22, 1982.

6. *The Challenge of Peace: God's Promise and Our Response.* (A Pastoral Letter on War and Peace by the National Conference of Catholic Bishops) May 3, 1983, pp. 36ff.

7. Moreland, J.P. and Norman Geisler, *The Life and Death Debate: Moral Issues in Our Time.* New York: Praeger, 1990, p. 133.

8. Ibid., p. 135.

9. Ellul, op. cit., p. 170.

10. Hauerwas, Stanley, *The Peaceable Kingdom: A Primer in Christian Ethics.* Notre Dame: University of Notre Dame, 1983.

11. Ibid., p. xvii.

12. Ibid., p. 15.

13. Ibid., p. xxi.

14. Ibid., p. 24.

15. Ibid., p. 30.

16. Ibid., p. 80.

17. Ibid., p. 32.

18. Ibid., p. 47.

19. Ibid., p. 49.

20. Ibid., p. 76.

21. Ibid., p. 86.

22. Ibid., p. 87.

23. Ibid., p. 88.

24. Ibid., p. 123.

25. Ibid., p. 104.

26. Ibid., p. 114.

27. Ibid., p. 124.

28. John Howard Yoder, What Would You Do If?," *Journal of Religious Ethics.* no 2, 1 (Fall, 1974) p. 90.

29. Ibid., p. 94.

30. Hauerwas, op. cit., p. 128.

31. H. Richard Niebuhr, "The Grace of Doing Nothing," *Christian Century* (March 30, 1932) pp. 415–417; Reinhold Niebuhr, "Must We Do Nothing," *Christian Century* 49 (March 30, 1932) pp. 415–417.

32. H. Richard Niebuhr, op. cit., p. 379.

33. Reinhold Niebuhr, op., cit., p. 416.

34. Ibid., p. 417.

35. Niebuhr, Reinhold. New York: Scribner's, 1940 (Archon Books ed., 1969).

36. Ibid., p. ix.

37. Ibid., pp. 1–2.

38. Ibid., pp. 20–21.

39. Ibid., p. 4.

40. Ibid., p. 5.

41. Ibid., p. 6.

42. Ibid., p. 31. (Note: Christian conservatives basically refer to the liberal theology

of Reinhold Niebuhr, and correctly, although he dismissed the charge "liberal" in his later writings. Resurgence of interest in Niebuhr is coming from Christian conservatives, citing him at least as often as those on the left do, although admittedly his social commitments were to the left. Readers are encouraged to read the article by Michael Novak in the *National Review* (May 11, 1992), entitled "Reinhold Niebuhr: Father of Conservatives.")

Chapter 15

PROTESTANT-CATHOLIC SELECTIVISM

From the earliest era of Christendom, notably from Augustine's *The City of God*, the Church has been shaped by so-called just-war theory. This theory then became the rationale for legitimate killing in wars waged for what was judged just cause. Over time, these notions provided not only just-cause criteria for warring states but theoretical justification for defensively killing assailants threatening to harm or kill innocent individuals.

Just-war theory was adopted officially by Roman Catholicism and Eastern Orthodoxy, later on assimilated into the theological ethics of the Protestant Reformers and the churches historically succeeding them. There were then, as now, notable exceptions, in early Reformation times the Anabaptists, today the Mennonite Church.

Just-war criteria has been applied to (1) defense of one's homeland against aggressors from outside and (2) to the protection or rescue of oppressed peoples in other lands. In either case, lethal countermeasures sometimes included preemptive action. In more limited terms, the same rationale validates lethal defense against life-threatening home intruders. Defense of *one's castle* is similar to defense of one's homeland. So the parallels are evident, the heart of the rationale being *just cause* for the employment of whatever means necessary for preserving life.

As for personal self-defense, there have been widely differing degrees of permissiveness, Augustine himself being among the first who could not conscientiously equate individual self-defense with neighbor-love criterion. In recent times, some just-war theorists have somewhat backed away in concern over the use of modern weapons of mass destruction, indiscriminate killing with long-range weapons, and the complexities of determining questions of relative justice when competing causes precipitate armed conflict. Especially troubling are the conflicts motivated by economic considerations under the guise of just cause. Thus, within all branches of the Christian community, ethicists and activists have fueled the debate with ever-greater intensity.

Our concern is not to enter the just-war debate as such (although admittedly we find the rationale sound), but simply to suggest parallels, points of contact, affirmations within the church at large for the use of lethal measures against life-threatening home intruders.

For a scholarly analysis of all aspects and applications of just-war theory, an important recent work is that of Richard B Miller.[1] To his careful work the authors owe a particular debt.

At the outset we note that just-war criteria provide a number of terms applicable to our thesis, including the following:

(1) *Just Cause.* This term refers to the basic rationale, including specification of occasions and conditions in which defensive use of force is justified. *Just cause* suggests a range of instances where it appears not only permissible but even requisite that lethal means be employed in defense against outside threats to innocent life, threats to basic human values, or (in the larger view) threats to the present or future welfare of the community as a whole.

(2) *Right Intention.* The reference here is to legitimate aims (such as defense of innocent life or protection of human rights). It does not allow the intention of revenge or retaliation.

(3) *Relative Justice.* In the acknowledged inability of any party in a conflict, to claim absolute justice for its cause, relative claims must be weighed period to any decision to use lethal force. In moral discourse, it is increasingly commonplace (less so among pacifists) to make reference to relative justice.

(4) *Proportionality.* This term concerns whether the values attainable through lethal force are commensurate with or greater than the possible unintended (although perhaps foreseeable) losses.

(5) *Prima Facie Duties.* Pacifists and just-war theorists alike possess a fundamental bias against violence, against coercive force; there is no point at issue here. Within each perspective is the presumption, fundamental to human welfare, of doing no harm to others, that is, the moral obligation not to harm or do injury. While for the pacifist this duty is absolute, without exception, for the just-war theorist it is a prima facie duty, that is, binding unless overridden by a weightier prima facie duty (say, the necessity for protecting innocent human life against aggression or the preservation of basic human rights). As to the question of the relative weight of these prima facie duties, the burden is upon those who wish to override any one in favor of another *in virtue of the totality . . . of ethically relevant circumstances.*[2]

Where the prima facie duty *Do not harm another person* is one of two conflicting prima facie duties, that duty remains the moral high ground, the ideal pointing to what is presumptively right and duty-bound except when overridden. For the just-war advocate, the overriding consideration is the obligation to protect helpless others.

(6) *Last Resort.* Reflective of the moral presumption against harming others, the reference is to the moral requirement *that all reasonable alternatives of less-harmful consequences be pursued before the employment of the means of last resort resulting in greater harm.*

A PROTESTANT PERSPECTIVE

For the Protestant theologian Karl Barth, the ethics of killing are premised upon obedience to the revealed Word of God communicated through the Scriptures and ultimately by God's direct command to receptive Christian conscience. Revealed commands supersede all rational considerations, all merely human expectations. Not that God through direct command is ever capricious or devoid of an ultimately worthy purpose. For Barth, the Sixth Commandment most surely provides a strong fundamental presumption against the use of lethal force. Therefore, any justifiable killing lies at *the extreme margin* or moral existence, constituting an emergency, justifiable, yes, but only as a rare departure from scriptural command, and then only by God's direct command. For Barth, the scriptural commands are not absolute inasmuch as such absolutism constrains divine freedom, freedom essential to divine sovereignty. Rather, scriptural commandments are given to provide provisional directions for responsible human actions, governing situations where there are no overriding reasons for exceptional action.

For Barth, killing, at very best, follows only after every other means has been taken into full account, and where nothing short of lethal means presents itself as adequate to the objective. Even then there must be a sense of moral ambiguity. Barth continues, "should I have in fact to kill the killer before he actually becomes a killer, so that he is only responsible for the will to do it whereas I must bear responsibility for the actual deed."[3]

Thus, for Barth, self-defense is a case of last resort. He further construes such action to comply with *the divine resistance entrusted to him.*[4] Additionally, violence is justifiable when properly aligned both with right intention and when *just cause* appears in accord with God's directly commanded purpose.

As noted by Miller, Barth's criticism of pacifism is targeted toward the evil of war in the abstract rather than in the concrete and without due regard for those conditions of peace which precede war. In a similar vein, we would add that the same considerations prevail in any decision made by an individual to act lethally against an aggressor. Miller cites the term used by Michael Wlazer, *the supreme emergency.*[5]

ROMAN CATHOLIC TEACHING

Contemporary Catholic theory permits pacifism and just-war tenets as equally valid options for individuals facing conscription into war service. Somewhat ambivalently, official Catholic teaching continues to mandate just-war tenets for the morality needed to direct states involved in conflict. Frequent church pronouncements depart from formerly outright rejection of pacifism, so to this extent at least favor a more qualified theory of the just war.

Underlying traditional Catholic teaching is a natural-law conviction that the natural duty of the state is to protect its citizens. The more recent official reversal with respect to conscientious objectors emerged with the *Pastoral Constitution of the Modern World* of the Second Vatican Council, later refined in the pastoral letter of the U.S. Bishops, *The Challenge of Peace: God's Promise and Our Response.* Like the Protestant Barth, Catholic scholar David Hollenbach insists that the presumption against violence does, however, contain an accompanying theory of exceptions. In emergency situation, the duty not to harm is relativized by conflicting duties toward different individuals.

The issue is reducible to the question of prior presumption: Is the prior presumption the duty to *do no harm* or the duty to *prevent harm from being done* a passive or active response? Is it active—that is, to protect those who are either being harmed or under threat of harm? Just-war theorists grant that the duty not to harm is fundamentally higher, although it may be *trumped* by the emergency which renders it a necessity to do harm in response to another individual's move to do harm.

The difference here is between negative and positive duties. Curiously, the just-war theorist generally accepts the negative premise that to refrain from inflicting harm is the more stringent duty, hence takes precedence over the positive duty to protect from harm. Nevertheless, in actuality, the duty to protect the innocent turns out to be relative to the victim's helplessness in the given situation, and thus the dominant presumption becomes the positive duty to protect. As Miller points out, "Rather than provide a reason for action which follows straightforwardly from the duty not to harm, just-war tenets furnish a rational for violence that must overcome the presumption established by the duty not to harm. . . . "[6] That is, justification for the use of force must hurdle over the obstacles presumed by the duty not to harm.

Into this complex equation comes the matter of human rights, which some theorists are attracted to, others not. Miller notes the perspective of Henry Veatch, who sees human rights as intelligible only as they refer to objective interests that clearly define human well-being. Veatch is quoted:

> Given the notion of an end or goal or perfection of human life that is determined by man's nature, it follows that the business of living, for a human being, must consist of an ongoing enterprise of trying to become and be simply what one ought to be . . . by nature that end will be obligatory. . . . My being under obligation to do thus-and-so implies that I have a right not to be interfered with or prevented from discharging my duty.[7]

Veatch's view, it should be noted, is not merely a variant of the more orthodox Christian view that *not self-protection but fulfillment of God's purpose for individual life is what is not to be interfered with or prevented.*

The more liberal position, both in Protestant and Catholic thought, accentuates the unconditional nature of neighbor love as literal non-preferentialism — as love that does not discriminate between neighbors, some near and others remote, between family and stranger, etc. Understandably, the liberal aim is to efface all differences — especially, say, between social or ethnic backgrounds, and particularly those which imply value judgments between individuals. But here the danger is failure to properly classify social relationships in terms of behavioral patterns which are either acceptable or not acceptable to society. It is a failure, in other words, to legitimately assess relative human values.

Recent refinement of Roman Catholicism's classical approach is attributable to the pontificate of Pius XII. For one thing, he reduced *just-cause* requirements to that of self-defense and the defense of others who are unjustly attacked. He emphatically denied a place for pacifism in Catholic moral theology. Pacifism's place was to appear later in the pontificate of John XXIII, at the Second Vatican Council, later still in the post-conciliar writings dating from the early 1960s. This led to the Bishop's

Pastoral Letter in 1983. But even in John XXIII's language there is no energetic support for the pacifist position. That breakthrough came with *The Pastoral Constitution,* the final document produced at the Second Vatican Council, opening for the first time an official sanction for pacifism as a legitimate option for Catholics in war situations. At the same time, however, explicit endorsement is given to just-war tenets, legitimating the right of self-defense whenever other means of peaceful settlement have been exhausted.

Somewhat typical of the trend away from the new pacifist option that emerged in the turbulent 1960s, especially with the anti-Vietnam war sentiment, Catholic doctrine continued developing just-war tenets. This proceeded until the broader sweep of opinion that came with *The Challenge to Peace* in 1983.

Responding to pacifist charges of preferentialism, just-war advocates correctly drew upon the notion of moral tragedy, noting the dissonance between ideal norms and the tragic realities of everyday living and decision-making. These advocates contended realistically that no human achievement can fully meet the requirements of indiscriminate, disinterested, non-preferential love. The U.S. bishops found justification under certain conditions as an unfortunate yet inescapable necessity in the histories of nation states. Likewise, in the case of the householder threatened by an intruder, it is clearly the case of taking preferential defensive measures for the good of some over the good of others, in this case the good of innocent victims over the good of victimizers.

PROTESTANT ETHICIST PAUL RAMSEY

Paul Ramsey understands just-war theory in light of the principle of *agape* (unconditional love). Love directed toward the protection of innocent persons, albeit by way of the necessary use of lethal force, requires no exceptional authorization or even any special conceptualization, inasmuch as it is a positive expression, not of compromise but of agape love towards objects of care. Thus no duties are overridden, no exceptions are in need of justification, so long as force is employed in the positive effort of rescuing victims of aggression.

Miller cites theologian Paul Tillich to the effect that "the Protestant principle contains the divine and human protest against any absolute claim made for a relative reality."[8] Once again, indeed, the name of

Reinhold comes to mind—Reinhold Niebuhr for whom love relativizes all historical accomplishments, love standing always as the *impossible possibility*. When all is said and done, love is ever the ideal nonetheless, albeit only a partially reachable ideal. It remains the absolute standard for measuring relative claims to justice, the standard that judges all our acts.

Ramsey vacillated on the issue of self-protection, despite his insisting on the protection of others. He was following the logic of Augustine, that the use of lethal force to protect oneself violates the requirements of disinterested neighbor love. This logic was predicated on the premise that the enemy is also our neighbor, hence to be treated in a non-preferential way. But then, as Miller notes, in other instances Ramsey does not find love and violence mutually exclusive. So this is the key: we are forced to rank the duties acquired by the principle of neighbor love. On behalf of innocent victims, agape love requires that care first be directed to those whose concrete needs are either seriously neglected or under great duress, hence the justification of preferentialism in the distribution of love.[9]

Pacifists, because they fail to recognize the preferential requirements of agape love in the face of multifaceted need (preferentialism aimed toward those in need yet helpless to protect themselves), proceed to compromise those requirements. On the other hand, protective coercion can be expressed as *force for love's sake,* hence *not really an "exception" but rather a determinate expression of justice and mercy.*[10]

Ramsey appeals to the principle of double effect, a principle we review in detail elsewhere. He also supports the argument that self-protection is a duty insofar as the Christian's continuing existence is a necessary condition for relieving the burdens of others. At times, says Ramsey, failure to protect either oneself or one's own may actually involve greater burdens or injury to others. Surely, then *self-defense may be but an extreme instance of those "duties to self" which are part of Christian vocational obligation,* adding that this may not only be an unnecessary acceptance of injustice but *also to start down the steep slope along which justice can find no place whereon to stand.*[11]

Thus, for Ramsey, the criterion of just cause, the logic of prima facie duties sometimes overridden, the reality of emergencies occasioned by another's action to do harm—all these in reality mean that self-defense is not exceptional, nor is it *last resort.* Rather, it is proper response to just cause and the necessity for agape care. In Miller's words, the logic of prima facie duties, then, is designed to give the ethics of war an idiom that (even more fully than *agape* love) expresses the context and the moral tensions occasioned by the phenomenon of violence . . . the presumption is to restrain evil and protect the innocent.[12]

He throws his weight on the side of the positive presumption. So do the authors!

Just-war tenets, while a matter of continued debate, clearly translate to the quandary here being examined. Both duties—the duty not to harm, and the duty to prevent harm—are correlative, the latter at times taking precedence over the former—a powerful supporting argument for the position taken in this book.

NOTES

1. Miller, Richard B., *Interpretations of Conflict: Ethics, Pacifism, and the Just-War Tradition.* Chicago: University of Chicago, 1991.
2. Ross, W.D., *Foundations of Ethics.* Oxford: Clarendon, 1939, p. 86.
3. Barth, Karl, *Church Dogmatics,* III/4, trans. A. T. Mackay, et al., Edinburgh: Clark, 1961, p. 432.
4. Ibid., p. 435.
5. *See* Walzer, Michael, *Just and Unjust Wars: A Moral Argument with Historical Illustrations.* New York: Basic Books, 1977, pp. 251–268.
6. Miller, op. cit., p. 41.
7. Quoted by Miller from Henry B. Veatch, *Human Rights: Fact or Fancy?* Louisiana State University, 1985, pp. 163–166.
8. Tillich, Paul, *The Protestant Era.* Chicago: University of Chicago, 1948, p. 163.
9. Ramsey, Paul, *The Just War: Force and Political Responsibility.* New York: Scribner's, 1968, p. 143.
10. *See* Ramsey, Paul, *Christian Ethics and the Sit-In.* New York: Association Press, 1961, p. 102.
11. Ramsey, Paul, *War and the Christian Conscience.* Durham: Duke University, 1961, 205.
12. Ramsey, Paul, *Speak Up for Just War or Pacifism: A Critique of the United Methodist Bishop's Letter "In Defense of Creation,"* State Park: Pennsylvania University, 1988, p. 83.

Chapter 16

ETHICS POSTSCRIPT

From philosophical ethics, three concepts assist our understanding of the responsibilities we have for the use of lethal defense against a violent intruder. These three are compatible with theological ethics.

(1) Prima Facie Versus Actual Duties

Understanding the Sixth Commandment as apodictic and casuistic law is enhanced by a widely accepted distinction first proposed by W.D. Ross.[1] Ross distinguished two forms of duty: *prima facie* and *actual.*

Prima facie duty is an obligation which is binding *on the face of things* (literally, *on first appearance*). While it contains no exceptions, it is nevertheless qualified by *all things being equal* (*before further examination*). Prima facie duty becomes actual duty provided no other moral considerations intervene to change the priority of obligation. No duty is the actual one when, upon full examination, other moral considerations outweigh it. A second prima facie duty more stringent than the first can take precedence over the first. Thus, actual duty is the binding obligation *all things considered,* after every possible competing obligation has been taken into account and given relative weight. The weightier value then assumes prior claim. Although both prima facie duties remain absolutes, one takes precedence.

In the quandary of how to effectively confront a violent intruder in the interest of saving innocent people, there is a genuine conflict of prima facie duties. One moral imperative pulls in one direction, another pulls in another direction. If, then, not every individual's interest can be fulfilled, whose interests are most deserving?

Inaction is a form of action; *no-decision* is a specific decision not to act and represents responsible choice or, as Richard McCormick says, *to omit to take a preventive action.*[2] Inaction may turn out to be a truly irresponsible form of responsibility.

Two biblical stories are illustrative, one from the Old Testament, one from the New.

RAHAB THE HARLOT

According to Joshua 2:1–6:18, during Israel's invasion of Canaan Rahab the harlot shifted her allegiance from the king of Jericho to the God of Israel. She lied to the soldiers in order to save the lives of God's people and bring about the fall of Jericho. She breached a prima facie duty, but saving lives was also a prima facie duty.

Bible scholars generally agree with John Jefferson Davis of Gordon Seminary:

> Her higher duty to protect the lives of the servants of God suspended the prima facie duty to tell the truth, and her course of action was acceptable to God. In the New Testament, Rahab is cited as an example of faith for receiving the spies and sending them out in a different way (James 2:25; Hebrews 11:31). Nowhere in Scripture is Rahab condemned for her action in lying to the soldiers. On this construction, Rahab fulfilled the moral absolute that applied in this wartime context, namely, to save the lives of God's people; and her actions, rather than being the lesser of two evils, were actually good.[3]

Donald Bloesch remarks, "Rahab was honored not because she lied but because she heeded the command of God to preserve the life of the two spies. She was honored in spite of her lie, which was covered by the righteousness of her faith."[4]

A New Testament illustration of the irresponsibility attached to inaction is recorded in Mark 3:1–5. On a Sabbath day, Jesus healed a man who had a withered hand. Immediately the legalistic Pharisees accused Him of violating the Sabbath law. Jesus replied, *Is it lawful on the Sabbath to do good or to do harm?* (inaction here equated with doing harm).

Jesus could either have healed the man or refused on the grounds of keeping the Sabbath law (divinely appointed prima facie duty). Jesus' choice is a forced one. The Pharisees looked on to see what He would do. Whichever way Jesus chooses to go, He cannot avoid taking direct responsibility for the outcome. If He heals, He does good. If He refuses to heal, He contributes to the harm that dominates the man's life. Jesus' presumption is that healing is the higher value, hence the value taking precedence. One prima facie duty, that of healing, overrides another, the Sabbath law.

Ethics professor Stephen Mott observes that responsibility is never to a single value but to a total system of values. He reminds us that even where a person is unable to fulfill a prima facie duty because competing values take precedence, that duty remains a relevant standard nonetheless. Thus the obligation embodied in the Sixth Commandment ought always to be taken into account as part of the *all things considered,* even when it is unenforceable because an obligation of greater weight preempts it.[5]

In summary, prima facie duties do not stand in isolation from one another; they are interrelated. When two or more are in tension, making it impossible for each to be fulfilled, we need to (a) look to God's express command, (2) examine extenuating circumstances and their relative weight, (3) determine the duty having the greater weight, the more substantial claim, and (4) seek to discern the will of God through prayer and the counsel of the Christian community. In this way we come to the most assured actual obligation.

John Harris points to an extraordinary illustration in the Gospels, the familiar parable Jesus told of *The Good Samaritan.* If ever the neglect of beneficence was blameworthy, it was the inaction of both priest and Levite toward the man who fell among thieves. He was left half dead by them and might have perished had the Samaritan followed their inaction.

> To see this is to see a causal connection between the failure to tend the man and his death. And it is because we understand this connection that we see the point of the parable, that we realize why it is that the priest and the Levite ought to have tended the man. We do not need to postulate a duty of benefi- cence to explain how the neglect of the passersby might well have resulted in the man's death, rather we need to understand the causal connection between neglect and death to see why anyone might be required to tend him.[6]

Whatever might have prevented harm is likely to have valid causal status. Harris places emphasis upon the point that omission adds to irresponsibility when it constitutes a departure from normal expectation (normal expectation is the protection of self or others).

Harris concludes that morally, killing is no worse than letting die, that between acts and omissions there is no moral difference.[8] This implies that to willingly refuse to save an innocent victim (by refusing to harm the victimizer) can be morally equated with actively killing the innocent person.

(2) **Principle of Double Effect**

A second concept moving us forward is what ethicists call The Principle of Double Effect. John Harris states it precisely: "The doctrine of the double effect distinguishes between what a man foresees will result from his conduct and what in the strict sense he intends." Harris explains as follows: "While one may not bring about a forbidden result intentionally, that prohibition may not extend to the result when that result is the second effect."9 R. M. Hare further refines the idea, saying,

> If an act, not sinful in itself, has two consequences, and if one of these consequences is something which normally it is sinful to bring about, yet this consequence is a necessary condition of the other good consequences, it may not be sinful to undertake the original act, for the reason that only the good consequence is intended, the other not.10

The principle may be summarized in seven propositions:

(1) The act must not be morally evil in and of itself.

(2) The act produces two effects, one good and one evil.

(3) The evil effect, although foreseen, is not intended.

(4) The good effect is not the result of the evil effect.

(5) The intended good effect substantially outweighs the unintended evil effect.

(6) There is no alternative action perceivable that can achieve the good effect without causing the evil effect.

(7) The value preserved is in all likelihood incapable of being subverted by later developments.

Germain Grisez points out one further necessity, that the two effects be concurrent, the evil effect being incidental and unavoidable.

Here, then, is a single act with a double effect, one effect intended, the other not. The act itself is indivisible insofar as its effects are concerned. Killing an assailant would be an intrinsic evil, but not as the unavoidable second effect—*the tragic duality of the single act, the double effect.* We conclude that the second effect does not render the actor culpable.

To take life in order to save life has its illustrations outside the arena of criminal threat. Doctor C. Everett Koop is best known as the crusading Surgeon General during the Reagan administration. Less known is his international fame as a pioneer in the field of pediatric surgery. I first knew Doctor Koop when I was co-pastor of Tenth Presbyterian Church, Philadelphia, where Doctor Koop had come to faith in Christ and was an active member. He was then chief of surgery at the world famous Children's

Hospital, already internationally renowned for surgical methodology for normalizing children born with hydrocephalus, surgical correction of children born with spina bifida, and for separating conjoined twins. From the start, his life was devoted to saving the lives of children other physicians regarded hopeless. Then, in 1977, Doctor Koop faced an operation he has since characterized as the hardest day in his life.

Conjoined twins, born of Orthodox Jewish parents, shared a single, normal heart that could not sustain life for the conjoined twins for long. If they were separated, the heart would have to go to one or the other. For 11 days a group of rabbis and Talmudic scholars sought to determine a course of action—whether to do nothing, in which case both babies would die, or operate so as to take the life of one that the other might live. The latter course was found consistent with Judaism's ancient body of law and tradition.

Doctor Koop said it took him only 10 minutes to decide that intervention was the moral course consistent with his Christian understanding. Having assessed the relative chances of survival of one twin over against the other, the die was cast. As the table with Baby B who was granted the heart was pulled away, Koop stopped the twenty-nine team members. Then he himself took the ultimate responsibility, clamping off Baby A's carotid arteries. Baby A's life was taken, Baby B's saved. In this heart-rending conflict of values, the higher value was chosen.[11]

Historically, the principle of double effect has been held by Roman Catholic moralists over a long history. Today, Protestant and Catholic ethicists alike appeal to the validity of the principle, Paul Ramsey and Richard McCormick being notable examples.[12]

Richard McCormick opens his essay by noting:

> The issue becomes much more complex when one questions the decisive moral relevance of the direct/indirect distinction, and yet maintains that it is still morally right at times to perform actions inseparably joined with causing harm or death.[13]

We can speak of *dominant intentionality* (stopping the intruder poised to kill innocents) and *subdominant intentionality* (stopping the intruder even if this action results in his death).

James Gustafson cautions:

> Does the actor sincerely not intend the evil effect, the death of the intruder? Are the good and evil effects caused simultaneously so that the evil is never a sequential means to the good? Is there a proportionately grave reason for permitting the evil effect?

Having asked the question, Gustafson answers,

> "Whether the outcome could decisively avoid the moral ambiguity of the act, however, depends upon one's confidence in the principle of double effect to resolve all doubt.[14]

One final observation by Paul Ramsey:

> Killing may be tragically necessary in the fabric of life that restrains and sustains others for whom Christ died. . . . Killing a human being must surely be classified with moral evil as something that Christians ought never to encompass with direct voluntariety . . . only indirectly intended or permitted.[15]

The Principle of the Double Effect certainly illuminates our quandary, separating as it does the intention of stopping the intruder from an unintended, yet possible death. Culpability is clearly that of the assailant, not the victim.[16]

(3) Consequentialism

In commenting upon consequentialism as an element in nearly every modern ethical proposal, James Gustafson notes that we equate consequentialism with the purposeful actions of moral agents, that as Christians we are to act purposefully, thus consequentialism will figure in any adequate Christian ethic.

The consequentialist takes the position that if the end result of an action achieves the greatest conceivable good, then the choice is a right one. Or, if the intended result appears reasonably certain of bringing about the greatest good—maximizing the potential good and minimizing the potential evil—it can be considered right.

We previously made the point that consequences are of utmost importance to Christian decision-making, but not everything that matters? Is it not equally important that consequences also meet the criteria of the two biblical absolutes, justice and love? What about God's commands and admonitions? Can we know for sure which results will be *good?*

One problem with making everything depend on consequences, it is then deceptively easy to justify the use of bad means in order to achieve good ends. Not all means can be justified by good ends. Some ends justify some means, but no end justifies every means.

Another problem is that along the whole spectrum of human values, not all values are equal; we've seen that values are relative. Some are good, others bad, some better or best, others less or least good. Some ends combine both good and bad elements. If two things are good, for example, which is the greater good? If two things are bad, which is the least bad? What price must be paid to achieve a certain good? Is the end worth that price? Is the good on one occasion the good for every similar occasion? How is the good or bad affected by mitigating circumstances? Would other people judge the same consequences the way I do? Can we accurately distinguish personal preferences from what is genuinely the good?

In the larger picture of human relationships, good consequences are those that make life in community good (sustaining what is now good, making life better, or keeping life from getting worse than it now is). What we do as individuals affects the whole community.

To the Christian, end results are indeed important. Think of scriptural admonitions: Proverbs 3:27: *Do not withhold good from those to whom it is due, when it is in your power to do it.* While we make judgments as to the good from a limited perspective, we also sense the need for having God's perspective and that of the Christian community. When we think we see a certain end filling a certain need, we need to ask if God sees the need differently and desires it filled by achieving a different end? Do we earnestly seek to distinguish His purposes from our own?

Consequentialism judges solely by the utility gained, not by the instrumentality of its achievement. The *greatest good for the greatest number,* this is the general theme of all utilitarianism. But for the Christian there are other matters to consider, especially what standards any and all consequences themselves must be measured by.

One weakness of consequentialism is its tendency to get caught up in the immediate consequences, losing sight of long-term consequences. Often a person is not even in position to foresee long-term consequences. James Gustafson adds a reminder:

> Consequentialists are always reminded of the difficulty in predicting consequences, especially over a long range of time and those in very complex circumstances in which many persons are interacting. The reminder is always appropriate, for it is one of the truisms of moral experience that the effects one intends from a course of action often do not follow, and that the further one looks ahead the less secure one's predictions and forecasts are likely to be.[17]

In fact, one's very intentions may be unrecognizably mixed. Gustafson then expresses a balanced view: "Certainly, the calculation of probable consequences of various courses of action is part of the process of discernment."[18] So while the calculation of probable consequences is not the whole of discernment as the Christian understands it it is a relevant, important part of that process.

Donald Bloesch writes:

> Theological ethics gives place both to consequences and to moral rules, but stands above both as revelational. Its appeal is never to an abstract good (as that good may be assessed by human reason alone), but appeals to the concrete good as revealed in the commands and principles of God's Word, and as dynamically and contextually applied by the word of the living Christ to His people in their particular situations.[19]

To this we add the perspective of Richard McCormick: "The problem is rather to do all we can to guarantee that our calculus will be truly adequate and fully Christian."

We conclude that determining probable consequences is relevant, necessary, and a biblically endorsed part of ethical decision, but not all we need for the most assured decision-making.[20]

NOTES

1. Ross, W. D., *The Right and the Good*. Oxford: Oxford University, 1930, pp. 20–21, 38.
2. McCormick, Richard A. and Paul Ramsey (eds.), *Doing Evil to Achieve Good: Moral Choice in Conflict Situations*. Chicago: Loyola University, 1978, pp. 93ff.
3. Davis, John Jefferson, *Evangelical Ethics: Issues Facing the Church Today*. Phillipsburg, PA: Presbyterian and Reformed, 1985, p. 16.
4. Bloesch, Donald A., *Freedom for Obedience: Evangelical Ethics In Contemporary Times*. San Francisco: Harper & Row, 1987, p. 206.
5. Mott, Stephen, *Biblical Ethics and Social Concerns*. Oxford: Oxford University, 1982, p. 157 (*see* also chapters 3, 4).
6. Harris, John, *Violence and Responsibility*. Boston: Routledge & Kegan Paul, 1980, p. 33.
7. Ibid., p. 35.
8. Ibid., p. 47.
9. Ibid., p. 48.
10. R. M. Hare, "Intention," *Dictionary of Christian Ethics*. John Macquarrie (ed.), Philadelphia: Westminster, 1967, p. 171.
11. Easterbrook, Gregg, *Surgeon Koop*. Knoxville: Whittle, 1991, pp. 43–44.
12. McCormick and Ramsey, op. cit., p. 35.
13. Ibid., p. 5.
14. Gustafson, James M., *Ethics from a Theocentric Perspective* (*Ethics and Theology*, Vol. 2), Chicago: University of Chicago, 1984, p. 197.
15. Ibid., p. 198.
16. *See* Anscombe, Elizabeth, "Modern Moral Philosophy," *Ethics*. Thomson, Judith

J., and Gerald Dworki, (eds.), New York: Harper & Row, 1968; Divine, Philip E., *The Ethics of Homicide.* Ithaca: Cornell University, 1978; Richards, Norvin, "Double Effect and Moral Character," *Mind* 93 (1984) pp. 381–397; Duff, R.A. "Absolute Principles and the Double Effect," *Analysis* 36 (Jan. 1976) pp. 68–70; McCormick, Richard A., *Ambiguity and Moral Choice,* Milwaukee: Marquette University, 1973.

17. Bloesch, op. cit., p. xviii.

18. On strengths and weakness of Consequentialism: Lyons, David, *Forms and Limits of Utilitarianism.* Oxford: Clarendon, 1965; Slote, M., *Common Sense Morality and Consequentialism.* Boston: Routledge & Kegan Paul, 1985; Smart, J.J.C., and Williams B., *Utilitarianism: For and Against.* Cambridge: Cambridge University, 1973.

Chapter 17

IT'S YOUR OPTION TO CHOOSE!

I t's time to consider options as we propose some final thoughts. We recall the wisdom of the late Henry Stob:

I am a fallen man living among other fallen men in a broken world existing under the power of death. Death stalks me and those for whom I have been appointed guardian. It also stalks those whom the Prince of this broken world has recruited in the cause of death — the murderers who may assault me or my wards. Under these circumstances killing will certainly occur. In the matter of killing, therefore, I am normally not placed before the alternative of preserving or terminating life. Normally I must choose between preserving this life or that, one life or many lives, many lives or more. The moral question to which commandment is relevant and for which it is determinative, is therefore this: How shall I, under the conditions of my existence as a fallen creature in a fallen world — and in this particular situation — act Christianly? Or, what shall be the shape of my obedience and the sign of my love?[1]

Stob's reply:

When I face the existential question, Whose life, here and now, shall be preserved, or what is the same thing, Whose life shall be terminated, I must draw upon the resources available to the Christian — love and law. Killing, in the situation contemplated, will occur; and in that situation I must act. The law will demand that I so act as to make, by my action, the greatest possible contribution to the preservation and enhancement of life.[2]

Reflecting upon the realities, Stob continues:

Meanwhile, of course, I will have killed, for in a world out of joint I cannot avoid killing, directly or indirectly, either myself, or my wards, or my assailant. Have I, then, violated the law? Quite possibly not. It all depends on whether I have succeeded, under the tutelage of love, in preserving the right life, or the greatest amount of life, or the highest degree of life which it is the intent of the law to safeguard. . . . To meet the needs of men the law does not need to be suspended, but it does need to be opened up by love, and thus made relevant to the situation.[3]

That's it — law under the tutelage of love!
Stob's conclusion?

We must obey God's law, but always and only in such a way as to make us our brothers' keepers. . . . God reigns over all and will, we trust, one day perfect our feeble attempts both to obey and to be compassionate. But today he puts a double burden upon us. He bids us both to remember the commandments and to seek the welfare of the neighbor.[4]

The Christian prays as Paul prayed for the Colossian Christians, that they might have *the knowledge of his will in spiritual wisdom* (Colossians 1:9). In other words, that God's will might be known in the present situation, that wisdom might be imparted from above, knowing that God is able to make clear the ends He wants served, the outcomes He wants brought about. To Him, all relevant factors are perfectly in view. Whatever action is taken, He knows precisely what consequences will follow.

We the authors are personally drawn to the words of contemporary Christian philosopher, William Frankena:

It remains true, nevertheless, that a man must in the moment of decision do whatever he thinks is right. He cannot do otherwise. This does not mean that what he does will be right or even that he will not be worthy of blame or punishment. He simply has no choice, for he cannot at that moment see any discrepancy between what is right and what he thinks is right. He cannot be morally good if he does not do what he finally believes to be right, and even then what he does may not be what he ought to do. The life of man, even if he would be moral, is not without its risks.[5]

When there is no avoiding a forced choice, no escaping responsibility for commitment to one option or another, then the greatest possible good is to be sought even if it involves an otherwise unacceptable act. This assumes a proper consideration of the laws and admonitions of Scripture. When only bad choices are available, the Christian must discern which choice is the least bad, a choice aimed at maximizing the good and minimizing the evil.

A Christian's decisions are gauged by considerations more stringent than those of non-Christians because they are made with the sense of ultimate accountability to God. He knows his actions will eventually be judged by the Sovereign Lord of all. With such accountability, the Christian proceeds to make tough decisions and carry them through.

CHRISTIAN SOCIAL RESPONSIBILITY

The Christian's primary social responsibility is outlined in I Timothy 5:8: "If anyone does not provide for his relatives, and especially for his own family, he has disowned the faith and is worse than an unbeliever." Strong words! Specific obligations! Can we imagine not providing protection for the very lives of family members? We recall James 4:17: "Whoever knows what is right to do and fails to do it, for him it is sin."

Next in order comes fellow Christians. Galatians 6:10 reads: "So then, as we have opportunity, let us do good to all men, and especially to those who are of the household of faith." What *especially* is our responsibility when we have Christian guests in our home and an intruder threatens? Is it not full protective responsibility?

The Apostle affirms our responsibility to all, but two classes are singled out, using *especially* to give priority to family and fellow Christians. The sociologist might ask, *Isn't it sheer ethnocentrism that caused Paul to use the word "especially" to favor close-of-kin affiliations?* No, not really; he was faithfully responding to divine orders, giving credence to the biblical order for setting priorities.

So *especially* confers the right of precedence, first upon our immediate kinship circle, then upon those within the body of Christ. At that point love reaches out to the larger circle of *all persons.*

Don Kates calls attention to a sermon of Gilbert Tennent, preached at the birthplace of our nation, Philadelphia, in 1747. Tennent was one of the most noted of the eighteenth century American preachers. He said in part,

> He that suffers his life to be taken from him by one that hath no authority for that purpose, when he might preserve it by defense, incurs the guilt of self-murder since God hath enjoined him to seek the continuance of his life, and nature itself teaches every creature to defend himself. . . .

(Incidentally, Mr. Small served for a brief period in the historic church in Philadelphia known to Gilbert Tennant.) Not only the sons of John Calvin have consistently held this position.

In summary, the Christian seeks more than what is right by law or good in terms of consequences. His standard is the Word of God. Violence is to be avoided except where necessary to preserve life and the values of a morally ordered society. In any given situation the Christian is to seek the will of God. Neither one's own life or the life of any other is the ultimate value; the purposes of God are the final consideration and it is this the Christian must seek earnestly to perceive. But in principle we sustain the view that lethal self-defense against a dangerous intruder is justifiable, even when stopping him results in his life taken, and unless God clearly directs otherwise.

Christian selectivists implicitly put their trust in God, but for them the prudent thing is to presuppose that the solution requires human action as well. So they trust God for the right decision, the right action, and the right outcome for everyone.

The Christian must always keep in mind that what one fellow Christian deems right for himself is not necessarily what other Christians find right for themselves. Each one's primary responsibility is to have first given thought and prayer to the issue for himself or herself, and only then have come to an honest conviction before the Lord. Every Christian is responsible to act on his or her own convictions.

Some Christians may be convinced that the use of lethal force is legitimate, yet find it personally impossible to actually use a deadly weapon no matter what the situation. Action would not be congruent with something intangible yet real. If something inside tells them they must not act, we dare not see this as weakness, much less inconsistency. Each person is to be true to himself or herself and with no need for explanations. For that person the various security measures available may be the final line of defense. This is not a decision based merely upon logical analysis, even pragmatic considerations; it is a personal spiritual decision, one of conscience which speaks profoundly of one's personal relationship with the Lord.

We've come to the end of a long route, necessarily so because the issue is both complex and grave, what with a nation in a state of crisis because of mounting violence and every individual a potential victim. Perhaps the best word with which to close would be to suggest that the issue become the study for church discussion groups. What better course than to have this critical moral dilemma enhanced by the input of Christians of every conviction. To this end we commend the present study.

NOTES

1. Stob, Henry, *Ethical Reflections: Essays on Moral Themes.* Grand Rapids: Eerdmans, 1978, p. 148.

2. Ibid., p. 148.
3. Ibid., Ibid., p. 148.
4. Ibid., p. 150.
5. Frankena, William K., *Ethics* (second edition), Engelwood Cliffs, NJ: Prentice-Hall, 1973.

Part III
SOCIAL POLICY ISSUES

Chapter 18

CONTENDING AGENDAS

We come to a crucial issue—social policy as it relates to private gun possession and use. The controversy over gun control is one of the heated issues of our time, with an almost bewildering variety of political positions ranging from extremists on the left to extremists on the right. There are those who would ban all guns from civilian possession and others who resist regulation in any form whatsoever. Among moderates are those who would ban only certain types of guns, those even more moderate who stress a waiting period or instant police check before a firearm can be purchased. Still others call for gun registration. Strong advocacy is represented in each camp.

Actually, two major orientations stand in major conflict. On one hand is a powerful and vocal group truly convinced that society would be better served by the elimination of all privately owned firearms.[1] Opposed are those who believe the heart of the issue is keeping firearms out of the hands of certain classes of citizens—juveniles, convicted felons, the mentally impaired, and drug users. Moderates generally concede that a sensible compromise is desirable between individual and societal rights, and hence want only reasonable restrictions protective of the public good together with an improved criminal justice system and better law enforcement. They see crime control as a far larger issue than gun control.

WHERE THE AUTHORS STAND

Authors Furnish and Small share their thinking about most aspects of this subject, yet have their individual perspectives. As to the major quandary being addressed, both authors firmly believe in the legitimacy of lethal force in defending against intruders having the potential for violence (never the preferable course should any other be genuinely open). Nevertheless, the authors have a few significant differences, generally ideological, reflective of Furnish's more conservative social orientation,

211

Small's somewhat more liberal social orientation. Differences do not extend, however, to the theological, since both authors are biblically conservative.

Furnish is persuaded that the historical analysis of Hallbrook and other scholars substantiates the belief that the Second Amendment guarantees broad individual rights for citizen firearms possession.[2] Small is less sure of the interpretation of the amendment insofar as the Framers originally intended it in their time, primarily addressed as it was to the question of an adequate militia—a viable national protective force against enemies within and without in that early period when conditions were vastly different than today. We concur that a contemporary interpretation might broadly support citizen possession with appropriate exceptions, together with firearms regulation of an acceptable kind. Both authors find an urgent need for the Supreme Court to definitively clarify this debate with reference to the Second Amendment.

One simplistic view that reappears with regularity (and is anything but helpful) is that there are but two classes of citizens: criminals and law-abiding citizens; for criminals the restriction of gun use must be absolute, but for law-abiding citizens, absolutely no restriction. Whatever mitigating circumstances, whatever social dangers exist, whatever unreasonable proliferation of guns, nothing must be allowed to qualify our Second Amendment right. It is an argument that ignores all social theory that suggests the ways in which even *law-abiding* citizen gun owners might abuse guns for whatever reasons.

Fact is, legislation is in place restricting ownership and possession of firearms by criminals, juveniles, and mental defectives. And, of course, it was not the Second Amendment that imposed these restrictions or withheld them. Even anti-control advocates agree with restricting such classes of *law-abiding citizens* as juveniles and mental defectives. People are not divisible into two classes only: criminal and law-abiding. The Second Amendment makes no mention of ineligible classes of individuals; it is equally void of any mention of future regulatory necessity. The Second Amendment was not intended to comprehend every change, every contingency in a developing nation.

Just as certainly can it be argued that the Second Amendment didn't envision, hence wasn't concerned to qualify, which classes of firearms yet to be invented might be disallowed. Nowhere does the amendment hint that hand-carried missiles or machine guns are restricted (weapons then nonexistent). But Congress has found no incongruity in restricting these

weapons from citizen use. Congress does have the power of regulation—
and the responsibility to make such determination; it is the Supreme
Court's responsibility to render a contemporary interpretation of the
amendment.

There is the reasonable argument that if people have the right to life
and liberty, they also have the right to possess the means of defending
both. In a sense, the Second Amendment, as applied to individuals,
secures the preservation of First Amendment rights insofar as it preserves the very life to which such other rights belong.

Of course, gun control (as any other means of crime control) is only as
good as its enforcement. And when the law criminalizes law-abiding
citizens who possess guns for defensive purposes (as in Washington, D.C.
and New York City), or when the criminal justice system fails to deal
severely with gun crime—this is enough to discourage any hopes for
effective gun control policy. Admittedly, the results have so far not been
promising.

On July 11, 1990, Senate bill 1970, derived from a Senate Judiciary
Committee summary, the Omnibus Crime Bill, was passed by the Senate
by a vote of 94 to 6. Title IV bans the domestic manufacture and assembly
of 14 specific *assault weapons* and increases to 10 years the minimum
penalty for use of such a weapon.[3] Furnish makes the point that semiautomatics for sport shooting simply permit far more convenient reloads.
Hence, the problem is not the weapon's capability but keeping them out
of the wrong hands where such quick firing allows the greater ability to
inflict harm.

ADVENT OF *NEW CLASS* INFORMATION BROKERS

At a rather subtle level, a growing number of sociologists now believe
that a disproportionate amount of power has been abrogated by the
information brokers of contemporary society—a social phenomenon just
now being more broadly recognized. Furnish finds much of the present
opposition to private firearms generated by this new controlling elite,
their opposition contrived with their own ideological purposes in view.
Small agrees but cautions that this doesn't mean we can dismiss the
genuine widespread public concern about unrestricted firearms ownership.
Neither author would disagree that there is need for the public at large
to be more informed about the disproportionate influence New Class

thought is gaining upon public policymaking and how it dominates the media.

Admittedly, Christians are not bound to uniformity in their thinking with reference to social issues, and while the position of the authors is clear-cut, it is not intended that their views be imposed upon readers. Inasmuch as biblical ethics has nothing specific to say about such modern social issues as gun control, at best only deductions can be made from Scriptural principles. Having said this, let's examine some of the more salient elements of the ongoing controversy.

SOCIETAL RATIONALE FOR GUN REGULATION

For a variety of reasons, our media-driven culture depicts the ownership of firearms as somehow immoral, especially if the primary purpose is self-defense. For a number of years we have been indoctrinated into believing that the gun is an evil talisman which merits no place in a civilized society. With this comes exaggerated rhetoric concerning the need to pass ever-increasing restrictive legislation, if not outright bans, as guarantor for crime-stopping. In this thinking one detects a simplistic and one-dimensional focus.

One cannot but observe that New Class thought embraces a well-orchestrated plan to gradually abrogate the existing legal rights of gun owners, the goal being the eventual disarming of the entire citizenry. This scenario essentially follows the same process that occurred in England and Denmark.[4] Not that we wish to convey the notion of a sinister ideological conspiracy! Rather, we agree with William Tonso that more likely a group of people in this society, bent on bringing about an ever-maturing *modernity,* simply feel the good and just society would be that in which all weapons have been eliminated.[5] A noble ideal but less than universally accepted, and in practical terms unenforceable.

The most significant and articulate group of people involved in the ongoing effort to ban all guns is the *New Class,* an elitist clique occupying positions as society's *information brokers.* This elite consists of college professors, media persons, social welfare establishment professionals— anyone, actually, who influences the flow of ideas and information. Syndicated columnists and media pundits are, with a few notable exceptions, also high on the list. These persons are identified by Max Singer as *University-Oriented Americans.* He claims that the major launching pad for their careers, the focus for their ideas, is not society's pragmatic and empirical concerns but has to do with intellectual prestige and influence within academe. They are people who talk to each other and, through various media, to the public. Consequently, it is to this elite corps that the average citizen has been brought to look for *the articulation of ideas, for thinking about the world, for study and analysis, and for teaching....* [6] They are society's self-designated mentors.

Protestant and Catholic clergy of both liberal and evangelical persuasion, as well as many Christian lay leaders, constitute another important segment of the New Class. Curiously, as James Hunter observes, Evangelicals sometimes seem to have greater allegiance to the New Class cultural agenda than to biblical teaching.[7]

It needs to be said, however, that lay people in our churches are often in sharp disagreement with New Class denominational officials who often create the church's pronouncements.[8]

For the most part, the New Class greatly admires the First Amendment while holding the Second Amendment in disdain—and for their own good reasons. It is part of New Class conventional wisdom that by restricting and eventually eliminating the availability of guns to all citizens, criminal use of firearms would also be totally reduced if not eliminated altogether.

Interestingly, pacifists who do not base their concepts of non-violence upon religious thinking are among the New Class ideologues whose optimism rests in the moral perfectibility of man, a view biblical Christians find completely unwarranted.

This outlook, as Barry Bruce-Briggs observes, reflects a fundamental schism among American social classes, particularly a schism between the relatively inarticulate working class and the highly educated and articulate New Class. This latter group strongly believes (on the basis of ideology, not data-based studies) that uncontrolled firearms ownership—especially *blue-collar* ownership—is both dangerous and uncivilized. (*These working classes don't know, really.*) Accordingly, the New Class' ultimate goal is a total gun ban.[9]

Until the last few years, the speculative judgments of the pro-control elite were difficult to refute on empirical grounds. However, within the last dozen years, a voluminous body of literature has emerged, largely out of the fields of sociology, criminology and law. This now flourishes, partially in reaction to the intransigent conventional wisdom of society's spokespersons. More recent judgments—sociologically and criminologically well-founded—seriously challenge New Class notions regarding the whole issue of firearms ownership, usage, social policy, and the morality of citizen self-defense. Recent conceptualization reflects the rise of a powerful data base to inform and challenge the more speculative, impressionistic, and largely unquestioned views. Then, too, the continuing catastrophic crime surge has exacerbated this partial turnaround. Once again, citizen concern is on the ascendancy, bringing more pragmatic concerns to replace the purely ideological.

ARE GUN LAWS EFFECTIVE IN CRIME REDUCTION?

Sociologists James Wright and Peter Rossi, joined by a team of researchers, have compiled a large number of data-based studies, demonstrating that there is little or no evidence to indicate that existing gun laws—which are legion—have decreased crime to any measurable extent.[10]

Alarmingly, what gun laws have accomplished is to create an entire class of new criminals—normally honest, law-abiding citizens who elect to keep a gun in full knowledge that they are in violation of certain local and state laws.[11] Many of these persons belong to minority groups living in crime-infested inner-city neighborhoods, individuals only too aware that the police are not prepared to protect them from predatory criminal sociopaths freely marauding about. Moreover, these population segments have less concern for the intricacies of the law to begin with. Furthermore, for them gun ownership (often of cheaper models) is quite simply a desperate self-defense measure undertaken with little regard that discovery might lead to prison. Ironically, New Class opponents are generally of the class of citizens able to live in the safer environments and to afford security systems.

This phenomenon of the creation of a new category of criminals—a *victimless crime* category—has been well documented by Don Kates, Raymond Kessler, and others.[12] Not only is this a criminalization of otherwise law-abiding citizens, but it tends toward a substantial *erosion of respect for the rule of law and for those who make and enforce such law.*[13]

In places like New York City, for example, gun proliferation has become so widespread that it is estimated that presently as many as two million illegal firearms are held by private citizens in direct contravention of that city's very tough gun laws.[14] This was the case with Bernhard Goetz who was fortunate to receive a sentence of one year for the illegal possession of a handgun; he could have gone to jail for as long as seven years for violating New York's possession laws.[15]

Surprisingly, very few felons ever go to jail for violating possession laws. In almost all cases such charges are plea bargained away in pre-trial hearings (e.g., in a recent study of plea bargaining in the City of Los Angeles, none of the criminals convicted of assault with a deadly weapon was ever prosecuted for the illegal possession and use of a concealed weapon).[16]

Likewise, several recent studies indicate that in states where *enhancement* sentencing laws are in effect (mandatory sentence for using a gun in a crime), judges are known to find ways of subverting such laws in order to facilitate the setting of lesser sentences. It will be interesting to follow the new stiffer gun legislation in California to see if it has any effect on the sentencing of criminals who misuse guns.[17]

There are some unorthodox views circulating. For example, Black civil rights leader, Roy Innis, questions the conventional wisdom that New York City's gun laws retard crime, observing that such laws do not in fact disarm the criminal but only help to make the victim defenseless. He facetiously commented, *A well-thinking criminal will have to be a strong advocate of gun control.* Then, in a serious proposal, Mr. Innis suggested training and arming responsible black citizens as a practical way to make the inner-city environment safer.

Predictably, this novel but highly iconoclastic proposal was ill-received by New York's liberal political establishment. Nevertheless, Mr. Innis's observations regarding the ineffectiveness of New York City's gun laws are worthy of consideration.[18]

As a matter of fact, Innis is not alone in this thinking. Recently, the ranking member of the highest court of West Virginia, Chief Justice of the Supreme Court Richard Neely, published a book on, of all things, a concept of vigilantism: *Take Back Your Neighborhood: A Case for Modern-Day Vigilantism.*

Neely has been a judge for nearly twenty years and recognizes that police can no longer do the job on their own. He seems to think that fighting crime is someone else's problem anyway. In a long and sympathetic review in *The Wall Street Journal,* he is quoted as saying

> If the rich can hire private security from doormen to office guards, "ordinary" working Americans who live in declining urban neighborhoods or middle-class suburbs ought to be able to perform that function for themselves.[19]

A second allegation of New Class belief is that *the polls show that the American public is "fed up" with the "gun lobby" and demands* [increased] *gun control.* This has become a favorite theme of some well-known media pundits. Close examination of the survey data indicates, on the contrary, that what the public truly supports is regulation of firearms in the same way that automobiles are regulated. There is very little public support for the outright banning of weapons. Kates summarizes:

> The polls consistently show public support for regulation that is more stringent than in the least gun-restrictive states and less stringent than in the most restrictive (i.e., a permit system that would seek to disarm felons, juveniles, and the mentally unstable as far as possible without denying ordinary responsible citizens the right to choose to own a gun for family defense).[20]

Although an initiative in Maryland restricting the purchase of cheap handguns was recently approved by voters, two other state constitutional initiatives better illustrate the point that the public does not favor an outright ban.[21]

In 1975, the Massachusetts State Legislature passed a drastic gun permit law which mandated one-year prison sentences for anyone caught in the Commonwealth with an unlicensed firearm. Emboldened by success, a collection of anti-firearm ownership groups placed a State Constitutional initiative on the 1976 General Election ballot to totally ban handguns. The measure was overwhelmingly rejected by the same Massachusetts electorate.[22]

In 1982, an attempt was made to pass a statewide initiative in California. Proposition 15 would have required the registration of all handguns within the state and, additionally, would have frozen the stock of handguns at the number in the state on the date of the 1982 General Election. One likely effect would have been to significantly drive up the price of the existing stock of handguns. Proposition 15 was strongly supported by all the major media outlets in the state and to a significant extent by national TV networks. Interestingly, the proposition went down to defeat, losing by 4.7 million to 2.8 million. All of this confirms a variety of national poll results. Evidently, although most citizens favor moderate control of firearms, they are unwilling to disarm themselves or accept what they regard as unnecessary regulation. The proposed freeze on additional guns further rendered the proposition self-defeating.[23]

The truth is that there are approximately 20,000 various federal, state and local laws and regulations now in existence. More importantly, it appears that many of these laws are seldom enforced, particularly with regard to felons charged with other serious offenses. When firearms laws are enforced, the enforcement is frequently carried out in a highly selective manner.[24]

FIREARMS LEGISLATION

Having been generally defeated at the ballot box in terms of pressing for strong interdictionist laws, firearms opponents are now attempting to eliminate selected weapons in piecemeal fashion. We shall update this action in the next chapter.

One highly publicized incident became especially salient: the tragic shooting of school children in Stockton, California by a mentally disturbed drifter, Patrick Purdy. The *Purdy* case was the most famous firearms case of 1989 and deserves a brief mention inasmuch as the media continue to center primarily on semiautomatic weapons, not upon the assailant or upon the background of the crime. The case is also an excellent example of what New Class *information brokers* choose to keep before the public by accenting only the features that focus upon the *gun question.*

What the case truly exemplifies is the breakdown of the criminal justice system, which we dare to suggest must shoulder much of the responsibility for this crime and many others similar to it. Incidentally, it was a similar breakdown of the courts that made it possible for John Hinkley to purchase the gun with which he shot then-President Ronald Reagan.

It is pertinent to note that Purdy had a rather lengthy and aberrant criminal career. He was arrested no fewer than eight times, four of these for felonies. Each time, with the collusion of the criminal justice system, he *plea bargained* the felony charges into misdemeanors. This, for him, nullified the California handgun law which stringently prevents retail sale of a handgun to mentally unstable persons. Because his felonies were not prosecuted as felonies, Purdy could legally buy handguns, and in fact bought several.

The last time Purdy was arrested, prior to his assault on the school children, he attempted to commit suicide. Hospitalized in a psychiatric institution, he was eventually diagnosed as being mentally impaired. Indeed, his problem was adjudged to be severe enough that he qualified for federal government assistance money for the disabled. Although he was acknowledged by the mental health profession to be aberrant, no central record of this was made that the California Bureau of Investigation had access to. Whereas the Federal Gun Control Act of 1968 specifically prohibits *mentally ill* people from buying weapons, in the interests of *not stigmatizing* the mentally ill, who is so adjudged is not allowed! Thus a mockery is made of the law.[25] And it appears that it's the law-abiding gun owner who must suffer in the interests of providing an environment less threatening to mentally marginal people, the social misfits of our society.

FOCUS UPON A SINGLE WEAPON

In 1987 the Austrian-made *Glock 17* auto-loading pistol began to receive considerable media attention—but not for its highly advanced design or usefulness to law enforcement officers!

We note, first of all, that although this weapon utilizes a lot of plastic in its construction, its operable parts contain 19 ounces of gun steel. Some pro-control members of Congress alerted the media to the existence of an *all plastic gun,* which they alleged could *easily* pass through airport metal detectors. The media responded with hysterical hyperbole about the new *terrorist weapon,* despite the fact that both the FAA and BATF agreed that this particular handgun (as is true of all other currently manufactured weapons) is readily detectable by current airport security devices.[26]

MORE RECENT FOCUS: SEMI–AUTOMATICS

A similar debate is now raging regarding the admissibility of *assault rifles.* A true assault rifle is actually a military machine gun, a type of weapon normally prohibited to civilians.[27] There are, however, semi-automatic versions of these weapons available for civilian ownership. These have become fairly popular as sporting rifles. It is worth noting that a number of media figures have recently claimed that the conversion of these weapons to fully automatic machine guns is a cheap and simple procedure. In fact, it isn't, since the semi-automatic versions are designed, on orders from the BATF, to be configured in such a manner that only with difficulty could even a skilled machinist make such a conversion. Granted, such conversions do occur, but they are extremely rare. Additionally, conversions of this sort are usually dangerous to the shooter, all too frequently causing the gun to misfire in an uncontrollable manner. Furthermore, all rifles (long guns) are unwieldy in close-range shooting, far less desirable and effective than, say, a semi-automatic pistol or pump-action shotgun—weapons of choice among all classes of armed criminals.

As one follows this debate, it becomes apparent that the manifest reason for legislating increased control over this class of weapons is that they are intimidating. But then, what gun isn't? Thus much of the legislation proposed to eliminate the problem which these weapons are supposedly creating turns out to be, potentially, the eventual elimination of all auto-loading, semi-automatic firearms. In consequence of such a ban, perhaps one-half of existing firearms would be eliminated under the guise of their being *assault weapons.* Further, the real nature of the problem involving *assault rifles* is usually overlooked by most media commentators. Rival gang feuding is on the increase in every major city, and these gangs kill; you eliminate a rival by killing him. It is the phenomenal rise in street killings by rival drug gangs, almost invariably comprised of urban underclass black teenagers, that is the true threat. Occasionally, gang members are found to have semi-automatic weapons but not to the extent that the media would have us believe. Actually, gangs far more frequently use handguns or pump-action shotguns which are considerably more deadly than assault rifles. A ban on assault weapons would most likely encourage gang members to simply acquire the more deadly alternatives. Today, the weapon of choice for many is the readily available TEC-9 semi-automatic pistol. It does seem highly unlikely that any such bans would have any effect on such criminals. It is as easy to get weapons on the street as it is to get drugs on high school campuses! The current epidemic of shootings by school children only dramatizes this.

Surprisingly, data recently released from the California Attorney General's office show that *assault rifles* have seldom been used in criminal shooting incidents in this state.

In May, 1992, the Ninth U.S. Circuit of Appeals upheld California's first-in-the-nation ban on sales of semi-automatic rifles, stating that the court is bound by an 1876 Supreme Court ruling that any right to bear arms recognized by the Second Amendment was enforceable only against Congress, not the states.

Curiously, of the fatal shootings investigated by the Los Angeles Police Department in 1990 and 1991, less than two percent involved the so-called assault weapons. And incidentally, as of early 1992, of the estimated 300,000 to 600,000 assault rifles in California, no more than 70,000 have been registered as mandated by law.[28]

Given the fact that this number represents a very small fraction of all shooting incidents—less than one percent of the semi-automatic weapons legally owned in the state—recent legislation which bans new *assault rifles* may prove to have quite limited value in preventing crime. Not only are very few crimes committed with such weapons, but those few lawbreakers that do use them for crime purposes have evidenced little regard for law in general—let alone gun laws.

Since the criminal justice system has apparently had little effect to date upon the problem of street gangs and urban drug dealing, it is not surprising to find average law-abiding, but virtually powerless citizens responding in such a manner. Moreover, it goes against the grain of most men to have it known that they're motivated by fear to buy weapons.

LATENT REASONS FOR GUN CONTROL

As seen from these few examples, current efforts to bring about increased firearms control through additional legislation are often driven by a covert rationale. Indeed, the entire New Class focus on gun control may be an effort to mask the many other inadequacies in our society's dealing with crime and violence, and New Class' inability to successfully address issues such as the need for more prisons, a greatly improved criminal justice system, the problem of recidivism, plea bargaining and the like.

Former U.N. Ambassador Jeanne Kirkpatrick[29] has criticized the New Class for their role as cultural specialists in bringing about a shift in responsibility for social life—away from the individual, the family, and private groups, to the government. This shift occurred at the same time the New Class claimed that because of their collective expertise they were the ones who had the ability to develop an agenda to bring about social justice and with it an end to social ills. What is not readily understood is that while the New Class is now largely setting the social agenda, it also maintains the power to obscure their policy failures from previous attempts at social engineering.

The relationship between New Class social policy failure and weapons interdictionist policy is becoming more transparent, especially in terms of New Class policies toward the underclass. Is it not ironic that although the New Class can be characterized as having a quasi-socialistic, progressive orientation, it can at the same time be highly class conscious and surprisingly racist as well?

Blacks, for example, have often been treated by New Class policies in a condescending, patronizing manner. Still, the New Class would never be caught acknowledging that their policies have contributed to the disintegration of the black family and the alienation of vast numbers of the poor from the dominant culture. These failed policies have, in consequence, accelerated the enormous increase in violent crime.[30]

Similarly, New Class efforts to *de-institutionalize* the mentally ill have succeeded in creating a subculture of demented vagabonds who swell the ranks of the homeless and in significant measure have led to increased fear among average citizens. The massive failures of the social agenda for the underclass over the past several decades gave momentum to the frenetic New Class concern over gun control. A lot of smoke and mirrors!

Tolerance toward recreational drug use during the 1970s by significant elements of the New Class did much toward accelerating our contemporary pandemic of drug abuse. Moreover, it is passing strange that so little effort has been made to show the connection between urban drug wars and the widely recognized abuse of cocaine by New Class people in the entertainment industry.

With their vested interest in the welfare and criminal justice systems, the New Class elite, rather than concerning themselves with the structural reasons for minority crime, propose instead a *quick fix* in the form of more stringent gun control, as though legislation were the ultimate and guaranteed solution. To the contrary, the alienated poor and disadvantaged minorities would generally be the segment of the population least restrained by interdictionist law. Quite necessarily, for the disadvantaged self-protection is high on their priority list.

Under these conditions, interdictionist law becomes a form of what sociologist Joseph Gusfield called *symbolic law,* used politically in response to societal demand but without actually affecting the problem it is intended to curb.[31] The passage of symbolic interdictionist law merely provides an illusory resolution of the dilemmas plaguing a restless and increasingly violent underclass.

A final reason why the New Class favors an enlarged scope of firearms legislation has to do with the fact that such laws favor the development of large bureaucracies—one of the things Jeanne Kirkpatrick observes the New Class doing so well.[32] For example, we only need look at the number and type of New Class experts currently involved in the criminal justice system. Expanded gun control also expands the need for more *experts* since it creates an entire new category of *criminals* (formerly legitimate gun owners).

In this regard, we note that the City of Chicago now has one entire criminal court section devoted exclusively to firearms violations. In a similar fashion, California's Proposition 15 would have required an initial work force in excess of 800 employees.[33] Most likely this gun bureaucracy would have grown far beyond that number, serving to broaden the New Class power base by providing for an ever-increasing work force to implement and administer the burgeoning system of controls.

The authors take the position that as citizens of this democracy we should not willingly abrogate any of our individual rights unless there are strong compelling reasons for doing so. Among basic individual rights, we are persuaded that the private ownership of firearms is included. Of course, the welfare of the community sometimes requires that certain restrictions be placed upon basic liberties in order to sustain the citizenry's larger liberty to live in safety and security. There is no such thing in this world as unlimited liberty.

The point of the present discussion is that we should be alert to and wary of any elitist schemes to disarm the law-abiding citizenry, while at the same time recognizing that as reasonable people living in community we are facing pervasive problems in the existing pattern of gun legislation. No all-embracing solutions have as yet been forthcoming.

THE NATIONAL RIFLE ASSOCIATION AND GUN CONTROL

Discussion of firearms control cannot be complete without considering the role of one of the significant players, the National Rifle Association. Unfortunately, we are unable to give more than a brief account of this impressive organization.

Depending upon one's view of gun control, people either admire or loathe the NRA, and presently the nation seems polarized in its attitude toward this powerful organization. For those who would seriously understand the NRA, the most comprehensive analysis to date is the recent book by Professor Edward Leddy, *Magnum Force Lobby,* a thorough review of the history and policy positions of this powerful voluntary gun advocacy organization.[34]

The NRA traces its origin back to 1871, when it was established by Union Army veterans to train civilian marksmen as a way of improving the skills of militia members. By 1910 the NRA had begun to move in the direction of defending the rights of citizens to own firearms. Today, the NRA is probably best known for its remarkably firm positions on firearms legislation. With nearly three million dues-paying members nationwide, the NRA is the largest voluntary organization in the country. It also ranks as one of the most powerful lobbying groups in the nation. Just as interestingly, many important political figures are life members of the NRA, including recent presidents (currently, George Bush). Perhaps one of the most interesting facets of the NRA is the strong resolve to position itself as a single-issue lobby by consistently resisting pressures to involve itself in issues outside the scope of its perceived mandate.

Many information brokers, especially in the popular media, criticize the NRA as being intransigent about firearms restriction in any form, a criticism also heard among other citizen groups outside the New Class. The claim is that the NRA simply never seems willing to make reasonable compromises over the gun control issue. The response of the NRA is that they have tried on numerous occasions only to have the opposition attempt to take advantage by deceit and subterfuge. Notably, the NRA has recently begun to find it increasingly difficult to get their message across, even reluctantly conceding the possible good of some kind of police assent for purchase permits.

Unfortunately, the NRA has been made the convenient scapegoat for all who are opposed to guns for whatever reason. Extremists paint the NRA as the reckless promoters of gun possession whatever the cost. What is also lost among the opposition is any knowledge and appreciation of the NRA's educational efforts targeting the true problems of crime control, and the NRA's strong promotion of citizen education and practice of gun safety.

HANDGUN CONTROL, INC.

Although a variety of organizations oppose the NRA, the best known and best funded is *Handgun Control, Inc.*[35] This organization was founded by Pete Shields, a former Dupont Company executive whose son was the last person murdered in the so-called San Francisco *Zebra* killings. These murders were committed by a radical splinter group of Black Muslims who believed they received heavenly blessings by slaying white people. Although some of the Zebra victims were hacked to death by machetes, Mr. Shields chooses to blame guns for his son's tragic murder, not the disturbed fanatical terrorists who chose a variety of weapons, any one of which could be successfully employed.[36]

In recent years, Mr. Shields has been joined by Sarah Brady, the wife of President Reagan's press secretary James Brady, who was disabled in the Hinkley presidential assassination attempt.

HCI claims to have over one million members. Although they purport to be mainly interested in restricting handgun availability, they have tended to support strong interdictionist law toward all classes of firearms. Most recently, they've thrown their support behind the banning of semiautomatic rifles.

The rhetoric between HCI and the NRA is at times quite shrill. Indeed, one of the authors received a HCI mailing in mid-1991 which began with the words, *Now you can tell the NRA to go to hell.* [37] While such diatribes may be useful for fundraising and membership drives, they are not at all conducive to finding the resolution to an increasingly vexing American conundrum, i.e., how to allow responsible law-abiding citizens to retain firearms while at the same time precluding weapons possession from those who are incompetent by reason of age, a history of mental illness, known violent manifestations, or who have a criminal record. From reasoned analysis, we believe that strict interdictionist law accomplishes very little. Accordingly, the time has come for both sides to re-think their positions with mutual respect and seek to find some common ground. There are signs that this is taking place.

SOME STEPS TO ALLEVIATE THE IMPASSE

(1) Greater visibility of the Church in the moral issues having to do with crime control, not a narrow focus on gun control.

One of the outstanding ministries today is that of a para-church organization, Prison Fellowship, headed by Charles Colson. It seems that the Church, in its historic role as both peacemaker and champion of justice, could be a significant force in leading the way. Colson is an outstanding example of Christian thought and action. However, as divergent as the Church is in today's culture, with the issues strongly represented with adherents ranging from extremely liberal to extremely conservative, this task, unfortunately, is beset with all but insuperable difficulties. It seems evident that pacifist and non-pacifist ranks within the church would find common ground on policy difficult to come by. Our position is that the church ought not be held back by the minority who hold a pacifist position. At a minimum, one might hope for enlightened discussion around such guides as the present volume, granting latitude for individual belief.

(2) Clarification of the citizen's right to own private firearms.

One of the major sources of apprehension for many firearms owners is the real fear that the government will eventually confiscate all weapons. One can already detect on the horizon a well-coordinated scheme to eventually totally disarm the nation, the sole exception being police and military personnel. Many firearms apologists note that the same people who are leading the fight against semiautomatic rifles were until recently assuring the American public that they *only wanted to ban handguns* and were not interested in long guns at all. The picture is presently fluid.

Polls consistently show that a majority of citizens believe they have a constitutional right to own weapons.[38] Furthermore, a large segment of the population is suspicious of modern legal interpretations of their constitutional rights. Curiously, the Supreme Court has never ruled definitively on this issue, so no one is presently sure what ultimate rights are established for the individual by the Second Amendment.

Don Kates offers an excellent summary:

> At a minimum, gun owners would need the reassurance of a U.S. Supreme Court decision squarely recognizing that the Bill of Rights gives every law-abiding, responsible adult the freedom to choose to own guns for the protection of home and family. Also, gun owners would have to be convinced of the following. First, that the proposed gun laws are formulated in recognition of their legitimate interests and represent an honest attempt to accommodate those interests within the social necessity of rational control over deadly instruments. Second, the law's administration would not be so hostile or arbitrary as to deny law-abiding, responsible adults the freedom to choose to own guns for home and family defense.[39]

(3) Immediate and significant reform of the criminal justice system.

Recent studies have clearly demonstrated that one of the major reasons for the recent escalation in private armament is citizen's lack of confidence in the criminal justice system, and for good cause.

We need to listen more closely to Charles Colson, especially when he discusses alternative sentencing systems such as moving non-violent criminals from jails to appropriate alternate facilities in order to create much-needed prison space for the truly violent offenders.[40]

Likewise, there is the need to act more quickly to administer stern justice to those violent offenders who are the cause of such widespread fear and the resultant armament buildup among the citizenry. Expectation of a speedy trial along with swift and sure punishment has become a farce in our nation. One only has to notice that the alleged *night stalker,*

California serial killer Richard Ramirez, managed to delay his trial for four years! Similarly, several of the young men who accosted Bernard Goetz had been charged with multiple major felonies at the time, yet were out of jail *on their own recognizance* awaiting trial.

One disturbing reality from a political standpoint is the recognition that some of the same legislators who are champions of the most restrictive gun control measures oppose legislation which would enhance penalties for violent criminals who use firearms in the commission of crimes.

(4) Resolve the problem of care for the mentally ill so as to remove them from the streets.

Rarely even noted by New Class commentators, the truth of the matter is that all of the public massacres of the last few years have been perpetrated by people with significant mental problems. In the interest of granting full civil rights to the mentally ill, the citizenry has been exposed to substantial risk. We have also exposed the mentally ill to considerable risk. In large part, recent firearms' suicides are people identified as aberrant. Likewise, the buildup in armament is partly because citizens are becoming terrified of the wild-eyed insane who roam city streets as homeless people, and who, incidentally, cast suspicion upon the homeless who have no criminal proclivities. It is time that we acknowledge that *mainstreaming* and *de-institutionalization* of the mentally ill simply has not worked, and for quite understandable reasons will not work.

Is it not time we begin creating humane institutional environments where the helpless can once again experience adequate care and security. Might we not once again seriously consider a central state registration of people with significant mental disabilities—a registry accessible to those (and only those) charged with determining who is eligible to purchase a firearm? In the books, present federal gun control law makes it illegal for anyone with a record of mental illness to purchase a firearm, whereas the fact that no such registry exists makes the law virtually meaningless; there is no way at present to implement it. Thus we have a classic case of the conflict of rights—the right of society to preclude weapon's sale to the mentally unfit, the right to avoid stigmatization by being publicly labeled aberrant.

Complex issues are not conducive to simple solutions and we cannot afford to think this is ever the case. Eventually, incautious efforts or injudicious decisions can cause us to lose one precious liberty or another, and foreclose the stewardship responsibilities God has so graciously and generously permitted us to have.

NOTES

1. *See* Pete Shields, *Guns Don't Die—People Do,* New York: Arbor, 1981, pp. 48ff; Robert J. Riley, "Shooting to Kill the Handgun: Time to Martyr Another American 'Hero'," *Journal of Urban Law* 51 (1954) pp. 491–524.

2. Halbrook, Stephen P., *That Every Man Be Armed: The Evolution of a Constitutional Right.* Albuquerque: University of New Mexico, 1984.

3. *Congressional Digest,* Nov. 1990, Washington, DC, The Congressional Digest Corporation, p. 259.

4. *See* Greenwood, Colin, *Firearms Control: A Study of Armed Crime and Firearms Control in England and Wales.* London: Routledge & Kegan Paul, 1972; Colin Greenwood and Joseph Maggadino, "Comparative Cross-Cultural Studies," in Kates, Don B. Jr., *Restricting Handguns: The Liberal Critics Speak Out.* Croton-on-Hudson, North River, 1979, pp. 31–68.

5. Tonso, William R., *Guns and Society.* Washington, DC: University Press of America, 1982 (esp. chapters 1 & 2)

6. Bruce-Briggs, Barry, *The New Class.* New York: McGraw-Hill, 1979; Gouldner, Alvin W., *The Future of Intellectuals and the Rise of the New Class.* New York: Oxford University, 1979; Etzioni-Halevy, Eva, *The Knowledge Elite and the Failure of Prophecy.* London: Allen & Unwin, 1985; Isaac, Rael and Erich, *The Coercive Utopians.* Chicago: Regenery Gateway, 1983; Lebedoff, David, *The New Elite.* New York: Franklin Watts, 1981; Singer, Max, *Passage to a Human World,* Indianapolis: The Hudson Institute, 1987.

7. Hunter, James D., *American Evangelicalism.* New Brunswick: Rutgers University, 1983. *See* Young, Robert L., "The Protestant Heritage and the Spirit of Gun Ownership," *Journal of the Scientific Study of Religion.* 1989, 28 (No. 3) pp. 300–309.

8. An example is the independent monthly publication, *The Presbyterian Layman,* a critical review of denominational policies, serving as a lay voice for the church.

9. Bruce-Briggs, Barry, "The Great American Gun War," *The Public Interest,* 45 (Fall 1976) pp. 37–62.

10. Wright, James D., et al., *Under the Gun,* Hawthorne: Aldine de Gruyter, 1983; Wright, James D. and Peter H. Rossi, *Armed and Considered Dangerous,* Hawthorne: Aldine de Gruyter, 1986.

11. Joseph P. Magaddino and Marshall H. Medoff, "An Empirical Analysis of Federal and State Firearm Control Laws," in Kates, Don B. Jr., *Firearms and Violence.* San Francisco: Pacific Institute for Public Policy, 1984, pp. 225–258; Paul Bendis and Steven Balkin, "A Look at Gun Control Enforcement," *Journal of Police Science Administration.* 7 no. 2 (Mar.–Apr. 1979) pp. 439–448.

12. Zimring, Franklin E. and Hawkins, Gordon, *The Citizen's Guide to Gun Control,*

New York: Macmillan, 1987, pp. 101–107; Raymond G. Kessler, "Enforcement Problems of Gun Control: A Victimless Crime Analysis," *Criminal Law Bulletin* 16 (Mar.–Apr. 1980), pp. 131ff.

13. *See* Kessler, op. cit.; David T. Hardy and Kenneth L. Chotner, "The Potentiality for Civil Liberties Violations in the Enforcement of Handgun Prohibition," Kates, *Restricting Handguns,* op. cit., p. 156.

14. Don B. Kates, Jr., "Handgun Banning in Light of the Prohibition Experience," in Kates, Don B., Jr., *Firearms and Violence.* op. cit., p. 156.

15. Arthur Eckstein, "The Revenge of the Nerd," *Chronicles.* March, 1988, pp. 26–30; Edward F. Leddy, "The Ownership and Carrying of Personal Firearms and Reduction of Crime Victimization," in Tonso, William F. (ed.), *The Gun Culture and Its Enemies.* Belleview: Merrill, 1989, pp. 25–41.

16. Paul Dean, "Armed and Ordinary," *Los Angeles Times,* May 10, 1988, n.p.

17. Stuart J. Deutsch, "The Effect of Massachusetts' Gun Control Law on Gun Related Crimes in the City of Boston," *Evaluation Quarterly.* 1 NO. 4 (1977) pp. 543–68; Colin Loftin, et al., "Mandatory Sentencing and Firearms Violence: Evaluating Alternatives to Gun Control," *Law and Society Review.* 17 No. 2 (1983) p. 318; James A. Beha, "And Nobody Can Get You Out: The Impact of a Mandatory Prison Sentence for the Illegal Carrying of a Firearm," *Boston University Law Review* 57 (1977).

18. Quoted in Frank Borzellieri, "Arming Citizens to Fight Crime," *USA Today* July 1985, pp. 56–57.

19. L. Gordon Crovitz, "A Chief Justice Makes the Case for Vigilantism," *The Wall Street Journal,* December 12, 1990, p. A17.

20. Kates, Don B. Jr., *Guns, Murders, and the Constitution: A Realistic Assessment of Gun Control* (A Public Policy Briefing), San Francisco: Pacific Research Institute for Public Policy, Feb. 1990 (*see* footnote on page 6).

21. Lance K. Stell, "Guns, Politics and Reason," *Journal of American Culture.* 9 (1986) 71–85; James T. Wright, "Second Thoughts About Gun Control," *The Public Interest.* Spring 1988, pp. 23–39.

22. Brendan F. J. Furnish, "The New Class and the California Handgun Initiative: Elitist-Developed Law as Gun Control," in Tonso, William R. (ed.) op. cit., pp. 127–141; David J. Bordua, "Adversary Polling and the Construction of Social Meaning: Implications in Gun Control Elections in Massachusetts and California," *Law and Policy Quarterly* 5 (July 1983) pp. 345–366.

23. Fred Epstein, "California Sticks to its Guns: How the NRA Got Voters to Say No to Handgun Control," *Rolling Stone Magazine* 19 (Feb. 17, 1983); James D. Wright, "Public Opinion & Gun Control: A Comparison of the Results From Two Recent Studies," *The Annals of the American Academy of Political and Social Science.* (Mar. 1981).

24. *State Laws and Published Ordinances – Firearms,* Bureau of Alcohol, Tobacco and Firearms, Department of the Treasury, Washington, DC: USGPO (ATF P 5300.5), 1988, pp. 87–88.

25. *See* statement of David B. Kopel of Guardian Group International before the United States Senate Subcommittee on the Constitution of the Committee on

the Judiciary, Feb. 10, 1989, pp. 3ff. (Available from Guardian Group International, 21 Warren St., Suite 3E, New York, N.Y. 10007.)

26. *American Rifleman*, Sept. 1987, pp. 42–43; George Hackett, "The Battle Over the Plastic Gun," in *Gun Control*, Robert Emmet Long (ed), New York: H. W. Wilson, 60 No. 6, (1989) pp. 164ff

27. Wayne R. Austerman, "Those Deadly, Depressing, Syncopated Semi-Automatic Assault Rifle Blues," *Chronicles* 21, (Nov. 1989) pp. 21ff; Kates, Don B. Jr., "Guns, Murder and the Constitution," *Policy Briefing*, San Francisco: Pacific Research Institute for Public Policy, Feb. 1990, pp. 44ff.

28. John K. Van de Kamp and G.W. Clemons, "Assault Rifle Survey," Unpublished Report of the California Attorney General (# CJ-88-09-DLE), Sacramento, 1988.

29. Jeanne J. Kirkpatrick, "Politics and the New Class," in Barry Bruce-Briggs, op. cit., pp. 42–48.

30. Currie, Elliot, *Confronting Crime*. New York: Pantheon Books, 1985, esp. pp. 151ff; Lewis, Dan A., and Greta Salem, *Fear of Crime*. New Brunswick: Transaction Books, 1986; Hawkins, Darnell F., *Homicide Among Black Americans*. Lanham: University Press of America, 1986.

31. Gusfield, Joseph R., *Symbolic Crusade: Status, Politics and the American Temperance Movement*. Urbana: University of Illinois, 1969; Chambliss, William and Seidman, Robert, *Law, Order and Power*. Menlo Park: Addison-Wesley, 1976, pp. 14–16.

32. Kirkpatrick, op. cit.

33. Franchetti, Michael V., *Analysis of Handgun Initiatives*. Sacramento: State of California, Jan. 29, 1982.

34. Leddy, Edward F., *Magnum Force Lobby*. op. cit.; "Under Fire," *Time Magazine* (special report), Jan. 29, 1990, pp. 16–22.

35. Shields, op. cit.; "Handgun Facts: Twelve Questions and Answers about Handgun Control," pamphlet of Handgun Control, Inc., in Long, op. cit., pp. 76–79.

36. Howard, Clark, *Zebra: The True Account of the 179 Days of Terror in San Francisco*. New York: Richard Marek, 1979.

37. Handgun Control, Inc., general mailing, May 1991.

38. Bruce L. Benson, "Guns for Protection and Other Private Sector Responses to the Fear of Rising Crime," in Kates, *Firearms and Violence,* op. cit., pp. 329–360.

39. Kates, *Guns, Murder and the Constitution*, op. cit., p. 59.

40. Colson, Charles W., *Life Sentence*. Waco: Word Books, 1979.

Chapter 19

PROMISE FOR THE FUTURE

In May, 1991, the House passed the so-called *Brady bill*, named after James S. Brady, Press Secretary under President Ronald Reagan, who was shot in the head in the 1981 attempt by John Hinkley, Jr. on the president's life. Passage came after years of campaigning for a national waiting period provision for the purchase of handguns and after vigorous opposition led by the NRA and a group of congressmen.

In June, 1991, the Senate by a two-to-one vote passed an amended version which, unlike the House bill, requires a gun purchaser's check within five days instead of seven. The Senate bill would also lift the waiting period after 2½ years, following which time the government would be required to have set up a nationwide computer system for gun dealers to make *instant checks.* In view of the difficulties which different states would encounter, the bill aims at *sunsetting* the waiting period, one state at a time, as each is able to set up its own system of instant checks. No deadlines are set for that accomplishment.

This latter measure does set a deadline of 30 months for the Justice Department to complete a nationwide computerized system, a time period which Justice Department studies say is not long enough. The provision would cut the Justice Department's budget if the system is not implemented within thirty months. In addition, the bill authorizes $100 million to help states improve their criminal records and make them accessible, a figure many say is far too little.

In a recent volume of considerable significance,[1] Gary Kleck analyzes the central element of the proposed regulatory strategy, the federal *instant records check* at the point of retail gun sale, the outlines of which were set forth in considerable detail in a U.S. Department of Justice report in 1989.[2]

Option A of that report outlines the following system. A prospective gun buyer go to a licensed gun dealer, fill out an application, and show two pieces of identification, one having a current photo. The gun dealer would then make a toll-free call to a designated state or federal law enforcement agency for a criminal records check of the applicant. The agency would scan existing state and federal computerized master name indexes covering persons arrested for felonies and serious misdemeanors. As of 1990, 20 states participated in the FBI-operated interstate Identification Index.

Rejected applicants could go through a more extensive secondary verification procedure without charge. This might take several weeks. They would be required to present themselves in person to a law enforcement agency, presenting identification. He or she could submit to fingerprinting. Further inquiries might be made if information for final disposition was judged inadequate.

The Justice Department estimates that upwards of 88 percent of applicants could be issued Certificates of Purchase within minutes. It is also estimated that an additional 6–8 percent would pass a secondary verification process.

For auditing purposes, the telephone inquiry, together with an inquiry identification number, would be logged by the law enforcement agency to compare with gun dealer records, thus ensuring that dealers were not selling guns without such records checks and were not using inquiries for unauthorized purposes.

Names of applicants would not be retained on the system files. This precludes it from being gun owner licensing and registration systems. This is of critical importance to those who envision a list of gun owners that could conceivably be used for future confiscation purposes.

A critical element of the proposed system concerns requiring private transfers be routed through licensed gun dealers. This question was not addressed by the Justice Department's proposal. It is estimated that in the late 1980s there were over 3 million private gun transfers annually.

There is in existence the FBI-operated National Criminal Information Center resource, also the Interstate Identification Index III, a computerized index of persons with criminal records in twenty states. But records are far from complete. Many repositories have yet to automate all or some of their records. It is estimated that half of all felony convictions in the nation are available in automated form.

The toughened Senate version, in contrast to the House bill, mandates checks of criminal or mental records rather than leaving such checks to the discretion of police. Final action on the overall crime legislation has been delayed as of the end of 1991.

Attorney David Kopel, analyst for the Cato Institute and long-time student of gun control policy, has recently compiled a forward-looking analysis. By permission, this chapter excerpts and comments on his study.[3]

Kopel begins:

> Waiting periods: Many states already have them; most national police organizations, most people, and most gun owners are for them. In the 1970s, even the National Rifle Association supported the idea of a carefully crafted state waiting period.[4]

Two decades later, however, the NRA, by now rejecting a national waiting period policy, gave its support to Senator Harley Swaggers's alternate to the Brady bill, modelled after Virginia's present state requirement. This calls for a gun shop's mandatory instant telephone check.

The U.S. Justice Department supports the instant check, although cautioning of cost, time required to implement it, and the status of record keeping in many states. The Attorney General also voiced his support.[5] Many chiefs of police also support an instant check over, say, a national firearms identification card.[6]

Our consulting authority Don Kates supports the instant check as do the authors. Kates recently proposed one form of the firearms owner's identification card, writing:

> More promising would be to check for a criminal record by using the driver's license. Every license issued could bear the notation "eligible to own firearms" (except, of course, for juveniles, felons, and those with insanity records). Selling a gun to a person without a driver's license bearing this notation would be a felony and would make the seller financially liable for any wrong done by the buyer.[7]

Handgun Control, Inc. accepted the instant check in Virginia, opposed it in Ohio. In that organization today there are those who recognize the advantage of the instant check over the proposed waiting period, seeing it as the ultimate goal, yet wanting a waiting period policy for the interim.

In 1989, Virginia enacted its instant telephone check. Recently, Florida and Delaware followed suit. The first year the check was in effect in Virginia, there were 540 denials, leading to the arrest of 7 fugitives, including one wanted for murder, and at least one false arrest. About 16–20 percent of the phone applications resulted in denials which then required a secondary verification. This called for submitting fingerprints to the police to prove non-criminal identity.

Addressing police organization support for a waiting period, Kopel shows the selectivity by which HCI claims *every major police organization in the country.* Two that do not are The American Federation of Police, the second largest rank and file police organization in the U.S., and The National Association of Chiefs of Police, the second largest command rank organization in the U.S. (annual opinion surveys of command rank police officers).[8]

Granted, many important police organizations do support a waiting period. The Police Executive Research Forum, a Washington think tank comprising about 500 present and former big-city police executives, polled its membership and found 92 percent in favor of a national 7-day waiting period for handguns.[9]

As for public opinion, while the public favors a waiting period (probably by fewer than the 91 percent according to Gallup), it opposes *a law giving police the power to decide who may or may not own firearms* by 68 percent to 29 percent margin.[10]

Criminology studies are cited in depth by Kopel. (Curiously, congressmen debating the Brady bill rarely cited criminologists or their studies, and HCI lists no major criminologist on its national committee.)

Professor Matthew DeZee states: *I firmly believe that more restrictive legislation is necessary to reduce the volume of gun crime.* Yet his comparative study of state laws, including waiting periods, found "the results indicate that not a single gun control law, and not all the gun control laws added together, had a significant impact . . . in determining gun violence. . . . Gun laws do not appear to affect gun crime."[11]

The U.S. Senate Judiciary Committee found no evidence that waiting periods affect crime, and no correlation between a waiting period and lower crime rates.[12] This is confirmed by the chief investigators.[13]

Under the Carter administration, the National Institute of Justice offered a grant to the former president of the American Sociological Association and two colleagues to survey the field of research on gun control. Peter Rossi and his co-authors Jim Wright and Kathleen Daly began their work convinced of the need for strict national gun control. Indeed, Wright had already written about the need for more control. After looking at the data, however, the three researchers found no convincing evidence that gun control curbs crime.[14]

Wright and Rossi disagree with HCI's interpretation of their data, writing:

> . . . one quickly senses that the measure would have little or no effect on the criminal users whom we are trying to interdict and a considerable effect on

legitimate gun users. . . . The ideal gun crime policy is one that impacts directly
on the illicit user but leaves the legitimate user pretty much alone.[15]

In California, with its fifteen-day waiting period, in 1991 there were
5,859 permission requests rejected. Some 609 were of persons convicted
of drug law violations, 328 convicted burglars, 102 convicted robbers,
101 convicted of sex offenses, 7 kidnappers, 34 convicted of murder,
and 2,967 convicted of assault. Even Kopel concedes that there is
thus a *measurable value* to waiting-period provisions, pointing out, however, that there continued to be a rise in crime rates during this
period, with no data to prove that interdiction does or does not suppress
crime.

Illinois's experience is also cited:

> Prospective gun purchasers must obtain a Firearms Owners Identification
> card (FOID), which is valid for five years. (Such cards generally haves the
> individual's fingerprint, electronically embossed data, allowing unlimited
> purchases over a stipulated period of time). In Illinois there are about 5,000
> applications for the card every week. Over the weekend, a list of applications is
> run through the State Department of Mental Health, typically revealing about
> 10 applicants who are ineligible to buy because of mental disability.[16]

Illinois's automated licensing system often takes 60 days to authorize a
clearance. FOID cards are issued to about 78 percent of the applicants,
another 17 percent after follow-up of an initial rejection, for an annual
total of about 200,000 FOID cards issued. Roughly 5 percent of applications are ultimately rejected, or about 2.5 percent. About 0.8 percent of
previously issued cards are subsequently revoked due to felony convictions.
Professor David Bordua found that the administrators were not convinced that the system was effective.[17]

Kopel points to problems with the New Jersey system, the state with
the strictest firearms laws. While HCI acclaims *10,000 convicted felons
caught trying to buy handguns,* about one-quarter of the rejections are
actually based on a police hunch that it would not be a good idea for the
individual in question to own a gun, rather than specifying any disquali-
fying criterion.[18] For no apparently valid reason, some applications are
denied for years.

Kopel cautions that virtually no one who intends to commit a crime
seeks to buy a gun from a gun store. Incidentally, of the people denied
permission in all systems, a mere 1 percent are found to be wanted
individuals and are arrested.[19]

In any permissions system, a few persons with this background will slip through. This, however, does not weigh against the probability of a substantial number of others being caught.

One major fault of the Brady bill is that it contains no appeals process if a person is denied purchase permission—another indication that the entire matter has not been adequately addressed.

The argument that police who do not implement the background check would be subject to litigation is, of course, a possible liability in view of HCI's threat to sue. But departments such as Los Angeles City have paid out millions in suits of various kinds, and it stands to reason that legal provisions could be made to offset this threat, and does not render the cost of a waiting period as prohibitive as is made out to be. The American public seems overwhelmingly in favor of doing what is necessary to suppress crime and believes any slowing the flow of guns are worthy measures.

The possibility that permission systems can operate as de facto gun registration is anathema to all libertarians. For many, the real reason for opposition to registration is a significant distrust of the federal government's intents and purposes. Don Kates remarks that it is strange that gun owners can so vehemently oppose controls that are substantially similar to those they accept on automobiles and prescription medicines.

In fact, police in New York, New Jersey, California and other states now add the names of applicants to a list of gun owners.[20] The fear is that any check may be a prelude to gun confiscation, and the argument is that the government has *no authority to register people merely for exercising their Constitutional rights.*[21] But it is not a question of people being denied their Second Amendment rights but of jurisdictional regulation of those rights. Nonetheless, the courts would have to clearly limit any such use of national gun or gun owner registration to satisfy legitimate fears.

Kopel has a strong point in his wariness of the confidentiality of private medical records that could be compromised. He cites the case of California where legislators enacting a waiting period were told that mental health records would be kept strictly confidential. That same year, the California Department of Justice ordered public and private mental health clinics to report their clients to the state, then those names were placed with those of felons in a data base accessible to police check. Further compromising this procedure, non-violent persons who were not psychotic but voluntarily checked into private facilities for such problems as anxiety or stress were included.

New Jersey and Illinois are jurisdictions that presently require purchasers to waive the confidentiality of their medical or mental health records.[22]

One fear is that employers or others might have access to those records surreptitiously by asking a prospective or current employee to produce proof of eligibility to purchase a gun. On this count, it would seem that such fears could be alleviated by legislative requirements that made such requests illegal. This problem fits similar legislation that makes it illegal for businesses accepting credit cards to require a phone number.

A major argument of opponents to gun control systems is that police bureaucracies have the capability of obstructing and delaying the purchase of guns for indefinite periods of time and for arbitrary considerations. To some individuals, even the knowledge of isolated instances is sufficient to sound an alarm. For there is ample evidence to demonstrate that a few police bureaucracies have in the past indeed been guilty of deliberately delaying sales by holding up purchase permits. This is similar to the discretionary policies of some police departments in issuing permits to carry weapons, notably their granting permits to politicians with questionable carrying credentials.

In the case of police delays, this has occurred in localities in which police had no time limit imposed upon the purchase permit process, and so could exercise wide discretion as to how quickly or slowly to proceed. Such a situation is, of course, untenable and should be disallowed by any federal legislation.

In this same regard, there is one provision in California's 15-day waiting period statute that is important. If the local police and State Bureau of Investigation fail to complete the records check within the fifteen days, they cannot prevent the sale. Such a system protects both the public and the firearms purchaser and is worthy of replication at the national level. Abuse of the application procedure, whether by unreasonable delays or refusal on other grounds than what the law states, is a matter to legislate out of possibility and poses no valid argument against permissions systems per se.

Kopel's strongest argument is the disadvantage a waiting period imposes upon the individual who has a genuine urgency to possess a defensive weapon. It is here that he most finds the waiting period to *threaten public safety.* There is no question but that a neighborhood being terrorized night after night makes it urgent for the single woman to purchase a defensive weapon now, not seven to fifteen days from now (or in the case of the FOID card even longer). A woman whose ex-boyfriend is threatening to come over and batter her can seek a court injunction, but this is no guarantee.

Take the case of Catherine Latta of Charlotte, North Carolina. In September, 1990, Miss Latta, a mail carrier, went to the police to obtain permission to buy a handgun. Her ex-boyfriend had assaulted her on several occasions, raped her and threatened her with death. She was informed that her gun permit would take two to four weeks. So that afternoon she risked going to a dangerous part of town where she purchased an illegal semiautomatic pistol on the street for $20. Five hours later, her ex-boyfriend attacked her outside her house. She shot him dead. The county prosecutor decided not to prosecute her for either the self-defense homicide or illegal possession of a gun.

A waiting period system creates the need for waiving that period for exceptional circumstances, and if so, how such instances would be determined. The Brady bill proposal does allow a waiver if the chief law enforcement official or his designee issues a written order stating that immediate purchase is necessary to protect the life of the gun purchaser.[23] (Incidentally, by this concession supporters of the Brady bill have given tacit recognition of the value of private firearms for self-protection. The Fifth Circuit Court of Appeals has already ruled that *the right to defend oneself from deadly attack is fundamental.*)[24]

Of critical importance is the present inadequate state of criminal records in most jurisdictions, a fact that impinges upon any permissions system, whether it be a waiting period of so many days, an instant telephone check, or FOID card. The system is only as good as the records available. The Justice Department estimates it would take upwards of five years or more to complete an automated system with full records. Only about 40 percent to 60 percent of the nation's felony records are presently automated.[25] Another problem is the FBI's estimate that *approximately one-half of the arrest charges in their records do not show a final disposition.*[26]

Then, too, there is the problem of false information recorded on police *rap* sheets. As Kopel notes, courts have held that even after acquittal or dismissal of charges, a person has no Constitutional right to have an arrest purged from his record.[27] This is notoriously the case with minorities disproportionately victimized by arrests that are without proof leading to conviction.

According to the Department of Justice, performing a reliable background check under current data quality conditions would take 30 days.

The Department found that checks made within seven days (or California's fifteen days) were no more reliable than instant checks, a conclusion confirmed by police surveys.[28] The Justice Task Force concluded that approximately 50 percent of the cases where persons appear to have a criminal history are eventually found to be incorrect. In such instances, the secondary verification process to prove non-criminal identity takes from four to six weeks.[29] In some instances, as Kopel argues, this is critical to public safety.

We would respectfully reject Kopel's statement: "Most importantly, the waiting period is social conditioning; it sends the message that citizens do not possess a right to bear arms, but merely have a privilege dependent on police permission."[30] This is tantamount to saying that it makes the Constitutional right to bear arms reducible to whatever conditions the Congress or the Supreme Court determine are valid to regulate one's right, hence invalid. We would reply that ownership of deadly weapons (be they guns or automobiles) is certainly a privilege as well as a right, properly reserved to those who can qualify as responsible citizens. As rights imply commensurate duties, so do they imply responsibility. In a country such as ours, social responsibility is defined by consensus with regard to appropriate standards. Nor is it very likely that the Supreme Court would find any permissions system a prior restraint on the exercise of Constitutional rights. Leroy D. Clark comments that

> the Second Amendment is probably one that has become antiquated in its thrust due to the vast changes in the technology of the phenomena that it sought to control. . . . It is likely, therefore, that the Supreme Court will not find this amendment an impediment to federal arms control legislation that has some potential for increasing public safety.[31]

Kopel is wary of gun registration, also with Firearm Owner's Identification Cards, persuaded they would serve as a basis for gun-owner registration. But turning driver's licenses into *smart cards* involves normal accepted fingerprinting. Kopel insists that it *requires citizens to submit fingerprints to the government in order to exercise their Constitutional rights.* This is essentially the argument of the NRA.[32] The American Civil Liberties Union, while finding justification for limited criminal history records checks, for certain licensing and employment situations, opposes routine fingerprinting for all individuals who seek to purchase firearms as an invasion of privacy. On the basis of precedent, that would be difficult to argue. On the other hand, The National Association of Police Organizations favors the collection of fingerprints as the first step towards a comprehensive fingerprint system "not merely for its benefits in connection with felon identification concerning firearms purchases but also in connection with improving law enforcement in general."[33] Study and consensus is needed here.

Even Kopel reminds us that social security numbers are in effect a mandatory universal identification number demanded at all levels of government and by businesses as well (no national protest against this). And whereas in the past Congress has repeatedly rejected calls for a national ID card, there is not sufficient reason to believe this position might not be reversed as national conditions call for more compelling considerations.

Here, too, we need to recall that the First Amendment does not give us carte blanche the right to yell *fire* in a crowded theater. To imply that exercise of any Constitutional right can in no way be subject to conditions derived from court decisions to fit contemporary needs is difficult to comprehend. Despite Kopel's own arguments, he himself agrees that the so-called *smart card* poses no serious problems from a pure Second Amendment viewpoint.

In this connection, George F. Will, in a syndicated article entitled *Founders Didn't Envision Siege of Gunfire,*[34] cites yet another study, this one in the *Yale Law Journal* entitled "The Embarrassing Second Amendment." The author, Sanford Levinson of the University of Texas Law School, notes that James Mason said *the militia consists now of the whole people.*

Wouldn't Mason be astounded to see the changes in our day! Back then, just five years prior to the adoption of the twelve amendments, the militia had to put down Shay and his thousands of farmers rebelling against the government in Boston—the very same farmers who had helped win the Revolutionary War. From that insurrection evolved the militia of the several states under the command of the state governors in peacetime. But today we no longer have militias, no longer every able-bodied man owning a gun as part of a militia nor expecting to own a gun for the purpose of being part of a militia. Rather, state national guard units provide massive amounts of manpower and firepower to ensure peacetime control. Weapons themselves have evolved from single-fire muskets to automatics and semiautomatics, while the dominant abusers of firearms are not truculent citizens but criminals.

Will concludes that the Bill of Rights should be modified only with extreme reluctance, but that America has an extreme crisis of gunfire. He says: "Whatever right the Second Amendment protects is not as important as it was 200 years ago. . . . But whatever the right is, there it is."

Gun control, like crime itself, remains an elusive, changing target. Policy remains in the embryo stage of development. In this regard, this book serves as an introduction to an ongoing social policy issue. The issues addressed are complex and ever evolving. Social problems are not standing targets but moving ones. The nature of the solutions, like the nature of the problems, requires constant re-evaluation. What the authors have attempted to demonstrate is that social problems like the one addressed in this book demand ethical as well as pragmatic consideration. For solutions to be human, they must be ethically well-advised. If this book advances the ethical reflections which the mounting crisis of the violent home intruder deserves, the distance toward those solutions may have been shortened.

NOTES

1. Kleck, Gary, *Point Blank: Guns and Violence in America.* Hawthorne: Aldine de Gruyter, 1991.
2. United States Department of Justice, "Draft Report on Systems for Identifying Felons Who Attempt to Purchase Firearms: Notes and Request for Comments," *Federal Register,* June 26, 1989, 26901–41.
3. David B. Kopel, "Why Gun Waiting Periods Threaten Public Safety," *Independence Issue Paper,* Independence Institute, March 25, 1991.
4. Ibid., p. 1.
5. "The Attorney General of the United States insists that any verification system for firearms purchasers be at the point of sale, without further delays; he reasons that any check that would be significantly more accurate would take a month, and 'Such a delay would impose an unreasonable burden on legitimate gun purchasers.'" (Letter to Vice-President Dan Quayle, Nov. 20, 1989, p. 2), p. 61.
6. Members of the Police Executive Research Forum (a think-tank for major urban police chiefs) supported an instant check over a firearms license card by a margin of 49 percent to 46 percent. (Task Force, p. 113; Police Executive Research Forum, Comments on Justice Department's Draft Report on Systems for Identifying Felons Who Attempt to Purchase Firearms. July 26, 1989, p. 2) p. 61.
7. Kates, Don B. Jr., *Guns, Murder and the Constitution: A Realistic Assessment of Gun Control.* San Francisco: Pacific Research Institute For Public Policy. (Policy Briefing, February 1990), pp. 59–60.
8. Kopel, op. cit., p. 7.
9. Majority police organizations in support: The Federal Law Enforcement Offi-

cers Association, Fraternal Order of Police, International Brotherhood of Police Officers, International Association of Chiefs of Police, Major Cities Chief Administrators, National Association of Police Organizations, National Organization of Black Law Enforcement Executives, National Sheriffs Association, National Troopers Coalition, Police Executive Research Forum, Police Foundation, and Police Management Association. (Reported in *Congressional Record*, September 15, 1988, H 7639).

10. Kopel, op. cit., 11; *see* James D. Wright, Peter H. Rossi, and Kathleen Daly, *Under the Gun: Weapons, Crime and Violence in America.* Hawthorne: Aldine de Gruyter, 1983, pp. 223–235.

11. Kopel, op. cit, p. 12; *see* Matthew DeZee, "Gun Control Legislation: Impact and Ideology," *Law & Policy Quarterly* 5 (July 1983): pp. 363–379.

12. *Report on the Federal Firearm Owners Protection Act,* S. Rep. no. 3476, 97th Congress, 2nd session (1982), pp. 51–52.

13. Philip J. Cook and James Blose, "State Programs for Screening Handgun Buyers," *Annals of the American Academy of Political Science* 455 (May 1981) pp. 88–90.

14. Wright, Rossi & Daly, op. cit.

15. Wright, Rossi & Daly, op. cit., *see* Wright's chapter in Joseph F. Shelley, *Criminology.* Belmont: Wadsworth, 1991.

16. Bureau of Justice Statistics, *Identifying Persons Other than Felons Ineligible to Purchase Firearms: A Feasibility Study.* Cambridge: Enforth Corporation, May, 1990.

17. David Bordua, "Operation and Effects of Firearms Owners Identification and Waiting Period Legislation in Illinois," University of Illinois, unpublished paper, 1985.

18. Kopel (op. cit.) records complaints in endnotes 66–69.

19. Kopel, Ibid., pp. 18–19.

20. Kopel, Ibid., *see* endnote 101.

21. Kopel states: "The right to bear arms obviously includes the right to purchase them, just as the right to free speech includes the right to purchase printed matter." (endnote 156) Here Kopel's argument is facile and does not give regard to legitimate regulation of rights.

22. Kopel cites the example of Arlington, Virginia where handgun applicants are required to "authorize a review and full disclosure of all arrest and medical psychiatric records." (Form 2020-63 as of April, 1988.)

23. H.R. 7, (a)(1)(B).

24. *United States v. Panter,* 688 F.2nd 268, 271 (5th Cir. 1982).

25. Task Force Draft, 54 *Federal Register* 43528, Oct. 25, 1989. The task force stated that eleven states did not have automated records, ten other states had less than 65 percent of their records automated; *see* 54 *Federal Register,* 43545.

26. Task Force Draft, Ibid.

27. Kopel cites *Hammons v. Scott,* 423 F. Supp. 618 (N.D. Cal. 1976); *Rowlett v. Fairfax,* 446 F. Supp. 186 (W.D.Mo. 1978).

28. Kopel, op. cit., p. 32.

29. Task Force, op. cit., p. 15.

30. Kopel, op. cit., p. 32.

31. Leroy D. Clark, "Reducing Firearms Availability: Constitutional Impediments to Effective Legislation and an Agenda for Research," *Firearms and Violence: Issues of Public Policy.* Kates, Don B. Jr., ed., San Francisco: Pacific Institute for Public Policy Research, 1984, p. 15.

32. Kopel sees this as prior restraints on Constitutional Rights; *see* argument pages 33–36.

33. Kopel, Ibid., p. 37.

34. George F. Will, "Founders Didn't Envision Siege of Gunfire," *Santa Barbara News Press.* March 23, 1991.

NAME INDEX

A

Abel, Gene, 39
Abraham, 112–113, 117, 133
Alston, Judge Gilbert, 59
Alviani, Joseph D., 44
Amir, Menachim, 41, 42
Anscombe, Elizabeth, 202
Anker, Roy M., 21, 22
Aquinas, St. Thomas, 99, 173
Arendt, Hannah, 38
Aristotle, 134
Armstrong, Senator John, 176
Aukerman, Dale, 173
Augustine, St., 173, 187, 193
Austerman, Wayne R., 231
Avila, Karola, 9
Ayoob, Massad, 48, 83, 88

B

Balkin, Steven, 229
Bankston, James W., 91
Bankston, Thayer-Doyle, 91
Barclay, William, 126–127
Baron, Larry, 44
Bart, Pauline, 36
Barth, Karl, 109, 189, 190
Beha, James A., 230
Bendis, Paul, 229
Beneke, Timothy, 44
Bennett, John C., 151
Benson, Bruce L., 231
Bernbaum, John A., 174
Bier, William C., 106
Bigelow, Steve, 91
Bloesch, Donald A., 102, 138, 151, 158, 196, 202
Blose, James, 243

Bordua, David J., 236
Bordwell, Sally, 44
Borzellieri, Frank, 230
Bouthilet, Lorraine, 18, 26
Bowers, Wendy, 26
Brady, James, 226, 232
Brady, Sarah, 225
Bretall, Robert W., 148
Bronson, Charles, 21
Brownmiller, Susan, 41, 42, 78
Bruce-Briggs, Barry, 215
Bruce, L., 76
Brunner, Emil, 134
Burgess, Ann W., 44
Bush, President George, 225

C

Callahan, Charles M., 26
Calvin, John, 173
Carnell, Edward John, 158
Cassidy, Richard, 125
Centerwall, Brandon S., 18
Chaiken, Jan M., 27
Chaiken, Marcia R., 27
Childs, Brevard, 111
Chambliss, William, 231
Charnock, Stephen, 147
Chotner, Kenneth L., 230
Cicero, 176
Clark, Howard, 231
Clark, Leroy D., 240
Clements, R.E., 119
Clemons, G.W., 231
Cole, Alan, 119
Colson, Charles W., 226, 227
Cook, Philip J., 243
Copeland, Lorraine, 86
Coser, Lewis A., 30

245

SUBJECT INDEX

A

American Civil Liberties Union, 240
Assault, 4, 59–60
    by ex-husbands, ex-boyfriends, 85
    by intruders, 27–32
    by rapists, 32, 84–85
Assault weapons (see Guns)

B

Bureau of Alcohol and Firearms, 10

C

Commandment, the Sixth, 107–117
    as unqualified absolute, 107–108, 116–117
    case law, modifier of, 108, 117
    creation in God's image, basis of, 111–112
    God's righteous character reflected in,
        109
    Hebrew verb, key to, 110–111
    legal understanding of, 111
        apodictic aspect of, 114
        casuistic aspect of, 114–115
    Mosaic law, 108–110
        background of, 108–110
        intruders, application to, 117
    prescriptive aspect of, 109, 112
    proscriptive aspect of, 112
    superseded by direct command, illustra-
        tions of, 112–113, 117
Conscience, 97–105
    accountability and, 103
    autonomous, as unreliable guide, 98, 102
    characterized by acting out one's true self,
        105
    content, originally God-given, directly
        mediated, 98, 100

    criminal development of, 103
    formation aids
        Christian community, 102
        moral experience, 103
        prayer, 102
        Scripture, 101
        Spirit of God, 102
    limitations of,
        human finitude and sinfulness, 98, 100,
            102–103
    moral intuition, not innate aspect of, 97
    nature of, characterized by
        behavior monitoring aspect, 100–102
        lifelong socialization process, 98
        moral developmental process, 99–100
    New Testament references to, 99
    newly-formed convictions, effect upon,
        103–104
    spiritual transformation of, 101
    secular understanding of, 97
    theological understanding of, 99
    uneasiness, residue within, 102, 104
Crime, violent
    conviction rates for, 15–16
    disarming citizens, effect upon, 212–213
Criminals
    career, typology of, 27–29
    non-career, typology of, 29–30

D

Deadly force, 65
    proportionality rule, 66–67
    versus non-deadly force, 65
Decision Making Information, Inc., 82
Demographic Research Institute, 27

251

E

Emergency 911 calls for crime intervention
    relative ineffectiveness of, 12–13, 45–47
Eisenhower Commission Report, 83
Ethics, philosophical
    Consequentialism, 200–202
        christian decision-making aspect of,
            200–202
        limitations of, 200–201
        principles of, 200
    Double Effect Principle, 198–200
        intruders, application to, 200
        catholic/protestant acceptance of, 199–
            200
        defining aspects of, 198
        Koop, Surgeon General C.E., illustra-
            tion of, 198–199
    Prima Facie Duties, 195–197
        in conflict situations requiring choice,
            195
            biblical illustrations of, 196, 197
        theoretical principles of, 195

G

Goetz, Bernhard, case of, 13–14, 75
Guns
    accidents with, 49–52
        causes of, 51
        children, victims of, 49
        Children's Firearm Accident Protection
            Act, 51–52
        persons prone to, 52
        rates consistent over time, 51
        Ronald D. Stephens National School
            Safety Center, 51–52
        suicide, erroneous listing as, 50
        teens, victims of, 49–50
    assault rifles, 220–222
        as crime weapons, 221–222
        distinctive features of, 220
        Patrick Purdy, case of, 219–220
    burglars and, 27–28
    citizen possession of
        as crime deterrent, 12
        citizen disarmament, risks of, 60,
            74–75
        "evil talisman," phenomenon of, 48–49

fear, factor in, 14, 82–83
    perils accompanying, 48
    rationale for, 56–59
dealer sales, legal and illegal, 10
death by, 1–4, 8–9
handguns, 9–10
    banning proposals, criminalization
        effect, 28, 216, 218
    theft of, 9
    HCI misinformation, illustrations of,
        48
    high school youth, possession by,
        10–11
        carried to school by, 10
    private transfer of, 10
    theft of, 9
manufacture of, 9–10
plastic components, significance of, 220
"saturday night specials," 9–10
social order and disorder associated with,
    60
training and practice, women's special need
    for, 85–86
Gun Control
    Brady bill, 232
        appeals process, none provided by,
            237
        armed self-protection, tacitly recognized
            by, 239
        criminology input, lacking in, 235
        waiver provision, included in, 239
    California's Proposition 15, 218, 224
    confiscation, future attempt, fear of, 237
    crime control, effectiveness of, 216, 235
        Senate Judiciary Committee, findings
            on, 235
    enforcement of, 213, 216–217
    fingerprinting, purchase requirement pro-
        posal for, 240–241
        ACLU opposition to, 240
        police organizations favoring, 240–241
    firearms owners identification card, 234
        Illinois, experience with, 236
        Social Security card, similarity with,
            241
    gun registration, fear of, 237
        Second Amendment rights, no
            complication to, 237
    HCI, position of, 225–226, 234